Elements of
Interpersonal
Communication

Elements of
Interpersonal
Communication

John W. Keltner

Oregon State University

Wadsworth Publishing Company, Inc.
Belmont, California

For those beautiful students who leveled
with me about what they wanted and who
sustained me when I needed it.

Preface

Interpersonal communication is man's most significant behavior and consti-
tutes the basis of social interaction. A failure to understand its significance
and to seek effective development of the processes may inhibit the viability
of our society—a frightening, complex society of both technological advances and social disorder.

The purpose of this book is to help the reader to understand the significance of interpersonal communication, to help him develop his own
communication experiences, and to challenge him to change and improve
conditions in our society. While giving no pat formulas, the book develops
a concept of interpersonal communication that encompasses the utilitarian,
the artistic, and the therapeutic functions it performs. Self-awareness and
self-growth are inherent in the development of all three functions.

The book deals with the elements necessary for interpersonal communication. Each chapter deals with a specific aspect of the process. Objectives listed at the beginning of each chapter are intended to stimulate
the search for change. Short summaries appear at the end of each chapter
to aid the process of grasping the concepts and developing applications.
Following each chapter are a few annotated suggestions for further reading. In the concluding "Try This" section of each chapter are suggestions
for things to do that will help in understanding the ideas of the chapter, in
developing some of the applications of the chapter theory, and in creating
individual opportunities for personal development of interpersonal communication.

Underlying the book is the assumption that interpersonal communication is thoroughly interdisciplinary in every aspect of its form and function. The understanding of the self and the other in the societal context of
interpersonal communication is fundamental to this book. Through development of the processes, many of the individual needs and the group-
process needs of our society may be served. Our survival, our upward
mobility, our leadership, our decision-making processes, our management
of conflict, and our accomplishment of peak experiences in living are per-

ceived as being closely related to our interpersonal communication. Hopefully, the reader will find stimulation and seek ways to deal with problems of his own and of his society through communication interaction with his fellowmen.

Acknowledgments

Some wonderful people have made contributions to my efforts with this book. Whatever usefulness it may have is, in a great degree, the result of their efforts in my behalf. Whatever weaknesses or failures the book may have must fall to my account.

Credit for the greatest part of my desire to make this book something relevant and meaningful must go to the many students, of all ages, who have challenged, questioned, and tested me. I owe them much! Thanks, also, go to my academic colleagues and mentors who have given much of themselves with grace and goodwill. I shall always be in their debt.

Many fine people in the Federal Mediation and Conciliation Service and the labor and management parties they serve have made significant contributions to my understanding of people communicating with each other. I am particularly indebted to Regional Director Edwin W. Scott for counsel and advice.

I continue to owe special gratitude to a number of people for specific contributions to earlier versions of the original work that led to the publication of *Interpersonal Speech-Communication.* Bert Keltner gave much to the development of ideas and concepts from her depth of understanding, her creativity, and her refreshing excitement with teaching speech communication. Charles Goetzinger of the State University of New York at Geneseo, Alvin Goldberg of Northwestern University, Victor Harnack of the University of Illinois at Chicago Circle, Robert Kibler of Florida State University, Ben Padrow of Portland State University, and Milton Valentine of Oregon State University read and criticized early versions of the work, made useful suggestions for improving the manuscript, and gave me much encouragement.

I remain appreciative of the persistent encouragement and editorial direction of Rebecca Hayden and her belief in what I was trying to do. Similarly, I am thankful for the thoughtful and inspiring job done by Ellen Seacat, as manuscript editor, in helping to say what I wanted to say.

I am also grateful for the help and stimulation given to me by professional colleagues throughout the country. Through their use of the material in *Interpersonal Speech-Communication,* they have encouraged me to continue the necessary growth and development to keep this subject viable.

Contents

Prologue

I have started to write this prologue at least a dozen times, but each attempt just did not seem right to me, did not seem to have enough of what I want to put into it. I want to tell you some things of great importance to me; they are important to me because I hope they will help you experience this book as a part of your own growth and learning. I could make this prologue formal and could hide behind that formality, but if I did you would not really know much about me. Unless you know something about me, your experiencing of this book will not be all that it might be for you. Also, I want to do what I suggest that you do; that is, I want to reveal myself so that you may better understand what I am saying. Naturally, I do not want to go into all my personal history, with all its trials and tribulations. But I do want you to know something about me. In revealing something of myself, I know I am taking the chance that I may be hurt a bit as I let you in. But I believe that trust must begin, and so I trust you—to begin with—even though I am a bit scared about such a beginning.

You and your learning choices

I want to tell you, first, that there is nothing *I* can *learn for you.* If teaching is the imparting of information, I think I can do some of that. Information that I cast toward you does not really become input into your head, heart, and soul until *you* reach out for it and take it in *because you want it.* I would like for you to *want* some of the information I have tried to assemble here, but there is no way I can force you to want it. Above all, I could not live with the idea of forcing anyone to learn against his will, just as I despise a "rip-off" of anything by anybody to anybody.

I am convinced that everything I have learned I have learned myself. I think the same goes for you. Each of us has to do his own work of learning. No teacher can crawl into your being and control your *learning choices.* Learning takes some *effort* and before I expend that effort I need some *encouragement* to pay that price. Sometimes my own *curiosity* takes care of the matter, but sometimes I need the encouragement of others when I run up against things that seem too difficult or complex or that appear on the surface to be boring and useless. I also need help frequently in *sorting out* the things that would be more important for me to learn. The help I need, however, does not involve someone else making my decisions for me. I need the kind of help that provides me with stimulation, with more alternatives, and with emotional encouragement as I try to take hold of a problem. Really, no one else can make decisions for me about what I am going to learn.

In 1963, I returned to teaching after spending five years in a quite non-academic world of labor-management relations in American industry and government. I had not planned to return to the campus; in addition to thoroughly enjoying my work as a mediator, I had left the teaching business in full retreat before what I felt to be shallow, wasteful, inhumane, unscholarly, and unwise processes and attitudes in the system of higher education in our country. In that "outside" world I encountered considerable disdain for the education process and a lot of hardheaded and realistic demonstration of how learning can take place anywhere, anytime, for anyone who *wants to learn.* At the same time, it became obvious to me that a lot of people who were coming out of our schools had not learned in those schools very much that the schools intended or that was of great significance to them. The important learning had taken place outside the schools in the stream of daily living.

So why did I return to education? I guess it was because I felt a kind of responsibility to try to do something about the sorry state of affairs existing in education. I know that I am not going to create a revolution or upset the academic scheme of things. I also know that inside my own classroom I may be able to stimulate, to encourage, to support, to love, and to be present while people like you get in touch with their desire to learn about and improve themselves as communicators. When you reach out to me and others like me for support and stimulation and information, we (those others and I) can be ready—ready to share with you our own growing and becoming and our discoveries in communication. *But you have to reach for it!*

I have been making some assumptions about myself and my own way of facilitating learning: (1) The accumulation of factual knowledge is a very small part of being educated. (2) Learning comes when I seek and struggle and dig for myself in the areas of my own greatest needs and desires. (3) Absolute truth may not exist—or at least I can never know it. There are many, many ways of viewing any given fact. In any event, is that fact "the truth"? Even if it is, it will never be really known because each of us will have a different way of seeing it and it will tell us different things. (4) Learning is an active thing, sometimes violent. Sometimes traumatic events are essential to bring about a condition in which change and learning can take place. I have recently endured such a trauma in my personal life; and, in consequence, I feel myself reaching out for opportunities to learn, for new experiences, and for new ways of living with high excitement and activity. In fact, the days and nights are too short. The pleasure of discovery is so intense that I can hardly wait to see what will happen next. At the same time, I am involved with great awareness of the things that are happening in the here and now, and these things seem to have no limits. (5) Judgments about the *value* of the learning I have accomplished can be made only by me. No one else can grasp the whole set of conditions, standards, and needs under which I came to reach out for any particular set of learnings. Only I can truly evaluate myself. Only you can truly evaluate yourself.

If you look carefully at these assumptions, you can see that they might very well "freak out" some administrators, most teachers, and many students. Under these assumptions, *you, as a student or reader, cease to be perceived (by yourself or others) as a plastic bucket into which information is to be dumped.* You cease to try to put together things that have already been put together but start looking for ways to deal with the things that, for you, have not yet been put together (including yourself). You cease to be awed by the idea that truth is sealed in a big vault to be viewed only by perfect beings and begin to discover that your truth is not someone else's truth or mine but that each of us has a piece of the substance—and of the action. You cease trying to copy down the words of the teacher or memorizing sections of this book to regurgitate on an examination. Instead, you try to find in this book things that will be *useful* to you in the process of becoming a more humane and pleasure-full being. You are willing to allow others to find for themselves things that may be different from what you find. In other words, you begin to deal with your own needs—and you get "truckin' " along!

I hope that you will begin to initiate and generate *your own learning* conditions. I hope that you will become entranced with the excitement and the action of learning, of self-involvement, of change, and of growth. For me, I cannot separate ideas from things from feelings from me from you from information. They are all part of me and I am a total unit, not separated into heads, tails, and in between. My thinking is hooked up to my feelings. My feelings are part of my thinking; information coming in to me hits upon a very human mass of feelings, ideas, thoughts, needs, desires, hopes, wishes, and the like and I want to deal with that information in terms of the total constellation of me.

Bernice Marshall, in her excellent book *Experiences in Being*, strikes to the very heart of the whole matter, and what she says for her goes for me too.

> I want to be a part of a society which is geared to transcend survival; I want to participate in creating a society in which to live is to grow, not a society embodying fragments of splits and pieces of human protoplasm. For me this tends to perpetuate feelings of alienation and aloneness. I want to identify and accept

my own responsibility for creating and maintaining that which we do not have, that which we had and still want; my own need to relate in my humanness to the humanness of others, while retaining my own sense of my self. I reject the pace and the stance which so many of us assume as we exist in our age of advanced technology.

There is just so much that I can contemplate, explore, do by myself. I treasure my inner dialogues, my inner transactions. But I want more than that. I want and need others. I want to learn. . . . I want to grow—as a person. And in the saying, I confront myself. For to grow is to change, and in order to change I have to know myself. Can I be real? Can I know and be my real self? For if I cannot be real, know my thoughts, feelings, fears, desires, attitudes, and values, what is my criterion; what do I have against which to measure, how can I evaluate my experiences and, in process, identify my own learnings?[1]

If you really dig what has been said above, you may be ready to begin beginning to get on to the interpersonal communication trip.

Beginning the beginning:
The old and the new

I want to share some history with you in order that you may understand your own communication present. Our speech-communication past is a combination of rhetoric, drama, poetry, physical and biological sciences, psychology, sociology, history, and a host of other so-called academic disciplines. That past also consists of ages of effort by man to establish a bond and to create the *engagement* of speech communication (see pp. 24–26 for discussion of this concept). We could enjoy the delights of living in the past and let our imagination dwell with the ancients and how well or how poorly they dealt with their times through speech; but, while such reflections might be useful at certain stages of human development, they are not basic to the function or purpose of this book.

The time of our present demands a greater separation from the past than ever before. Issues of our here and now are not readily solved by reference to the past. We can enjoy the beauty of the past, but we cannot create our own new beauty by passive reflection. Our job is to become agents and participants in creating change in our contemporary society. Speech communication is one of the most powerful and most used of all the processes in the engineering of changes and growth in the person-group-society complex. We have an ethical responsibility to develop our effectiveness in the process to the highest possible degree. That responsibility comes as a simple result of just being alive. For, being alive, we bring with us the potential of *becoming* something more than what we now are. It is that process of *becoming* that determines our responsibility. In our

---

[1] Bernice Marshall, *Experiences in Being* (Monterey, Calif.: Brooks-Cole Publishing Co., 1971) p. 12.

times, too many of us have ignored, forgotten, and suppressed this responsibility.

Open yourself up to this responsibility. Assume an active and useful
role in the development of change. Too many of us have operated on the
tacit assumption that society is more or less static and nondynamic. That
this assumption is not only wrong but also dangerous is vividly described
by Dan Fabun.

> At exactly 5:13 a.m., the 18th of April, 1906, a cow was standing somewhere
> between the main barn and the milking shed on the old Shafter Ranch in Cali-
> fornia, minding her own business. Suddenly, the earth shook, the skies trembled,
> and when it was all over there was nothing showing of the cow above ground
> but a bit of her tail sticking up.
>
> For the student of change, the Shafter cow is a sort of symbol of our times.
> She stood quietly enough, thinking such gentle thoughts as cows are likely
> to have, while huge forces outside her ken built up all around her and—within
> a minute—discharged it all at once in a great movement that changed the con-
> figuration of the earth, and destroyed a city, and swallowed her up. And that's
> what we are going to talk about now; how, if we do not learn to understand and
> *guide* the great forces of change at work in our world today, we may find our-
> selves like the Shafter cow, swallowed up by vast upheavals in our way of life—
> quite early some morning. [Italics added.][2]

Our speech-communication present is like Shafter's cow. We have
tended to stand quietly and chew the cud of stuff that was gathered some
time ago. Our texts and handbooks have all too often presented no more
than reorganizations of the old materials, renaming them and sometimes
shuffling them up a bit. This may soon be past. Our communication present
involves the *artistic,* the *therapeutic,* and the *utilitarian* functions merged
into an organic unity. The theatre is as much a part of our speech communication today as are radio and television. What happens in Jerusalem, Saigon,
Belfast, Cape Town, Berkeley, Cairo, Chicago, Hattiesburg, Boston, and San
Francisco is as much a part of our speech communication as what is happening on our own campuses. The compression of time and space through the
mechanical devices of transmission and reception has made it possible for
us to extend our interpersonal speech communication more widely and more
rapidly than ever before in history. How well will we use it? To what end
will it be used? I hope that most of us will intensify use of speech communication in a deeply committed effort to deal with the issues and the
frontiers of our here and now.

[2] Don Fabun, *The Dynamics of Change* (Englewood Cliffs, N. J.: Prentice-Hall, 1967), p. 1.

Chapter One

Speech Communication and Human Society

Objectives

After studying this chapter, you should be better able to do these things:

- Perceive the communication bond between you and others.

- Be aware of others' attempts to communicate.

- Identify speech interaction outcomes as utilitarian, aesthetic, or therapeutic, or combinations of the three.

- Create models of the speech-communication event that clearly describe the process as you see it.

- Increase your attention to your own speech-communication interaction.

- Begin to cope with the transitory nature of speech communication by intensifying your efforts to make each moment more effective.

On a clear evening in spring, I stood on the deck outside my study and watched the sun fall away from my day. The clouds rising over the Coast Range seemed to be trying to decide whether to hide the departure or to allow it to occur in full view. The sun and the clouds, interacting, created great washes of color behind the mountains. My senses were aroused, my emotions became involved, and the feeling of infinite self-smallness surrounded me.

The sun retreated and I became enclosed in darkness. I turned to the house to seek someone with whom to share my experience and the strange feeling. No one was there. During my preoccupation with the close of the day, my family had dispersed to meetings, library, and shopping. With no one around, I felt suddenly bound up, inhibited, restricted. I felt some unreasonable anger at my family for not being there to hear of my experience. I had already formed phrases in my mind that I would use. I had anticipated how I would explain the wonderful happening. I had communicated with myself; but that self-communication was insufficient. I was stirred to want to communicate with another person.

My experience was a personal matter. *As long as it remained a singular personal matter wrapped up inside me, it was not complete.* I felt that until I was able to share the experience with someone, it would never be complete. Through the sharing with another person, I would be able to develop greater meaning and understanding of the experience itself. When I finally was able to express my experience and to interact with a friend about what I had seen and how I had felt, it seemed that the experience then, and only then, began to acquire its fuller meaning. Until I could interact with someone about it, the image and the reaction were almost like dusty clothes in a locked closet. Speech communication can be a way for us to unlock ourselves to each other.

Speech communication as spoken symbolic interaction

Through the stimulation of speech communication we are able to discover, explore, test, express, and stimulate meaning. *Speech is a unique process of symbolic communication that involves interaction between persons.* Because of its predominance among the forms of communication, speech is almost the essence of our life as social beings.

According to Joyce Hertzler, communication, while not an end in itself, is the elemental social process; and all social processes depend on communication as a social technique. She points out that without communication there are no interstimulations between people; no common meanings and concepts; no action which provides information, instruction, and provocative imitations. Without it there is no invention, recording, accumulation, or transmission of knowledge. Without it there can be no social organization, reorganization, and/or planning.[1]

Meanings of things experienced may arise as a result of the interaction of people through communication. This effect of speech interaction occurs frequently and is most powerful. Further, the control of things that have been experienced, that are happening, and that are anticipated may result principally from human speech interaction. The "miracle" of speech was vividly described by Charles Brown and Charles Van Riper.[2]

I agree with them that speech is the most universal of human functions,

[1] Joyce O. Hertzler, *A Sociology of Language* (New York: Random House, 1965), pp. 26–27.
[2] Charles T. Brown and Charles Van Riper, *Speech and Man* (Englewood Cliffs, N. J.: Prentice-Hall, © 1966), pp. 1–2.

unique to man. Few of us appreciate its power and potential, they claim, because it is so common in our society. While it is our most effective tool, most of us have not learned much about how to use it or about the extent to which it can be used. To those who have learned more than the primitive skills are given the fruits of the earth and our adoration. What great people have said enlivens the history of our civilization. Brown and Van Riper point out the incredible fact that so important a skill receives very little attention or training. If we taught people to read as we teach people to talk we would be illiterate.

Any sound and practical study of communication must take into account the primacy and the basic importance of speech as the fundamental human communication system. When more people become aware that speech is the most used and the most significant of the communication forms used by man, we may then begin to increase man's effectiveness in relating to his fellows.

All the factors that are brought into play upon and by a person as he attempts to establish communicative relationships with others are involved in speech communication. Any communicative relationship between two or more persons involves a unique *reciprocal bond* with another person—a bond that is at once the beginning of, a result of, a cause of, and concomitant to the interaction.

Thus, my experience at sundown had only limited meaning to me until I shared it with another person through communication interaction. That sharing of an experience enabled me to increase my understanding of its meaning to me. That communication interaction was almost totally dependent upon the establishment of a reciprocal bond between us, that other person and me. This *reciprocal bond* allowed us to relate to each other so that our meanings could develop. As this bond permits communication by speech, it becomes a cornerstone of a social structure. On such basic relationships between persons, whole social systems are built.

Outcomes of interaction

Three significant needs of people are met through the reciprocal relationship of speech communication: the need for *utility* in our daily life, the need for pleasure and enjoyment (*aesthetic*), and the need to treat illnesses (*therapeutic*). These various needs are often answered simultaneously by a single communication. For instance, a theatre performance may yield all three results in that it makes money for the producers; the cast and staff give pleasure to viewers as well as performers; and the experience may be therapeutic for some viewers and players.

The *utilitarian* result is some practical accomplishment of value to one or more members of the interaction. According to Miller, speech communication allows us to understand, control, and alter our environment and is one of the most effective means of maximizing rewards and minimizing punishment from our environment.[3]

The *aesthetic* result is enjoyment, pleasure, or entertainment for one or more members of the interaction. Speech that is used in a television or theatre performance, in reading literature aloud, in storytelling, and in various other forms of artistic expression becomes a tool to create pleasure.

The *therapeutic* result is a treatment, a cure, the removal of an inhibition, the diagnosis of a problem, or the reestablishment of the communicative personality. Speech becomes therapy when it allows a person to release tensions and to find himself, when it assists a person to explore and examine personal problems that affect his communicative bond with other people, and when it aims specifically at rehabilitating, restoring, and perhaps creating the instruments of human communication.

Speaking, listening, reading, and writing

Speaking, listening, reading, and writing involve different functions of the body and accomplish different objectives. From the very early stages of his existence on earth, after he graduated from the use of signs, man has used speech and listening as his principal means of communication.

The effective interaction of speaking and listening requires a particularly close relationship between the participants. David Riesman reports that in some of the isolated islands of the Philippines, where writing is unknown, messages are transmitted by speech alone. The accuracy of transmission is much higher than in civilized societies: "For these tribesmen, words are like buckets in a fire brigade, to be handled with full attention, while we feel we can afford to be careless with the spoken word, backstopped as we are by the written one."[4] Riesman points out that the written word becomes a private and isolating type of experience for a person. Conversely, as many of us assert, the spoken word is an interpersonal and socializing experience for a person.

Writing and printing have had a tremendous impact on the recording of ideas, but *the key interaction that forms the base of our society is still*

[3] Gerald R. Miller, *Speech Communication: A Behavioral Approach* (Indianapolis: Bobbs-Merrill Co., 1966), p. 2.

[4] David Riesman, "The Oral and Written Traditions," in Edmund Carpenter and Marshall McLuhan, eds., *Explorations in Communication* (Boston: Beacon Press, 1960), p. 111.

spoken language, or speech. There is close agreement in findings of a number of studies of the relative amounts of time we spend in use of the four communicative behaviors. The breakdown of time spent in normal communicative discourse by the average American falls into the following pattern:[5]

Listening	42% ⎫	
Speaking	32% ⎭	74%
Reading	15% ⎫	
Writing	11% ⎭	26%

We should use these data carefully. They tell us nothing about the relative *amounts of information* transmitted and actually received or the generation of meanings by means of writing and reading as compared with speaking and listening. We have no research findings on this question, but it seems probable that in any given time more information could be acquired on a precise subject through written words than through spoken words. The key to the matter may lie with the precision of the information transmitted and with the use of the language. In speech, the total message includes much information in addition to the actual spoken words and the imprecision and redundancy characteristic of speech do not normally occur in written material.

We cannot compare the two forms in terms of the relative *amounts of meaning* that can be developed from them, since the meaning is a function of the person. Writing seems a more precise and explicit way of transmitting information because it can be studied and reread as necessary. As personal tape recorders are more and more widely used, more and more spoken material can be reheard. The capability of replaying recorded speech may increase precision of transmittal of specific information through speech. As people become more skilled in speaking and in listening, with or without tape recorders, we can expect greater efficiency in meeting the human needs in our system.

Much contemporary cultural and social lag relative to our technological advancement stems from our grossly inadequate mastery of the face-to-face speech-communication processes. The culture lag threatens to become ever more pronounced. The printed page is already subject to computerization. Information, but *not* meanings, can be stored in, retrieved from, and manipulated by computers faster, more accurately, and more economically than it can be processed in written form by human beings. Computers have been programmed to "write verse," to "write music," and to produce translations from written Russian into written English. Written words can be stored in computers; meanings can be stored only in people.

[5] Ralph G. Nichols and Leonard A. Stevens, *Are You Listening?* (New York: McGraw-Hill Book Co., 1957), pp. 6–10.

More and more of the interaction between people will depend on speech and less and less on written words. Increasingly, people "correspond" with each other by tape recordings and telephone, rather than by letters, and, increasingly, business transactions are conducted by telephone rather than by written memos and letters. This tendency has become international, thanks to the fantastic growth of intercontinental communication as a result of the telecommunication satellites.

This growing importance and significance of the spoken word is not matched by equivalent emphasis and development in school curricula, from kindergarten to university. The nearly universal lack of speech training in our schools is probably based on the faulty assumption that, because most children can speak and listen by the time they enter preschool and primary programs, they need no special instruction in that area. Much of the speech behavior that a child has learned by his fourth or fifth year has been conditioned by what he has heard. In the most favorable of home environments, this conditioning is not sufficient to make him fully effective in speaking and listening.

Instruction in speech communication could profitably begin in primary grades in order to break bad habits acquired during preschool years and to establish more useful and effective speech patterns. If we do not increase the training in speaking and listening, the speech-communication inadequacies of one generation will simply be passed on to the next; and in a period when effective communication may be vital to the survival of mankind, we may understand each other less and less surely.

Speaking and listening begin almost with birth

Early attempts of the infant to communicate are gross uncoordinated sounds and actions, which become stabilized and less generalized as the child becomes aware that certain sounds and certain movements bring specific kinds of responses (when he cries, he gets attention). A language of sound and visible movement soon develops. The standards and the forms of this language of the infant are developed through contact with those who respond to the communication efforts, in most instances, the parents. Children adopt those behaviors that result in the greatest satisfaction of their needs and desires.

Eric Berne has developed a theory of social intercourse which he calls Transactional Analysis.[6] Studies of sensory deprivation indicate that infants who are deprived of caressing and other normal human contact show signs of physical and mental deterioration. He suggests that prolonged emotional deprivation brings deterioration and that severe emotional deprivation may be

---

[6] Eric Berne, *Transactional Analysis in Psychotherapy* (New York: Grove Press, 1961).

fatal. While the stimulus-hunger of the infant is most effectively satisfied by physical intimacy (handling, fondling, caressing), the adult learns to substitute symbolic forms of stroking for actual physical contact. This symbolic stimulus-hunger is considered by many to be as important to survival as food-hunger.

Berne sums up his core theory with the striking observation "If you are not stroked, your spinal cord will shrivel up."[7] He suggests that the infant stimulus-hunger becomes in the adult a recognition-hunger.

> "Stroking" may be used as a general term for intimate physical contact; in practice it may take various forms. Some people literally stroke an infant; others hug it or pat it, while some people pinch it playfully or flip it with a finger tip. *These all have their analogues in conversation,* so that it seems one might predict how an individual would handle a baby by listening to him talk. By an extension of meaning, "stroking" may be employed colloquially to denote any act implying recognition of another's presence. Hence a stroke may be used as the fundamental unit of social action.[8]

The reciprocal bond, which is at the heart of speech communication, may very well *begin* with the need for strokes, as Berne uses the term. Or, conversely, the bond may be developed by applying the stroking. Obviously, the child learns behaviors that lead to stroking in order that his stimulus-hunger can be fulfilled; and the behavior of the adult is also determined to some degree by his stimulus-hunger.

Speech also has fundamental physiological and psychological associations with the mouth and oral cavity and with the whole body system. René Spitz calls the mouth the bridge between the inside and outside of the human personality: "The mouth as the primal cavity is the bridge between inner reception and outer perception; it is the cradle of all external perception and its basic model; it is the place of transition for the development of intentional activity, for the emergence of volition from passivity."[9] Current investigations of the whole body-mind system are showing that speech is closely affected by body states.

Since early infantile learning is strongly influenced by the physiological interchange between parent and child, the first learned communication

---

[7] Eric Berne, *Games People Play* (New York: Grove Press, 1964), p. 14. Copyright © 1964 by Eric Berne.

[8] Berne, *Games,* p. 15.

[9] René Spitz, "The Primal Cavity: A Contribution to the Genesis of Perception and Its Role for Psychoanalytic Theory," in Ruth S. Eissler, Anna Freud, Heinz Hartmann, and Ernst Kris, *The Psychoanalytic Study of the Child* (New York: International Universities Press, 1955), p. 238.

behaviors could come from the stroking behaviors of the parents made in response to efforts of the infant to satisfy his needs. The parents inevitably determine which infant efforts will be rewarded, and the child soon learns to stimulate the stroking by creating the kind of oral behavior that satisfies the stroker (parent). In other words, the child strokes back, and the first communication interaction bonds develop.

Speech communication, in any context, is a basic form of adaption to the environment. Spitz's reference to the mouth as the bridge between the inner life of the infant and the outer life of the older child and adult gives added significance to the speech base of human interaction.

If the first speech is learned almost at the first breath, then what of the nature and quality of that speech? The infant quickly learns to adapt to his own mother and to provide her with reciprocal strokes that satisfy her needs. The standards of communication behavior between the two may be inadequate for settings beyond them. A mother can distinguish the cries of her child and can tell whether he is angry, sick, hungry, lonely, or simply bored. These messages, however, are not so easily understood by someone else.

Beyond these early stages, speech-communication habits of the pre-school child may be sufficient only for his limited and close environment. When the child enters school, he must develop new skills and new abilities if he is to deal adequately with his widening social contacts and with the competition for sensory and stimulus satisfactions. As his social world enlarges, he finds it necessary to adjust his speech-communication habits to entice, from that enlarging world, the greatest satisfaction he can extract. If the original standards of speech communication are poor and do not provide for the wider social interaction, the child almost certainly will become socially inhibited and deprived. This deprivation resulting from faulty speech-communication habits is more frequent and more universal than we realize or would care to admit if we did realize.

When we stop developing for ourselves new skills and new systems, we can no longer increase the potential of our social effectiveness. Old habits and behavior patterns, strongly established in a given environment, usually are not adequate for meeting new needs and desires in new situations. Change is a constant requirement.

In the classroom environment from primary grades into college, most students have learned that their social effectiveness is increased if they signal the teacher when they have something to say. In many seminars, a student participant need only find the appropriate moment and speak out; and students who continue the old behavior pattern of the raised-hand signal often lose their social effectiveness for a session or more, until they learn to use the new behavior patterns of the new situation.

The skills of speaking and listening

The multitudinous impacts of sensory stimuli and the social pressures experienced by each of us create strong desires to relate to others through the medium of speech communication. *We have to talk to each other.*

By its nature, speech communication is highly transitory. Although videotape and audiotape are now used to record many events, for the most part, words once spoken are lost forever, except as they can be replicated in the memories of those who were present when they were uttered. Furthermore, writing cannot replicate speech; the total message and the effect of the speech situation exceed any possibility of a complete and accurate written account.

Because of this highly transitory nature of the speech act, each effort at the communicative interaction through speech needs to be as effective as possible. Both speaker and listener must concentrate on grasping as much as possible of all that occurs in the moment of the speech act in order that maximum effectiveness can be achieved in the interaction.

The skills necessary to maximize speech-communication events are developed in many ways. The important skills in the use of language involve behavior that is at least bimodal, since language is composed of both verbal and nonverbal factors. Verbal skills relate to the spoken words and other vocal sounds that carry information and stimulate meaning. The nonverbal skills relate to the movements of the body and the nonverbal sounds (such as a snap of the fingers) that may occur as information-giving parts of the event. Gestures, bodily movement, and facial expression are nonverbal factors.

Language skills are needed not only for transmission but also reception. Keep in mind that *transmission and reception are two different processes and require different skills.* In learning a second language, for example, we often find that it is easier to receive than to transmit in our new language. Sometimes, but rarely, a student of a foreign language may acquire transmission skills more easily than reception skills.

A second area of skill development lies in the creation and construction of messages themselves. We must know what result we want from our effort to communicate an idea. Unless we clearly know what we want to accomplish, we cannot select effective content and materials for the message, nor can we properly evaluate the effectiveness of what we have said.

The *substance* of the message is central in the speech event and arises from the purpose of the communication. The *selection* and the *arrangement* of the materials and the emphasis upon them must meet the requirements of our intent and of the situation. *They must also meet the dynamic needs of our listener*. That is, we must select content that he can receive, can understand, and to which he can and, hopefully, will respond; and we must take care that arrangement and emphasis do not block his reception, understanding, and response.

Skills needed for perception and reception of messages are also important. Listening involves more than just hearing the sounds; observing involves more than just seeing what happens; and relating to the speaker involves more than just listening and observing. *The content of the message must be organized by the receiver as well as by the transmitter*.

Speech communication also requires skills in responding to ideas and to people. These skills enable us to provide adequate overt responses of physical and obvious nature. When we are skilled in responding, we can recognize the existence of covert reactions, which we can bring to the overt level or can suppress when necessary. We learn to accept the possibility of responses that are suppressed by our conditioning.

Berne's stroking behavior is actually a system of response. The response we give tends to reward or to punish the originator of the message. For example, children can and often do reward and punish their parents in the exchange of stroking behavior. A boy may respond with speechless obvious delight to a present from his father; his response is intended and probably is taken as a reward for his father for being all 'round a great guy. Another boy may respond to a present from his father with a coldly polite "Thank you very much, Father"; his response is intended and possibly is accepted as a punishment for his father's general indifference.

Communication models and patterns

You ask, "Why should I be interested in models?" We will find models more useful if we are aware that the communication process as a total event has been the subject of many studies. Models, or structural descriptions of the communication event, aid understanding of how the elements we have discussed fit into the general picture, or organization, of the total spoken event. Models may provide clues to us that will help us predict behavior of self and others and may stimulate us to further research and exploration of our own growth.

A model also provides us with a way to classify and to describe the parts of the process and to indicate how they fit together, and thus a model can contribute to an understanding of the total communicative event.

Now, you and I know that what we actually do does not exactly fit any predetermined model. There are too many dimensions to the self to include them all in any general model. The sample models discussed below range from the simplest form to one of some complexity. Consider how your behavior fits or does not fit into these models.

The simplest model consists of three elements: the sender, the receiver, and the message (see Figure 1–1). In the primary process of this model, a sender transmits a message to a receiver who sends it back. This description obviously omits much of the process, particularly the human factor. This model could be applied to a heat control system more effectively than to human behavior.

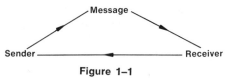

Figure 1–1

A more detailed model, which is still quite a general one, is described by Miller (see Figure 1–2).[10] Note that Miller's model incorporates several additional factors: the attitudes of both speaker and listener (which introduces human factors); the encoding skills of the speaker and the decoding skills of the listener; and feedback of both positive and negative nature. Many more aspects of the total process can be considered in examining this model.

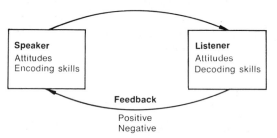

Figure 1–2

A third model of somewhat different form is based on David Berlo's concept of the major elements of the communication event: Source, Message, Channel, and Receiver (the SMCR model). Figure 1–3 represents an adaptation of the Berlo model.[11] Note that this model is *organizational,* rather than descriptive of the process. If it were process-oriented, there would be some reference to feedback.

According to Berlo's model, the source and the receiver are affected by the factors of communication skills, attitude, knowledge, the social system, and

[10] Miller, *Speech Communication,* p. 55.

[11] Adapted and reprinted from *The Process of Communication: An Introduction to Theory and Practice,* by David K. Berlo, p. 72. Copyright © 1960 by Holt, Rinehart and Winston, Inc. Adapted and reprinted by permission of Holt, Rinehart and Winston, Inc.

Source	Message	Channel	Receiver
Communication skills	Elements	Seeing	Communication skills
Attitudes	Structure	Hearing	Attitudes
Knowledge	Content	Touching	Knowledge
Social system	Treatment	Smelling	Social system
Culture	Code	Tasting	Culture

Figure 1–3

the culture. The message is developed by means of factors of elements, structure, content, treatment, and code. The channels are related to the functions of the five senses: seeing, hearing, touching, smelling, and tasting.

A more complete model developed by Miller and his associates takes into account physical behavior as well as verbal behavior in the communication situation. Figure 1–4 is an adaptation of this model.[12] Note that a number of other factors are identified more explicitly than in the other models we have noted. Miller has described his model in some detail:

It can be seen that the Source-Encoder constructs a message concerning some Referent. In order to avoid confusion, it should be pointed out that the term "Referent" is employed in a broader sense than is usual. Specifically, the Source-Encoder constructs a message that may "refer to" a wide range of objects, acts, situations, ideas, or experiences: the Referents. . . .

The total message that is encoded consists of at least three principal factors: Verbal Stimuli, Physical Stimuli, and Vocal Stimuli. Although these are

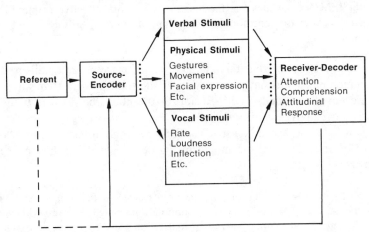

Figure 1–4

[12] Miller, *Speech Communication,* p. 73.

linked with the Source-Encoder by three separate arrows, the joining of these arrows with dotted lines indicates that all three dimensions of the message are encoded simultaneously, and that the message functions as a unit.

The message is transmitted to a Receiver-Decoder, who responds in some way to its verbal, physical, and vocal elements. As indicated, the first motive of the Source-Encoder is to gain the Receiver's attention. Once his attention is focused on the message, the Receiver-Decoder supplies a set of meanings for it, and certain nonevaluative (Comprehension) and evaluative (Attitudinal) responses occur. The extent to which these responses are consistent with the Source Encoder's purpose is dependent upon the total meaning resulting from the particular combination of the three types of stimuli. The arrows extending from the Receiver-Decoder to the Source-Encoder and to the Referent indicate that the Receiver-Decoder may respond jointly to at least two categories of stimuli: those linked with the Referent itself (primarily the Verbal Stimuli) and those associated with the individual who is encoding statements about the Referent (primarily the Physical and Vocal Stimuli). Obviously, the Receiver-Decoder's responses to both Source-Encoder and Referent will interact to determine the meaning he assigns to the situation. Whereas it would be psychologically difficult to respond to the Referent without also responding to the Source-Encoder, the converse does not necessarily hold; i.e., the Receiver-Decoder might focus his entire attention on the Physical and Vocal Stimuli encoded by the Source and largely ignore the Verbal Stimuli relating to the Referent.

The most obvious potential problem faced by the Source-Encoder consists of potential disparities in the meanings assigned by the Receiver-Decoder to the three sets of message factors. . . . In short, effective communication depends upon the harmonious blending of Verbal, Physical and Vocal Stimuli.[13]

We can readily see that this model contains many more details and provides a much more adequate description of the total process than any of the others we have examined. The inclusion of the nonverbal factors within the system is particularly significant.

One of the earliest models, devised by Wendell Johnson, consists of a sequence of activities as diagrammed in Figure 1–5, which Johnson explains as follows:

Stage 1, event, or source of stimulation, external to the sensory end organs of the speaker; Stage 2, sensory stimulation; Stage 3, pre-verbal neurophysiological state; Stage 4, transformation of pre-verbal state into symbolic forms; Stage 5, verbal formulations in "final draft" for overt expression;

[13] Miller, *Speech Communication,* pp. 72–74.

Stage 1′, transformation of verbal formulations into (a) air waves and (b) light waves, which serve as sources of stimulation for the listener (who may be either the speaker himself or another person); Stages 2′ through 1″ correspond, in the listener, to Stages 2 through 1′. The arrowed loops represent the functional interrelationships of the stages in the process as a whole.[14]

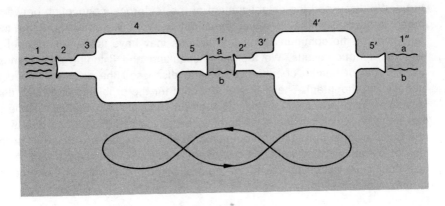

Figure 1–5

All the models have certain common elements. *They involve at least two individuals and the creation of messages into the form of physical stimuli that affect the behavior of the individuals.*

When we get to a more thorough discussion of meaning and the processes of the development of messages that stimulate meanings to occur, we will find some significant problems in relation to these models. The availability of people to each other, their common referents, their abilities to use the sensory systems, the character of meaning, the nature of a message and information, and the like are all involved in the process of building descriptive models. These elements are prerequisite to an understanding of the speech interaction event itself.

As we attempt to control and to increase the effectiveness of our speech-communication events, we discover that it is not enough merely to condition or to refine our skills of creating sound and visible stimuli. We must understand and become sensitive to *all* the factors that are operative in the event. Then we can examine the processes that are a part of the total event in order to find the fundamental problems that may be affecting our individual speech-communication effort.

[14] Wendell Johnson, "The Spoken Word and the Great Unsaid," *Quarterly Journal of Speech,* Vol. 32 (December 1951), p. 421.

Summary

We started this chapter with the idea that the reciprocal bond of the communicative relationship between persons is the base on which society is structured. We discussed the establishment of the reciprocal connection between persons that is essential to any communication event. We pointed out that the outcomes of the communication interactions may have utilitarian, aesthetic, and therapeutic results. We identified speaking and listening as the most used forms of human communication and discussed the origins of speech behavior in the infant. These origins account for the problems of growth and development of new speech skills throughout one's life. We identified some of the areas in which particular skills must be developed in order to deal with the basic elements of speech communication. We discussed the larger process of communication in terms of several models. In the next chapter, we will deal more specifically with the central binding elements of the speech-communication event.

For special reading

Keith Brooks, ed., *The Communicative Arts and Sciences of Speech* (Columbus, Ohio: Charles T. Merrill, 1967). The academic areas of speech are surveyed in this collection. The editor challenges you to note that the fundamental processes and principles of communication are applicable to each of the areas discussed. You will find here a provocative selection of articles that provide interesting support for interpersonal speech-communication principles.

Floyd W. Matson, and Ashley Montague, eds., *The Human Dialogue: Perspective on Communication* (New York: Free Press, 1967). The editors have collected an exciting array of essays from some of the most important contemporary writers on communication of our time. They seek to draw attention to what they call the third revolution in the study of communication. The emphasis reflects the growing interest in communication as a human activity rather than as engineering-scientific technology of the means and media. The wide interdisciplinary attention to the communication dialog makes this book highly useful as a source of added perspective on interpersonal speech-communication.

Ronald F. Reid, ed., *An Introduction to the Field of Speech* (Chicago: Scott, Foresman, 1965). This important series of essays, which demonstrate common and special elements of all areas of speech communication, should be useful for relating the various specialties to the core speech-communication concepts.

Try this

1   Keep a *speech-communication journal* in which you record your experiences and perceptions of the speech-communication activities involving yourself and your classmates. Take note of the development of rapport and bonds between you and your classmates that allow you to communicate with each other better. Watch for the nature of your interactions, for their purposes, and for their results. Try keeping track of your own and your classmates' growth and development toward more effective speech communication. If you keep your journal confidential, sharing its contents only with the instructor of your class, you can be absolutely frank and honest about your observations and feelings.

Make an entry for each class period with the following sections for each entry:

1. *Descriptive account* of the speech-communication behavior of others in the class.

2. *Descriptive account* of your own *perception of* and *reaction to* your classmates in relation to their communication efforts.

3. *Introspective account* of your own *feeling* about your own speech-communication efforts, problems, and results.

4. *Judgments* about the effectiveness of your class experience in assisting you to develop (a) insight into speech-communication situations; (b) insight into your own problems of speech communication; (c) understanding of the theory discussed in this book in relation to your actual experience; and (d) desire to improve and develop more effective speech communication.

You may wish to provide an introduction to your journal in which you include some information about *each* person in the class, including yourself.

2   Prepare an analysis of your communication activities during one school day from 8:00 a.m. until bedtime. First, write down an estimate of how much time you spend on each of the four communication behaviors. Then, keep a record for one day. Set up your work sheet on 15-minute intervals, with six columns:

	Speaking	Listening	Writing	Reading	Other	Remarks
8:00 a.m.						
8:15						
8:30						
8:45						
etc.						

Remember that "speaking" includes talking to yourself as well as to others. Conversations involve both speaking and listening. Use the "Remarks" column to note any particulars about communication activities of a given period.

Total the time spent for each activity. What percentage of your time was spent on each? How do your results compare with your previous estimates? How do your percentages compare with those shown on page 10?

3 Try constructing a model of communication using a binary system; that is, for each step in the process provide two alternative behaviors. Show the process (or breakdown or blockage) of communication for each possible choice of alternative. Thus, when you finish, you should have a model that could be programmed for a computer.

4 Talk with several persons about the relative time they spend in speech communication in their work activities. Try to select respondents representing a variety of work activities: for example, a social worker, a cab driver, a policeman, a school teacher, a barber or a beauty operator, a dentist, a salesman, a garage mechanic.

Prepare for these informal interviews by deciding what you want to find out and how you will tell your respondents what you are doing and what you mean by "speech-communication" (e.g., "I am conducting a survey on how much time people spend talking and listening in their work"). Then, block out the few specific questions you will ask each respondent, for example: (1) What kind of work do you do? (2) Do you deal with people in your work? (3) Does your work involve talking to people? Listening to them? Do you spend more time listening or talking? (4) In dealing with people on the job, is there anything in particular that you have to listen to especially closely? (5) Did you have any special training in what you should say in talking to people on the job? (6) During a working day, about how much time do you spend talking to people? Listening to people?

Set up your interview sheets so that you can make notes of answers (or use a tape recorder).

Analyze the answers. Which of your respondents spends the most time talking? listening? Think about the kinds of work done by your respondents. Do you think that special training in speaking and in listening would be helpful in any of these types of work? Why?

5 Try building a visual model of your own communication behavior. Make it in the form of a mobile or a "Rube Goldberg" machine or in some other visible and tangible physical form that will help others understand you. Bring the model to a meeting of your group and share it, giving whatever explanation you want.

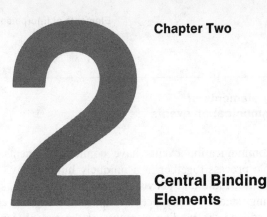

Chapter Two

Central Binding Elements

Objectives

After studying this chapter, you should be better able to do these things:

- Increase your own sensitivity as crucial to your speech communication.

- See that your world as you perceive it determines, to a large extent, the way you are.

- Be willing to become more emotionally involved with others as a way of coping with them through speech communication.

- Be able to separate what you *see* from what you *feel about what you see.*

- Build messages created from your own needs and your perception of others' needs.

- Consciously apply the central binding elements of speech in such forms of speech communication as small groups, public speaking, reading aloud, theatre, radio and television, and cinema.

Watch preschool children play alone and with each other. Their rivalries, affections, anxieties, hurts, and crises come through with astounding clarity. Small children communicate more openly and more directly with each other than do their elders—that is, until their elders condition them away from this behavior. Their verbal and nonverbal behavior reveals a particular awareness of themselves and of each other; they size up situations and begin to cope with what they find; they establish contacts with each other, and the bond of understanding is immediately connected. Their desire to communicate with each other is obvious; their recognition of the other's perception is realistic, and they translate their feelings into the speech communication that brings them together. All the binding elements of speech communication are at work in these early years.

The binding elements of
speech-communication events

All speech-communication events have common elements. These elements bind the whole process together in a uniquely human way. Wherever we are involved—theatre, radio and television, oral interpretation, speech correction, public speaking, small-group processes, speech education, and all allied performance areas—all the binding elements of the speech-communication processes are at work. Thus theatre in all its aspects is as directly concerned with the elements as any other area. The same is true of speech correction and any other specialization of the speech-communication process.

So, let's have a look at the key elements so necessary to all speech communication.

One: "S'engager": Coping with ourselves and other people through engagement

A bond between persons is necessary for a communication and *that bond must be activated before and during the interaction.* Two telephones may be connected by the necessary cables but will remain ineffective without power and without persons to use the connection. Similarly, the existence of a communication bond does not complete the elements necessary for interpersonal speech communication. To deal with each other, *the participants must arrive at a confrontation* and must produce a surge of energy between them.

Thus to confront and to activate is perhaps best expressed by the French verb *"s'engager,"* which can be translated in several meanings: "to engage oneself, to promise, to take upon oneself; to enlist; to entangle oneself, to get involved." To say "Je m'engage!" means more than our English "I am engaged" or "I am involved" or "I am committed"—the French expression incorporates all these and even more. We shall use here the participle, *"engagé,"* to mean "engaged/involved/committed/and then some." The word *"engagement"* will be used here in a sense derived from *"s'engager." S'engager* is to flip the switch that turns us on and activates transmission of our messages.

We are *engagé* in varying ways and with varying intensity or energy input and output. For instance, we can be *engagé* as actively with our enemies as with our friends or with ourselves. With friends, enemies, and ourselves, we have some degree of commitment; that is, we are expected to behave in certain ways. Our friends expect us to provide them some satisfactions for their needs; our enemies expect us to move against them or to behave contrary to their goals; our selves will expect us to move toward consistency with our self-perception.

For effective speech communication, *engagement* requires commitment, interaction, and energy. First, we must have a realistic *commitment*. It must have some intensity or strength; it must be meaningful or significant for all who are party to the communication; and it must establish the character of the support given by each to the other in the interaction. We may be committed to support each other or to oppose each other or to variations of support and opposition. Second, we must be *interacting* with each other. There must be both give and take. If we just talk, without listening for response and without adjusting to response, we are not *engagé*. If we are not *engagé* with what our body is saying to us, for example, we can do great physical harm to ourselves. Third, we must exert effort, we must throw energy into the encounter. If we are placid, unresponsive, uninvolved, and nongiving, we are not, we cannot be, *engagé*. I cannot deal with myself unless I actively seek *engagement* with me.

Each of us develops a unique and complex network, or system, of *engagements* on which we come to depend. In each of our worlds, we acquire many potential communication events in which we can become *engagé*. Our selves and our families represent the first array of *engagements*. As our contacts outside our family multiply, so do our potential *engagements*. Naturally, some *engagements* are more intense and have greater degrees and different kinds of commitment than others. In some marriages, for instance, there is intense *engagement* between the partners, with accompanying high degrees of mutually supporting intercommitments and interactions. Such marriages rarely end in failure or dissolution. In other marriages, where the nature of the mutual commitment is not very supportive, the *engagement* is different. Partners with mutually contradictory commitments are likely to be in constant and intense struggle with each other; the *engagement* is strong, but it is one of conflict rather than cooperation (see Chapter 11 on conflict). Still other marriages have very weak or limited *engagements*. Commitments of any kind between the partners are limited and rare. Little energy is directed from either toward the other. The communication is restricted and does not offer either partner a way to the other. Breakdowns are frequent in marriages characterized by conflict *engagement* or by weak *engagement*. And so with other significant relationships of our lives: Those of intense *engagement,* with intercommitment and interaction, endure—others do not.

Engagement is prerequisite to coping with others (adjusting and relating to others to maximize need satisfactions) through speech communication. Coping with others is the essence of social interaction. Our ability to cope with others can develop only as we interact with each other in *our here and now*. We do not and cannot communicate or cope readily with others or ourselves unless we relate through vital and dynamic confrontation.

Effective speech communication depends on our willingness to be *engagé* and on our effectiveness in fostering conditions that permit others to be *engagé.* We cope effectively with others, not by acting *upon* them, not by reacting *to* them, but by interacting *with* them—dynamically, with involvement and commitment; we must be *engagé.* Obviously, the most effective communication occurs under conditions of greatest desire and opportunity for *engagement.* Without *engagement,* it is truly impossible to communicate with and to cope with ourselves or those around us.

Two: Self-awareness

Of all our problems of today, knowing ourselves is probably one of the most serious. Too many of us are afraid to take a close look at ourselves. We are afraid to confront the various selves hiding behind all our various masks.[1]

In speech-communication processes, we are not being selfish or self-centered when we are sensitive to self. *The effective perception of one's self is essential for developing skill in any speech-communicative act.* No speech communication occurs without involvement of self. Without understanding of self, we cannot effectively control our communicative acts; and our objective here is to learn to control our communication so that it will accomplish our purposes.

Ask yourself: "Who am I? What am I? What do my actions say to others? What are my goals and intentions? How am I related to *this* situation? What is my function as I read this book? As I work in this class, what is my perception of and relationship to the others in this situation?" Probe into yourself with questions like these, which will help in your search for your self. We will deal at greater length with the self in Chapter 3.

Effective self-perception and meaningful sensitivity to self involve a keen sensitivity to and an acute awareness of others. Too many of us speak too often and say too much from within the boundaries of our own little limited worlds. While no one of us can truly escape his own world (or get outside his own skin), each of us can extend his contacts beyond the world of self sufficiently that he can perceive at least a small part of the world of others. This "reaching out" is the essence of humaneness.

Each of us, by nature, is essentially a highly selfish, or self-polarized, being. Whatever any one of us does is basically and essentially selfish—that is, related to the self as each of us sees it. Nevertheless, man's growth and development, perhaps his survival, require the ability (now almost totally ignored) to perceive other people as well as self. The will to perceive must be preceded by an intense desire to know and to understand people. *The desire and the ability to perceive other people as well as self are essential to effective communicative behavior.*

[1] See Kenneth J. Gergen, "The Healthy, Happy Human Being Wears Many Masks," *Psychology Today,* May 1972, p. 31ff.

Three: Sensitivity to other people

I may communicate with myself but through intrapersonal communication most of my communication efforts are directed toward other people. *A sensitivity to other people* is prerequisite to most of our speech-communicative efforts.

Henry Clay Smith defines sensitivity as "the ability to predict what an individual will feel, say, and do about you, himself, and others."[2] This definition indicates what sensitivity enables us to do, but it provides no insight into the *process* that allows us to predict behavior. Throughout this book, we will deal with the details of that process and with the development of a sensitivity to others. (The development of a *sensitivity to self* is basic to this process.)

The person who is sensitive to others is able to perceive much information about other persons. His perception involves a number of psychological elements—attitude, perceptual acuity, readiness, range of ability to experience several stimuli—but none of these elements can be effective if a person lacks the *desire* to perceive others and to gather information about them. For instance, it is unlikely that I can perceive you and your behavior if I am never with you or if I make no effort to watch you in action or refuse to communicate with you in any way. *We must be willing to become involved in the interaction with others.* Our sensitivity to others is related to this interaction. This means that if I would perceive you, I must *initiate* some interaction with you.

A sensitive person makes an effort to observe those persons with whom he wishes to interact, and he keeps his effort as unobtrusive as possible. He avoids, as far as possible, contaminating the other person's behavior primarily by his own presence and behavior. For example, to understand children's behavior, one must spend time with children as they pursue their routine activities. But an adult observer must "be with" the children in such a way that his presence does not cause them to act in a way that is significantly different from the way they act when he is not present. Naturally, there will be some contamination from the presence of an adult with children; but if the adult can maintain a position that is relatively nonintrusive, his information will be at least relatively uncontaminated.

Sensitivity requires an ability to judge, as accurately as possible, the significance of what we perceive. Too many of us evaluate the behavior of other people within a very limited range—as "good" or "bad," or as "proper" or "improper." I know a teacher who has never given an A in his course because, he says, no student can possibly meet the standards of excellence that he rates as A quality. When a student does meet these standards, the teacher then feels that he has not made his standards sufficiently high. He also rarely

[2] Henry Clay Smith, *Sensitivity to People* (New York: McGraw-Hill Book Co., 1966), p. 3.

gives an F grade, because, he says, it is utterly impossible for a student not to get something out of his course. He has left himself with a relatively limited range of grading possibilities. From the traditional range of five grades, A to F, he has subtracted the extremes, thus limiting the grading range to three. If this restricted range represents his actual ability to judge, he has contracted the area of his sensitivity. (This is in no way an argument in favor of a wide grade range or a narrow one. It is an observation about the ability of people to make distinctions.)

A sensitive person has *a wide range of possible evaluative positions from which he can respond to any one person.* The more he reduces the range of evaluative possibilities in any situation, the more limited his sensitivity in that situation becomes. If a person judges everyone as either "good" or "bad," we can assume that his sensitivity is limited.

In accurately evaluating what we perceive, *we must also understand the other person's set of values.* A car salesman must have considerable understanding of the values of his customer if he is to make a successful sale. If the salesman assumes that the customer places great value on size, model, and year, when, actually, the customer places greater value on durability and efficiency, the salesman is likely to fail in his sales effort.

Sensitivity involves the maximum use of our faculties of perception. Blind persons usually develop above-average tactile and auditory acuity. Many blind persons can, in fact, hear much that is not perceived by a normal person. One who has lost the faculty of sight must depend on his other four senses to give him information about the world around him. He uses his faculties of touch, hearing, taste, and smell much more and much more effectively than most of us who depend largely on our eyes. He pays much closer attention to the information he receives through his remaining senses. He not only receives sense impressions but also perceives them. We do not need to be blinded to learn to use our faculties of perception more effectively.

Our capacity to perceive is much greater than our use of it. The sensitivity and the awareness characteristic of childhood are locked up by the tensions and taboos imposed on the adult by our contemporary culture. Instead of expanding our capacity for sensory awareness, most of us begin to shrivel up as we leave childhood.

At the Esalen Institute in Big Sur, California, Bernard Gunther and others have explored many activities and programs that enable persons to experience greater sensory feeling and awareness of self and of others. One of the stated purposes of his "Experiments on Being Alive" is "to enhance direct sensory-reality in the here and now."[3]

The Esalen program provides numerous experiences whereby individuals,

[3] Bernard Gunther, *Sense Relaxation: Below Your Mind* (New York: Collier Books, 1968), p. 22.

by using and heeding their physical senses, may dimensionally increase their awareness of themselves, of another, of others, and of groups. The program is intended to demonstrate the total interconnection of mind and body. The Esalen program and others like it are experimental but are affecting many people. However, the significance of this type of experience to increasing sensitivity for speech communication is obvious. Constantin Stanislavski tried to teach his actors in the Moscow Art Theatre the essentials of mind-body sensory awareness. Others have approached the problem in various ways, yet too many of us are still locked up by our own insensitivity to ourselves as well as to others.

Each of our senses has a potential for revealing much more than we allow. The sensitive person increases the total use of *all* his senses in perceiving himself and other people. He *uses* his eyes, nose, tastebuds, and sense of touch. As a practical matter in developing sensitivity, all of us would do well to experiment with our several perceptual capacities in order to discover how much they can help us in the process of gathering information.

The sensitive person is able to relate what he has felt, smelled, heard, seen, and tasted to his own goals and purposes. He is always making judgments on the basis of his perceptions. *All of us relate to others with some intent.* We may not be able to identify this intent, but it does exist and it causes us to seek relationships with others or to continue relationships with others.

Bias and prejudice create screens to our perception that obliterate those things that do not fit our preconceived notions. *Sensitivity requires an ability to recognize our own biases and values and to account for these when we judge what we observe.* No one is fully aware of all his own biases and prejudices; many of us are not aware that we have any. We need the help of others in the tremendously difficult job of discovering our areas of bias. Once we are able to identify, at least in part, our own bias and prejudice, we can be much more sensitive to other people and can perceive them more accurately.

Parents tend to be biased, both positively and negatively, about their children. Mother's bias may cause her to see Junior as an academic genius, while his unbiased teachers grade him as an average student. Father's bias prevents him from realizing that, at eighteen, Junior is no longer a child and is sufficiently responsible to drive the family car. Bias is conditioned by the time and the place. If parents can recognize their bias relative to their offspring, can take it into account, and can therefore deal with it, their perception and judgment of all children, including their own, may be more accurate.

"Sensitivity" is often considered synonymous with the term "empathy"; however, I consider empathy an essential *part* of sensitivity to others but not the whole of that sensitivity. To be sensitive to others, one must be able to empathize with them; that is, *we must be able to perceive another person's feelings, thoughts, and behavior as if they were our own.*

Very few of us have *never* experienced empathy. How many times have you said, "Gee, I know just how he feels"? You may have seen someone smash his thumb with a hammer or heard that a friend has passed a test he had expected to fail or learned that someone's dog has been hit by a car. We empathize with characters in books, plays, movies, and television programs. Sitting in the football stand when two players clash head-on on the field, I can almost feel the shock down my own spine. There is value in such empathic responses; they help us to understand ourselves.

Four: Coping with the self

We have mentioned the necessity of perceiving the self and others in any given situation. But perception of self is not enough; we must also learn how to deal with what we find out about ourselves. Coping with self is a process that never ends. Time, space, and circumstances cause us to respond differently, because our accumulating experiences make all of us constantly changing people.

We must learn to deal with change, to encourage change, and to use it constructively. Those who are capable of productive change are probably the more effective people in our society. They are the ones who are always "becoming more of themselves."

Humor is an effective means of coping with self. If we can laugh at our own behavior and our own feelings when these are contradictory or inconsistent, we are perceiving ourselves and are using an effective tool for coping with our perceptions.

If we can realize, to some degree at least, our own rigidities and biases and can attempt to overcome or to account for them, we are coping with realities of self.

Trying to become more open in relationships with others adds another big dimension to self-coping. In becoming more open, we avoid blotting out thoughts, feelings, perceptions, memories, and the like, that are unpleasant at a given moment in the self-world. Instead, we examine these matters openly and frankly—being honest with self and with others.

Accepting the self we find we are is a very important part of coping. This is not to say that we necessarily like what we are or do not want to change. It *is* to say that to cope with self we must *start* by accepting who we are and go from there. In accepting self, we are willing to recognize that we do not always act consistently and that changing circumstances find us changing too.

Accepting other people becomes easier when we can accept ourselves. I know a young man who could not live with his parents' choice of vocation for him. Up to a point, he had passively accepted their determination that he would go into the family business. After a period of active and stormy resistance, he began to isolate himself from all those who loved him and began a series of associations that were superficial, casual, and (to him) apparently nonthreatening. His parents, his girlfriend, his sister, and others were deeply hurt by his behavior. *He actively rejected them by closing off all forms of communication with them.* He would not listen to what they said or read what they wrote to him. He initiated no spoken interactions with any of those who loved him most. When others initiated discussion with him, he kept the conversation completely away from any personal reference and talked only about abstract subjects like philosophy.

My young friend progressively rejected more and more people. During this period I was able to talk with him—briefly and inconclusively. It became apparent to me that at the heart of the matter was his *violent rejection of himself.* Through someone's crude brutality, he had come to believe that he was a cruel, self-serving, dangerous type of man who would lure people (like his parents and his girlfriend) into doing things for him and loving him and then would destroy them. He hated this image, but he believed it. The way he allowed himself to perceive his behavior tended to confirm, in *his* mind, this negative image of himself. As a result, he became emotionally ill, split the scene to wander over several states for months, and finally ended up under special care. Not until he was able to accept himself and to find some affection for himself was he able to overcome his difficulty and return to his loved ones without destroying his own self-respect.

Thus, when we can accept the experiences of others as being valid *for them* and avoid rejecting people because they do not act, believe, experience, or feel in the same way we do, then we are coping with ourselves.

Five: Identifying and recognizing responses and perceptions

Another essential element in the communication event consists of the identification and recognition of what we see, of our responses to what others do, of others' perceptions of and feelings toward us. For effective communication to take place, we must be able to identify and recognize these responses and perceptions and to place them in proper relationship.

Inadequate identification of responses and perceptions results in faulty communication. Whether effective or not, some form of communication event occurs when there is minimal recognition and identification of responses and purpose. A communication event based on erroneous responses and erroneous perceptions can have consequences ranging from hilarious to tragic. Our task as effective speech communicators is to reduce these errors.

Every week, there are a number of television productions in which comic effects depend on erroneous responses and erroneous perceptions. Some great comedies and tragedies of the theatre are developed from faulty identification and recognition of response and perception (Romeo, finding Juliet in coma, thought that she was dead, so killed himself). In real life, there are countless examples of faulty communications events.

A teen-age boy dressed as a hippie to conform with his group. He could not identify and recognize the perceptions businessmen had of him and could not understand why he could not get a summer job.

A teacher felt that everything was going well in her classroom because it was very quiet. She saw and heard a quiet and orderly class and identified what she perceived as proof of effective discipline. Actually, half the class was asleep and the other half preoccupied with reading comic books.

A policeman arrested a man as drunk and disorderly. The policeman saw that the other was staggering, heard incoherent speech, and identified the behavior pattern as drunkenness. At the time of the arrest, the man, a diabetic, was in insulin shock, was frightened, and was trying to ask for help. In the drunk tank at the jail, he went into coma and was close to death before he received medical aid.

Six: The strong desire to communicate

The communication situation demands that the parties to it have the desire to relate to each other. This, in turn, requires that they transmit and receive information, make interpretations of messages, then respond to these messages. Without the desire to communicate there would be no working relationship between persons. The desire and the need to reach out beyond oneself constitute a basic element of the communication event. Therefore, we can increase the effectiveness of our communication events by developing and intensifying this desire.

When there is no desire to communicate by one member of a pair and a strong desire by the other, consequences can be serious. A most effective way to disengage from or to alienate another person is to refuse to receive any communication from him. Alienation can be created or intensified by refusal to allow any communication interaction of any depth or significance. Most of us have experienced that sense of alienation that comes to us when a friend or loved one says, "I hear you," but by actual behavior shows that nothing that was said was either perceived or heeded.

A mutual desire of two people to communicate with each other is necessary for the maximum interaction values to develop. Where this desire is lacking, we need strategies to develop it—or we give up the idea of effective communication.

Seven: The state of readiness to respond to needs of those involved

A communication event occurs when those who are party to it are ready to respond to the needs of the others who are involved in the interactions. "Readiness" implies more than mere casual willingness.

A person is ready to respond when he is like the runner waiting for the gun to go off at the beginning of the race, when he is waiting for the moment to begin getting involved in the relationship of communication.

"Readiness" implies a willingness to bridge the gap between people. It is represented by increases of the "social feeling" within us. That "social feeling" consists of an ability to improvise freely with other people; to see them as they are; to hear them as they are; and to feel, with them, their experiences. One of the most exciting possibilities of this social feeling occurs when two people can sit face-to-face and each one can take the role of the other and describe the other's feelings and perceptions so adequately that the other recognizes himself in the description. When this can happen, people are ready to respond to each other's needs.

Eight: The creation and the translation of a message into speech communication

The seven elements of the communicative act that we have discussed so far have had little to do with the mechanical or physical performance involved in communication. We want to emphasize that speech communication is certainly much more than the overt, physical maneuvering of voice and body.

The overt maneuvering, while important, is a minor part of the total process of communication. Without the mechanics of speech behavior, the speech-communication system cannot exist, but the mechanical aspects of speech behavior (control of the voice, of articulation, and of the body) constitute only one part of the communication event.

Some kind of message is created in your mind whenever you respond to any outside stimulus. After you have experienced a response that includes perception of other persons and an identification of what has been said or done as it relates to yourself, you have a message in your mind about your response. The message may be an emotional reaction or a thought and not organized yet in words. When you speak, you translate your thought-feeling into a system that permits you to transmit your message to others; *you encode the message itself into the total language of speech.*

The language of speech is not the language of writing. The language of speech involves the total person physically, emotionally, and socially; the language of writing does not. The ability to organize the messages and the translations that we have created, the ability to extract the substance of our feelings and put that substance into the messages we are creating, depend upon our ability to use the language of speech and on our skills in the mechanics of speech behavior.

The elements in all types of speech communication

The central binding elements of all speech-communication are found in many settings. They are found in face-to-face interpersonal action, in small-group interaction, in front of large groups or in large-group interaction, in front of the camera, in front of the microphone, in front of the radio or television set, in front of the movie camera, on stage in the theatre or in the audience or behind the scenes, and even in solitude. In every realm of human speech activity the central binding elements of speech communication occur. For too long, we have thought of the many speech-communication activities as unrelated to each other. In fact, they are all forms of the human interaction that is basic to all types of speech. Let's look at some of the more obvious relationships of the binding elements to some of the speech activities.

Small groups

The informal conditions of conversation and other small-group discussion situations involve all the basic binding elements and all the basic values and purposes of speech communication. Obviously, small-group discussions and conferences, staff meetings, small-group decision-making and problem-solving, and encounter and sensitivity groups are utilitarian processes. In them, interpersonal interaction may reach a high level of sophistication.

The therapeutic functions of small-group processes are widely utilized in psychiatry and other social service situations. The programs of Alcoholics Anonymous, Synanon, and the Gestalt Institute incorporate modifications of group-therapy principles. It is through the small-group therapeutic process that self-revelation and interpersonal interactions are perceived. In small-group therapy, a vital part of the small-group discussion conversation is centered on the process itself. This focus on the process enhances the significance of the central binding elements to the therapeutic process.

Small-group activities involving the "spontaneous" theatre, sociodrama, and even aspects of the old *commedia dell'arte* rely on group processes in the creation of the participation in art.

Public speaking

Public speaking, long considered the only legitimate area for speech training, is but one small part of speech communication. Certainly, public speaking requires all the binding elements and may have utilitarian, aesthetic, or therapeutic purposes. The effective public speaker is directly involved in interacting with the audience, which he must perceive and understand. Interaction is more difficult in a public-speaking situation than under small-group or face-to-face conditions, because the audience is more fluid and more ambiguous, less precisely defined and definable.

Reading aloud

Reading aloud can be either a performance of a public nature or an interaction of a private nature. In either situation, it involves translating or transforming written language into oral language. As nothing else can, the process of reading aloud reveals the differences between the two forms of language.

The speech reader has the *utilitarian* purpose of transforming the language of writing into the language of speech. He has an *aesthetic* purpose in the application of the standards of art through his selective emphasis of the basic or central binding elements and as he attempts to create an entertaining interaction with his audience. He has a *therapeutic* function when he stimulates his audience to become more objective in viewing and perceiving the art forms of language behavior.

Theatre

The theatre and the enactment of drama are essentially concerned with aesthetic purposes. For the player, the producer, the stage manager, and others who make their livelihood through it, the theatre performs a very utilitarian function. Much practical and instrumental communication is involved in the development and production of a theatrical performance. The director himself, as he directs the players, uses communication for a utilitarian, or functional, purpose. The composite of the total utilitarian development of the production itself and the aesthetic factors of the performance results in an aesthetic experience for the audience.

All those who know theatre realize that the moment when the curtain rises marks the end of a long chain of events that involves all forms of human speech communication. The actual performance, consistent with the aesthetic purpose, arouses emotional responses and pleasure. It may also bring a utilitarian response from the audience if it conveys special messages of political, social, or religious nature and sets in motion a chain of prepared or designed responses.

The theatre, as represented by the works of such playwrights as Henrik Ibsen, Tennessee Williams, Bertolt Brecht, and Arthur Miller, carries particular social messages, which, as some have pointed out, also have political consequences and political overtones. In the period before the American Civil War, the old play *Uncle Tom's Cabin,* adapted from the novel by Harriet Beecher Stowe, carried a powerful instrumental, or utilitarian, message.

There are also therapeutic values in the theatre. It is often used as an instrument for self-development, as an outlet for feeling, and as a testing ground for behaviors not yet learned. Its value as a vicarious experience is especially demonstrated in educational theatres, where students find themselves playing roles that help them to gain insight into themselves and to overcome some of their own problems.

The binding elements of communication are inherent in the theatre function, for in that operation the role of the self, the ability of people to perceive others, to use the information, to relate what is observed, to empathize, and to use the mechanical skills of speech behavior are all essential. These elements are constant factors backstage in the preparation of the drama, on the stage as the enactment is taking place, and in the audience as it views the enactment. These binding elements of speech are always present and are always necessary to the full communicative event. Theatre *is* communication —the costumes, the scenery, and the lights are means of creating a mood and an atmosphere wherein a communicative event may take place with the greatest impact. Indeed, the intent and purpose for any show are to intensify the impact of a particular communicative event. Whether consciously or unconsciously, the producer, the director, the player, and the technician interact as a team in developing a very special communicative experience. Those in the theatre must understand the elements of speech communication so well that as they prepare for this exciting moment of enactment to an audience, they prepare with the foreknowledge of their dependence on the central elements of the communicative act.

Radio and television

Radio and television involve special applications of the central binding elements and are extensively used for utilitarian and aesthetic purposes. The therapeutic functions of radio and television, however, are less obvious than those of the theatre. Probably the most useful functions of radio and television are utilitarian in that they provide information and serve as avenues for persuasion. Much radio and television programming serves aesthetic purposes, in that it brings pleasure, entertainment, and enjoyment. In a sense, television is a kind of theatre.

Therapeutic values of radio and television are evident when people use them to establish relationships with the world around them. For the shut-in, the television set becomes his eye to the world and provides him with some insight into the world around him that he could not otherwise perceive; this insight has certain therapeutic values. Television sets are part of the standard equipment of most hospitals and nursing homes.

The binding elements in radio and television are found in the organization, management, and production of radio and television stations and networks. We talk about the design and development of a program that is to be aired and viewed or heard. The development of sales campaigns to sell time involves an understanding of the interactions between persons that are necessary to make the communicative event persuasively significant. The preparation of scripts for radio and television has as its inherent purpose structuring of speech-communication events and thus must take into consideration all the factors, or central elements, that make up unique speech-communicative experiences.

Cinema

The motion picture applies the central binding elements selectively in order to produce instruction, pleasure, excitement, and motivation. Its aesthetic values are much the same as those of the theatre. Its utilitarian values are exploited in sales and other propaganda films, in technical training and other educational films. Its therapeutic values are realized in special applicational functions, in which the motion picture is used for education and for providing information for therapeutic purposes. As in the theatre, and in radio and television, the central thrust of the productive effort, and of all those who are involved with a given production, is directed toward the development and the enhancement of the speech-communicative event. While the choice of setting, the camera angles, the editing of the film, and the like may not be directly involved in a speech-communication event, they enhance the event as it is eventually experienced by human beings. At the time of the communication event itself, unlike radio and live television or especially the theatre, movies do not involve any form of direct interpersonal interaction, but they serve as a device for transmitting messages from human beings to human beings (but not for interaction between persons).

Summary

The central binding elements of speech that are common factors of all speech communication that may lead to effective human interaction are (1) *"s'engager:"* coping with ourselves and with other people through *engagement;* (2) self-awareness; (3) sensitivity to other people; (4) coping with the self; (5) identifying and recognizing responses and perceptions; (6) the strong desire to communicate; (7) the state of readiness to respond to needs of those involved; (8) the creation and the translation of a message into speech communication.

In this chapter we have pointed out the central purposes and the central binding elements of the speech-communication event. We have tried to relate these briefly to some types of speech communication and to show how these activities rely on the central elements. We now turn to a closer examination of our personal involvement in the speech-communication event. Our next task is to find who is really the target of our talk.

For special reading

Edmund Carpenter and Marshall McLuhan, *Explorations in Communications* (Boston: Beacon Press, 1960). This collection of essays, dealing with communication in relation to several different media, is useful to give you the feeling for the great variety of applications of communication elements in speech—as well as non-speech-communication events. The book includes some of the more controversial contemporary essays regarding the place of communication in our society.

Marshall McLuhan, *Understanding Media: The Extensions of Man* (New York: McGraw-Hill Book Co., 1964). This is undoubtedly one of the most controversial books in the communication field in our time. McLuhan, in this book, describes his concepts of "The Medium Is the Message," "Media Hot and Cold," and others. His survey of communication media includes speech-communication but does more for an understanding of the modern application of the principles of communication to the several media.

Jurgen Ruesch, *Therapeutic Communication* (New York: W. W. Norton & Co., 1961). Ruesch is one of the several psychiatrists who, in their therapeutic theory and practice, have focused on factors of speech communication. In his approach, therapy is merged with the development of effective communication. He considers disturbed communication as indicative of the distorted social and intrapersonal orientations of his patients. In this book he describes in detail his concept of the principles of communication and their application to the therapeutic situation.

Curt John Ducasse, *The Philosophy of Art* (New York: Dover Publications, 1966). Ducasse begins his work with the concept *"Art is not a quality of things—but an activity of man."* This approach to art as an active and living affair opens up a series of stimulating statements concerning beauty, communication, and expression. While the central thrust of these essays is for art criticism, it can have great value to you if you would understand the role of speech communication as an aesthetic experience.

Try this

1 The next time you go to the student health center, try to discover the views of some member of the medical staff on the problems of speech-communication that he encounters in his professional work. You might suggest to the doctor who takes care of your sore throat or headache or sprained ankle that you want to be sure that you understand the instructions he gives you. Then ask him if he ever feels that patients do not understand his instructions and how he tries to be sure that they do. Ask him if there are any special problems in getting information across to very sick patients. Do technical terms help the patient understand, or is it better not to use them? Does he rely more on examination and observation or on information given by the patient? How does he get information from the patient? Can most patients answer his questions adequately?

2 Arrange an interview with an artist (e.g., painter, sculptor, musician) to discover his views on "Art as Communication." Report the results of your interview to the class.

3 We all have biases and prejudices—we lean toward or away from aspects of our life and we prejudge pro and con. How many of your own biases and prejudices can you list?

4 Close your eyes for a period of ten minutes and listen to every sound you can perceive. List the sounds you heard. Try this in various surroundings; for example, in a cafeteria, in a city park, in your room, in a library.

5 Select a partner from the class. Standing face to face with eyes closed, touch hands. Do not talk to each other. Try to send a message to or respond to your partner through your hands.

Then describe to your partner what you *meant* by your hand communication and listen to what your partner tried to communicate to you. How close did you come to communicating with each other? Were there things your hands said to your partner that you could not later put into words?

6 Sit alone and close your eyes. With your hands and body, explore the world immediately around you. What does it *feel* like? Is it different from the experience you had as you worked within the same space with your eyes open? Why?

7 For one day, pay particular attention to what your sense of smell reveals about the world around you. List the odors you were aware of during the day.

8 While riding as a passenger in a car, bus, airplane, or other vehicle, close your eyes and concentrate on your perceptions of movement. What sensory impressions inform you about changes in speed and direction, about the vehicle itself? List your sensory perceptions.

Chapter Three

Who Is Talking to Whom?
The Many Faces of You

Objectives

After studying this chapter, you should be better able to do these things:

- Recognize the difference between your perception of yourself and the perception others have of you and its effect on your communication.

- Be able to understand and identify dimensions of yourself that you were unable to recognize before.

- Discover that the process of self-revelation, though difficult, is important to your effectiveness as a speech communicator.

- Seek a relationship with others, based on trust, that will allow you to reveal yourself, in order to communicate more effectively.

- Be able to tolerate the ambiguity of speech behavior and, despite it, to accomplish communication with others.

- Realize that you can never perceive another person exactly as he is.

For a seminar on self-confrontation, students were asked to bring to one of the sessions some physical object or objects that would represent how they saw themselves. Sam brought a little black box that contained about a dozen postage stamps of different nations. The pictures on the stamps included a stern-looking person, an athlete, a humanitarian, a military hero, laborers, and others. In Sam's box was also a stamp with a picture of a snake on it.

During the session, Sam carried his box in both hands, holding it out for classmates to select the stamps (or images) they desired. He explained that he was a man of many faces.

Around Sam's neck were two chains holding large pendants, which had a face on each side. Along the chains were smaller medals bearing different astrological characters. One chain hung in front and one hung on his back. When asked about the one in the back, Sam said, "That's the me I cannot see."

The self and self-concept

Have you ever tried to tell someone what or who you think you really are? Have you ever thought about what distinguishes you from others so that when you say, "This is me!" you understand what you mean? When you say, "This is me!" you think of yourself as more than just a physical organism. Calvin Hall and Gardner Lindzey describe the self as "the awareness of one's being and functioning. In other words, it is the self-as-object, a set of experiences that have the same referent, namely, the 'I' or the 'me.' "[1] To understand the self, we need to examine those experiences that have the "I" as the main referent.

Clues to self-understanding are provided by our interactions with our total environment, which includes everything we experience, consciously and unconsciously, of the physical, intellectual, emotional, and social world we live in. Self-understanding is the basis for the self-concept. Each of us has certain beliefs about himself. The collection of beliefs about who and what we are goes to make up our self-image or self-concept. *The self-concept is composed of those physical and social perceptions of ourselves that we have acquired through our interaction with others and that have been validated by our own experience.*

Some guidelines for our search for self can be derived from Carl Rogers' propositions about personality[2] as follows:

> Each of us is the center of his own world, and that world is available only to him. Your reality, therefore, is what you perceive, mine is what I perceive.

> How each of us responds to what he sees in his world is guided by the desire to enhance and to maintain the self that he accepts and also to permit that self to express itself to fullest capacity. Everything in us strives to attain these goals within the world as each of us sees it.

> To understand ourselves, each of us must understand his own way of looking at the world. To understand others, we must, as best we can, understand how they see the world.

> We derive our self-concepts by judging the satisfactions we get from our interactions with other people and with the material factors of our environment. Some perceptions we have of ourselves seem more satisfactory to us

[1] Calvin S. Hall and Gardner Lindzey, *Theories of Personality* (New York: John Wiley & Sons, 1957), p. 483.

[2] Adapted from Carl R. Rogers, *Client-Centered Therapy* (Boston: Houghton Mifflin Co., 1951), pp. 483ff.

than others; that is, each of us has a value system which helps to order and to characterize his interactions.

Development of our values, or standards of usefulness, results from experiences that have satisfied or have failed to satisfy our needs, as well as from the experiences of others that we relate to ourselves.

All experiences do not have the same impact upon us, because some are accepted as consistent with our values and self-concepts, while others are seen as having no relationship to self and are therefore rejected and still others are interpreted or rationalized to fit our needs and goals even though they may be inconsistent with our perceptions of ourselves.

On the whole, a person's behavior provides clues to his self-concept.

Generally, we perceive experiences that do not fit our self-concepts as personally dangerous, and we tend to build defenses against them for the self as we see it.

We can examine those experiences that do not fit our concept of self by removing or reducing the conditions of threat that may be associated with changing the self-concept. Then we can more readily revise the self-concept to fit the actual experience.

As we open up and become responsively aware of our sensory and physical experiences, we become more understanding and accepting of others.

Acceptance of actual experiences and reactions into the self-concept will probably effect changes in previously held rigid value systems—thus we become more open to changing values and to changing concepts of ourselves. In other words, we can find happiness in discovering that we are constantly changing.

Self and other

Since our self-concepts derive principally from our perceptions of our own behavior in response to experience, it is important that others' perceptions of us be brought into our experience. However, we cannot discern their full perception, nor can we readily accept very much of it when it is inconsistent with our own perception.

Knowledge of self is developed in part from the experience of learning how other people perceive us. *If we are to understand ourselves, we must get information from other people about ourselves.* Indeed, it would be helpful if others could get to our center of the world we live in and see that world as we see it. Their vision of that world might help us to understand ourselves better. Conversely, *if we are to understand others, we must get to the center of their world and see it as they do.*

Whenever two or more of us are interacting, we have numerous opportunities to discover information about each other. The way we perceive another person responding to us reveals something about him. The things another person does for and to us convey information about us. His response gives us some clues about his perception of us, about what we seem to him to be.

A department chairman discovered that the members of his department always waited until he had suggested an idea before they made any contributions to staff discussions. He perceived thereby that the staff was hesitant to initiate ideas for fear of his disapproval. This, in turn, led him to examine what his behavior said to them about him. For several months, he carefully encouraged, reassured, and supported the members of his staff; finally, some of them felt sufficiently secure to express openly how they perceived him. His desire to open up his colleagues so that they would not hold back ideas and impressions led him to hold back on his own suggestions and to find opportunities to support suggestions others made.

A teacher was shocked and disturbed when a survey of students revealed that his students felt he was talking down to them in his lectures. What he felt was a useful simplification of ideas was viewed differently by his students. Upon closer examination, however, he discovered that his students were missing the more subtle ideas because the simple ones seemed so obvious that they turned off their listening.

Through the whole process of speech communication, the interaction between self and other is vital. From this interaction as we confirm or deny some of the perceptions we have of ourselves and some of the perceptions we have of others, we can help each other toward mutual understanding. Our perceptions of others come from different levels and from different points of view.

George Kelly gives an example of how much we seem to be willing to stake our lives on our ability to predict what the driver of an oncoming car will do and how others will behave in complex traffic systems. His point is that on one level we can predict fairly accurately about another's behavior but as we go higher in the total personality of the other we must get closer to him to find out what he will do.[3]

Abraham Maslow, in his book *Toward a Psychology of Being,* states that "the best way of understanding another human being, or at least a way necessary for some purposes, is to get into his Weltanschauung and to be able to see *his* world through his eyes."[4]

[3] George A. Kelly, *The Psychology of Personal Constructs* (New York: W. W. Norton & Co., 1955), Vol. 1, *A Theory of Personality,* pp. 95–96.
[4] Abraham Maslow, *Toward a Psychology of Being* (New York: Van Nostrand Reinhold Company, 1962), p. 13.

Dimensions of the self

We may be aided in our efforts to discover ourselves and to become ourselves if we seek to understand the self within the framework of some defined areas of behavior. Let's look at some of the dimensions, or factors, that may be describable units of an individual self.

The self as idea images (the cognitive self)

We may understand ourselves in terms of our ideas and thoughts. My view of the world is unique to me and is an idea that is representative of me. In turn, my rationalizations and justifications for what I do in my world as I see it represent characteristic ideas that reveal what I am. The late Martin Luther King's policy of nonviolence represents an idea that served to identify the man. His view of the world led him to believe, as did Mahatma Gandhi, that such a method of dealing with societal injustices is highly useful and moral. Their behavior was determined by their ideas about nonviolent resistance, which were in turn consistent with their views of themselves.

Our characteristic method of decision-making and reasoning in the abstract are factors of ourselves. Our ability to deal with facts and to evaluate their usefulness are factors of the "idea" self. Our sum of knowledge applicable to our situation is another aspect of the cognitive self.

The self as feeling

What do you feel like when you are afraid? In love? Happy? Hurt? All those responses that seem to be tied into the autonomic and endocrine systems as emotion are very important aspects of our self. Feelings and affections are very important to the understanding of any person. For too long our society has discouraged us from expressing the feeling part of ourselves. The result seems to be forms of frustration and anxiety that break out in many ways. If nothing else, the encounter-group movement has helped us to recognize the great importance of permitting expression of our feelings and of recognizing them. The suppression of feelings in early childhood has caused many people much anguish and hurt. When we can recognize that our feelings are real, legitimate, inescapable, and expected, we can more easily recognize a very important part of ourselves.[5]

Psychologists generally agree that the emotions are basically important in that they help us protect ourselves. This is particularly true in the newborn child. Fear of strangeness and the unexpected helps the baby to adapt to his

[5] See Anthony L. Rose and others, "The Feel Wheel," *Psychology Today,* May 1972, p. 45ff, for an excellent game that opens us up to our feelings.

environment. Our adult emotions and the manner in which they are expressed or repressed are significant cues to our personalities.

The self as body images

Hold your hand out and look at it—do you recognize its topography? Look in the mirror—do you see something familiar? Move your arm—does the movement feel the same as it has felt before? Each of us has a particular view of himself as a physical being. We may not be entirely conscious of the movements of our bodies as we walk, yet the feeling of movement represents a unique concept of self. Most of us set the boundary of our own unique individual being at the limits of the physical self; everything external to the physical unity of the body is perceived as being other than self. One significance of this dimension is that my physical self that I see and feel is not the same physical system that you perceive in me.

Millions of dollars are spent daily to cover and modify the human body with clothing, jewelry, cosmetics, tattoos, and the like. Each person attempts to provide some representation of his physical self with the help of these "addons." Certain parts of the body are not very well perceived because they have been tabooed by a strict social control. In most educational experiences, we have been conditioned not to rely upon body experiences. Instead, we are pushed to rely more on our idea self.

Because of taboos on the body, most of us have grown up with some irrational and alien ideas about our bodies. Seymour Fisher points out that "although an individual experiences his body more often and in far greater depth than he does any other object of his environment, his perceptions of this, his dearest possession, remain distorted throughout his life."[6]

Apparently, most of us have only a vague knowledge of our bodily appearance. The image I have of my body influences the way I behave. Thus if I see my body as fragile, I will be more protective of myself in dealing with the "outside" world than if I see it as husky and strong. Also, it appears that each of us has a special set of parts of the body that receive greater attention or concern than other parts.

Ida Rolf has experimented with adjustment of the body balance and center as a way to treat psychological disturbances.[7] Those who engage in physical therapy and massage have, for many years, recognized that our body awareness is closely related to our interaction with others. As a masseur, I have realized that areas of physical tension in different people seem to be clearly hooked up to their behavior not only at the time of massage but also generally.

[6] Seymour Fisher, "Experiencing Your Body: You Are What You Feel," *Saturday Review*, July 8, 1972, p. 28.
[7] Ida P. Rolf, "Structural Integration: Gravity, An Unexplored Factor in a More Human Use of Human Beings," *Systematics*, Vol. 1, 1963, pp. 66–83.

The self as vocal images

A young man appealed to the speech clinic for help with his voice, which, he had been told, was unpleasant to others. He himself had never perceived the high-pitch stridency until he heard a tape recording of his own voice at the clinic. Coming from an external source, the sound of his voice was not associated with himself; and while he could scarcely believe it was his voice, he heard it as others did and realized why it was unpleasant. After a few lessons, he learned to drop his tone to a well-modulated baritone. For several months, he frequently slipped back into his high voice, because, perceived from inside, it was what he associated with himself. However, as he became more accustomed to speaking in the new voice pattern, he came to accept it as part of himself, and also began to use it much more than he had used his original high-pitched voice pattern.

Each voice has unique characteristics. Recent studies validate what we all know intuitively—we can identify others by the unique energy components of their voices. A person's fingerprints are unique to him, and so are his patterns of vocal energy.

A person's voice is part of his self. The tone, the inflection, the feel and sound of its production are significant dimensions of the individual when viewed either from the inside by himself or from the outside by others.

The self as movement images

Each person has a characteristic way of moving. Human movement is essentially rhythmic; and the rhythms of walking, of handling objects, of gestures, represent for each of us a unique pattern of accent and pause in action. The way we reach to lift an object, the manner in which we sit down or stand up are inherent dimensions of the self. Like all the other dimensions of self, the movements that we feel and perceive are not the movements felt and perceived by others. Each person has an individual rhythm, and each phase or aspect of his mood, emotion, or other state of being seems to be accompanied by identifiable modification of rhythmic patterns of action.

Standing on a long deserted stretch of beach one day, I watched a man come from behind a large boulder more than a mile away and walk toward me. Before he came within a half mile of me and long before I could make out his features, I knew by his walk that he was a friend whom I had not seen for years. Reason told me that my friend could not be on this beach because he was supposed to be on the other side of the world. My senses were right—it was indeed my old friend. The movements and the manner of walking could not be identified with any other person.

The self as relationship-with-others-image

Each of us has formed a pattern of relationships with other people. Each has a set of interpersonal relationships within his own family. Other sets exist in the work group, in living groups, and in social groups. In every group into which we go, we establish networks of relationships with the others in those groups. The nature of these networks and the way we view ourselves in our relationships with the people in these groups are important dimensions of the self.

In fact, how we perceive our relationships with others has heavy significance in development of the self-concept. Some of us perceive that we are liked and in turn like most of the people in our group. Others feel that they are rejected by some and accepted by others. In a family, there are many possible interpersonal combinations. How do you view yourself in relation to the others in your family? Are you the most influential? least influential? Which other member of the family are you closest to in respect to your personal feelings? Such perceptions of our family relationships provide us with very significant dimensions of self.

Our relationships with close friends and lovers are unique and personal for each of us. The self-image of a person whose interests are focused almost exclusively on one partner obviously will be quite different than if his interests are scattered among several partners. Thus a girl who is engaged has a different relationship image than one who is "playing the field."

Self₁, self₂, self₃

Our relationships with our own selves determine dimensions of self. B. F. Skinner talks about a private self and a public self. Other writers and research scholars refer to various levels of the self. Freudian adherents refer to the superego, the ego, and the id as three different levels of the personality. Each of the levels plays a different role in personality development and in behavior.

Conditions and circumstances affect the nature of the self. Thus, in your speech-communication class you may be an alert, vocal, and influential member of the class group. In your philosophy class, you may be an indifferent, silent, and confused isolate who prefers to avoid contact with others in the class. At home, among your siblings, you may be hot-tempered and quarrelsome. At school, among your peers, you may be noted for your even disposition and cooperative attitude. We must realize that we are various selves as we move from one set of conditions to another. We can infer that the nature of the self at any given instant is a composite of all factors involved in that instant of time, space, and behavior. A person who has an unchanging and rigid self-concept may have difficulty in relating to varieties of people and experiences.

The self from different directions

The self is perceived from many directions, and we should understand its dimensions from many viewpoints. You, as an individual, may be perceived by others as you actually see yourself. You may be seen by yourself as you want to be seen, which may not be as others actually see you. You may want to be accepted by others as a jovial, friendly, likable person; if so, you probably will see yourself as an extroverted friend to everyone.

You may see yourself as you think you are seen by others. Or you may try to deny the self as you think others see you. Either one of these unrealistic perceptions ignores the real needs and desires of your self, and either one, carried to extremes, is unwise.

Not infrequently, others see you, not as you are to you, but as they expect you to be to them. Parents often cannot see their children as they are but perceive them, for better or for worse, as the parents expect them to be. Conversely, it is a rare person who can perceive his parents as they really are. Remember that some others see you as they expect you to be; remember, too, that you tend to perceive others as you expect them to be.

This expectation may be created by past experiences, not with the person perceived, but with others who may have similar functions or characteristics. A student who was humiliated as a child by a teacher may expect all persons who function as teachers (including college professors) to be hostile, antagonistic, and unreasonable.

The expectation may result from preconditioning or from previous relationships with the person perceived. An off-campus little theatre group in a university town included faculty members and undergraduates. Students who enrolled in a course taught by a fellow member of the group expected him to be as easy-going and fun-loving as they had seen him at rehearsals—after the first test, they were able to see him, not as they had expected him to be, but as he really was in the classroom situation.

What others find you to be may actually be partly what they expect you to be, partly what you are, partly the way you see yourself, and many other things. However, it seems sufficiently distinct that we can identify it as one of the ways in which you are seen by others.

Shared and unshared self-perception

The part of ourselves that we and others share is the whole arena of perception where we see ourselves as others see us; we can call this the *shared perception area.*

In each of us, there is the self that no one sees—that hidden portion of our behavioral potential, that source of actual behavior that is mostly unknown even to ourselves. If we are aware of its existence and if we pay careful attention, we may sometimes glimpse evidences of this unknown self in what we do, in what we think, in what we say, in what we are; and particularly in the way others respond to us. These glimpses often reveal aspects of our selves that surprise us.

Now, which of these selves is the real self? Which "you" is really you?

They all are. The real self is many selves; the real you is many yous. The knowledge of ourselves comes from these many different directions and is never complete. We need to understand as much as we can of what we really are. *The expanding of this understanding of ourselves is vitally necessary to our effectiveness as communicators.*

Gordon Allport has emphasized that you can begin to find yourself when you recognize how you differ from others so that you are a unique person; and the knowledge that you are unique, that you are different from others in some respects, will protect you from assuming that everyone thinks and feels and reacts as you do.[8]

Allport further suggests that each of us may explore his own uniqueness in such areas as inborn dispositions, culture and environment, consciousness of self, concerns, style of expression, experience with making choices and the freedom to so do, the manner of dealing with conflict and anxiety, and the nature of values, interests, and life goals.[9]

Understanding of ourselves is highly important to our speech communication. This self-awareness must be sought consciously and realistically.

The self as a factor in communication

How I talk to myself

One of the most significant concepts about personal and interpersonal communication, in relation to our discussion of the self, is the hypothesis that no one really talks or communicates with the total other or even with the real other person. *What we actually do as we speak with and to each other is talk to ourselves.*

Unless I can transport myself completely into your world, so that I can see the entire world exactly as you see it and can respond to the things around you as you respond to them, I really cannot deal with the world exactly as you do. When I speak to you, I am talking to a hypothesis or an estimation that I have about you and about what you are. In a sense, I really am talking to my image or my hypothesis of you. My image, or hypothesis, of what you are may be far different from the reality of what you are. I may not be able to understand, as I speak to you, what you might do or think or feel, how you might react, or what would cause you to respond. Obviously, the more I know about you, the greater the probability that I will be able to talk to *you*, rather than to *my image* of you. It seems impossible I will ever know enough about anybody

[8] Gordon W. Allport, "Becoming: The Dilemma of Uniqueness," in F. W. Matson, ed., *Being, Becoming and Behavior* (New York: George Braziller, 1967), p. 164.
[9] Allport, "Becoming," p. 164.

else (or even enough about myself) to be able to talk to him with a complete understanding of his world and of his possible reactions to what I say.

When I talk to your you

There is a serious question about the degree to which I can really talk to *your* you. That is, what are the chances that I can talk to you in terms of *your* image of yourself? Let's assume that you tend to view yourself as you want to be veiwed by others and that the character of your self-perception conditions your behavior. Then certainly, the effectiveness of my communicating with you would depend on how much I know and understand about how you perceive yourself. If I am to be effective, as I speak with you, *I must attempt to talk to as near your perception of yourself as possible instead of to my perception of you.* In order to talk to your perception of you, I need to know more about that perception.

The self as a total unit

Whenever we speak of the self ("my self," "your self," "his self," "her self"), we are referring to the total human organism, which, as nearly as we can determine, operates as a unit. Thus, all factors that are at work on an individual affect the total behavior of that individual at any given moment. What you had (or did not have) for breakfast, the weather, worry over an unpaid bill may affect your performance on an examination or the way you speak to your friends.

Numerous experiments have demonstrated that worker production is affected by modifications in the total working environment. The results of these studies indicate a payoff in better production from investment in pleasant working environment. Business and industry increasingly provide well-lighted, brightly colored work areas; background music; adequate time for breaks. Psychological environment has in some instances been modified by providing opportunities for employee discussion and participation in managerial decision-making. Business and industry have thus utilized the concept that an individual's behavior, at any given moment, results from the total function of that human organism at that moment. His behavior to some degree is determined by all that has happened before and whatever is happening at that moment.

Thus, what you do on a driving test, for instance, may not be a true measure only of your skills in driving a car. Everything that has been happening to you will affect your behavior of the moment and thus will affect your performance on the test. It is impossible for you to isolate any of your skills from all the factors surrounding you at a given moment.

Alteration of a single aspect of the behavior of an individual affects all behavior of that individual. If you change your way of walking, that change will affect, to some degree, your total self, your total personality. If you improve your vocal skills and your articulation skills, you will change your way of talking, which will affect, to some degree, your total personality. *We cannot compartmentalize elements of human behavior; we cannot deal with aspects isolated from the totality of behavior of any individual.*

Bringing your you and my you together through self-disclosure

The more I know about you and the more you know about me, the more effective and efficient will be our communication attempts. Just how do I find out about you, and just how do you find out about me? If we are to influence each other's behavior through communication, I must know about your self as you perceive you and you must know about my self as I perceive me.

Note carefully what Sidney M. Jourard says about self-disclosure:

> You cannot collaborate with another person towards some common end unless you know him. How can you know him, and he you, unless you have engaged in enough mutual disclosure of self to be able to anticipate how he will react and what part he will play? . . .
>
> Self disclosure, my communication of my private world to you, in language which you clearly understand, is truly an important bit of behavior for us to learn something about. You can know me truly only if I let you, only if I *want* you to know me. Your misunderstanding of me is only partly your fault. If I want you to know me, I shall find a means of communicating myself to you. If you want me to reveal myself, just demonstrate your good will—your will to employ your power for my good and not for my destruction.[10]

Jourard and others suggest that real self-disclosure is a means of achieving healthy personality and also a symptom of a healthy personality. Jurgen Ruesch, a psychiatrist, has described various of his psychiatric patients as persons who have forms of atrophy and overspecialization in certain aspects of their communication processes. Such atrophy and overspecialization lead to disability in the processes of knowing others and of becoming known to others. Jourard notes that "neurotic and psychotic systems might be viewed as smoke screens interposed between the patient's real self and the gaze of

[10] S. M. Jourard, *The Transparent Self* (New York: Van Nostrand Reinhold Company, 1964), pp. 3, 5–6.

the onlooker. We might call these symptoms *'devices to avoid becoming known.'* "[11] (Italics added.)

As we speak, and particularly in the face-to-face situation, our total physical and emotional state of being is exposed to some degree. No matter how good we may be as actors or how effective we may be at covering up our feelings, we reveal a great deal of ourselves as we engage in the face-to-face speech-communicative event. However, we probably do not reveal enough of ourselves in speech communication to enable our co-communicators to understand us better. The complexities of the world we live in demand better communication than we have known. *To communicate better, we must understand each other better. To understand each other better, we must reveal more of ourselves through speech and speech-communication events.*

Self is revealed through speech not only in the words we speak or use but also in mannerisms, behavioral conditions, posture, facial expressions, tone of voice, substantive context of the ideas about which we speak, manner of using the language with the person to whom we are speaking, and the like. By these means, we reveal ourselves to the sensitive listener or co-communicator. The person who is sensitive to all aspects of speech communication can know more about people and can understand their communication better than is possible for a person who is not so sensitive.

What can we reveal?

At the prospect of self-disclosure or self-revelation, most of us begin to build our defenses. We immediately identify those parts of self that may be revealed and those parts that we must never let anyone see. We may begin to sort out people in terms of who is to know what about us. We will allow certain people to see certain things about us and certain other people to see other things. We just don't feel that we can permit all people to see all things about us.

These reactions are perfectly normal. Indeed, *our whole culture seems to require a kind of behavior aimed not at self-disclosure but more commonly at self-encapsulation or nondisclosure.* We are still trying to live by an ethic that forces us to subscribe, both consciously and unconsciously, to self-sufficiency behavior patterns, which are essentially nonrevealing of ourselves, which tend to hide us from each other, and which simply are not fitted to meet the demands for interdependency in our present world.

What then, if we are to turn the tide in another direction, should be the beginning of disclosure for you and me?

Look carefully at Samuel Culbert's definition of self-disclosure:

> . . . an individual's explicitly communicating to one or more others some
> personal information that he believes these others would be unlikely to

[11] Jourard, p. 25.

acquire unless he himself discloses it. Moreover, this information must be "personally private"; that is, it must be of such a nature that it is not something the individual would disclose to everyone who might inquire about it.[12]

In self-disclosure, there are a number of things we might profitably reveal to each other:

Attitudes and opinions

Tastes and interests

Work perceptions

Money perceptions

Personality choices

Physical likes and dislikes (bodily activities)

Loves and hates

Fears and anxieties

Reactions to this moment

Feelings and perceptions of each other and others

Self-perceptions

Read that list carefully. Suppose that you and I are to meet face to face to engage in an exploratory discourse in which we would reveal ourselves to each other along those lines. The question immediately arises: "Do we have the 'guts' to do it?" And if we don't, why don't we? What inhibits this move to understanding one another?

Let's take this one step further. Can we really expect to communicate with each other with full effectiveness unless we know more about each other at least in terms of the above list?

Before we can engage in any such interaction of self-disclosure, we must be assured about certain conditions that will allow us to proceed. Jourard makes the point several times that self-disclosure can be made only in a setting of goodwill and that it sometimes takes a form of self-disclosure to stimulate goodwill in other people.[13] In other words, a little self-disclosure establishes your goodwill, which encourages the other to some self-disclosure, thus establishing his goodwill, which reassures you about further self-disclosure, and so on.

No one is likely to engage in much self-disclosure in a situation that is full of threat to him personally or to anyone with whom he is closely asso-

[12] Samuel A. Culbert, "The Interpersonal Process of Self-Disclosure: It Takes Two to See One," *Explorations in Applied Behavioral Science,* Number 3 (1967), p. 2. Washington, D. C.: NTL Institute for Applied Behavioral Science, associated with the NEA.

[13] Jourard, *The Transparent Self, passim.*

ciated. The situations in which we can most efficiently engage in speech communication are nonthreatening.

The interaction event of self-disclosure through speech is closely connected to the development of self-esteem.

When we speak we expose part of ourselves, either intentionally or unintentionally. We reveal a lot of what we are, of what we think we are, and maybe of what we hope we are. When someone responds to what we have thus exposed of ourselves, he or she may respond in an approving or disapproving, an accepting or rejecting, manner. The response then reinforces, either positively or negatively, the exposure we have made.[14]

The process of self-disclosure is not without difficulty or danger, and an atmosphere of goodwill is essential to its development.

Bennis and his colleagues point out that we are profoundly concerned when we think about the possibility of someone knowing everything about us. That concern seems to center around a fear that if someone knew all about us they could not love us, accept us, or want us. Three effects seem to develop when we begin to feel this way. (Keep in mind that—no matter what—no one is *actually* going to know *all* about you; however, we all too often begin with the *false* assumption that someone will and thus gain control over us.)

The first effect of this anxiety is a tendency to hide those parts of ourselves we feel are less than totally acceptable. This results in our relating to others only as "part persons" rather than whole persons.

The feeling that parts of us are unlovable leads us to *pretend* we are someone we are not. We put on masks, erect façades, build walls between us and others. As compared with hiding, this behavior has some advantages in that while it includes hiding it also allows us to do things or to play roles that are not like what we consider bad in ourselves. Doing this, then, makes it possible for us to expose the "bad self" as part of the role we are playing rather than a part of us. So, when we are rejected while playing a role that is not our self, we are comforted by the false belief that it is not our "real" self that is unacceptable. Take a real hard look at this in your own experience. When was the last time you did this? We all do it.

Doubts about our own worth often cause us to behave very cautiously and tentatively. We also may tend to conform to ritual in our behavior. We may thus remain aloof or only *minimally involved* in a situation with others and act with great caution and deliberateness. Or, we may simply perform the ritual tasks required of the setting, by, for example, simply saying "good morning" rather than greeting a person in the way our feelings would prompt us to greet him. The result of these self-doubts, then, is to stifle spontaneity and

[14] Warren G. Bennis, Edgar H. Schein, David E. Berlew, and Fred I. Steele, eds., *Interpersonal Dynamics: Essays and Readings on Human Interaction* (Homewood, Ill.: Dorsey Press, 1964), p. 208.

naturalness because we are unwilling to take the risk of unintentional exposure of the "worthless" parts of ourselves and are also unwilling to face the possibility that our own feelings of worthlessness will be confirmed.[15]

When we speak with each other, most of us hide behind masks or in "black bags."[16] We try to be something we know we are not. We fall back on ritual and formal procedures because we are afraid that we will be revealed as inadequate to cope with a situation if it is open and free.

The fear of exposure inhibits speech communication more directly than any other kind of behavior. Yet we must reveal ourselves if we are to communicate effectively. Our problem can be stated more simply than it can be solved: *We must discover how to remove the fear of self-revelation!*

Perhaps the most effective beginning is through an overt and conscious attempt to reveal something of yourself to someone else. *Until you make the first move, the other cannot follow.* There is no need to bare the innermost secrets of your soul to a casual acquaintance; but as you deal with people, consciously reveal yourself in terms of the list on page 53.

Those of us who can create conditions wherein mutual self-disclosure is possible will communicate effectively—others will not.

The different roles of you

We have mentioned that at any given moment, each of us responds as a total unit; and we noted earlier that we do not respond in the same way to every situation. Variations of time, place, and condition not only affect our perceptions of ourselves and others' perceptions of us but also affect the manner in which we behave in those circumstances. Indeed, the person whose behavior remains unchanged in all situations and circumstances is generally considered pathological.

Obviously, if you behaved at a protocol dinner as you do at a football game, your behavior would be unacceptable to your fellow diners. If you dealt with your professional colleagues and with your young children with no modifications of your behavior, you would encounter considerable difficulty, particularly with your colleagues.

Each of us plays many roles as he goes about his business of living from day to day; and the wider the repertoire of honest roles a person has, the more effective he will be as a communicator. It should be quite obvious (although it often is not) that the role played within the family is somewhat different from the roles played at work or school. Behavior at work or school is somewhat different from behavior exhibited in a recreational setting or in a social setting. Activities with peers are usually different from activities with

---

[15] Bennis and others, pp. 211–212.
[16] See Appendix, "The Black Bag," pp. 270–274.

superiors or subordinates. Behavior under conditions of threat differs from that in situations in which there is support. Behavior in response to love is different from behavior in response to animosity or hate.

Each of us appears as many different images to the various people he encounters. Generally, we more or less successfully adjust our role-playing to these images. The person who cannot accept the necessity to play many roles and who tries to maintain a constant image or role runs into difficulty. The same role cannot be used in all situations because the images are different. The same facet of self, or image, cannot be shown to all people; some persons simply do not see the same image that others see. Attempts to sustain a singular role may lead to stereotyped behavior and very limited effectiveness.

In short, we might say that the effective self is a multivalent personality, which has been discussed by Alfred M. Lee.[17] The effective self honestly changes behavior to meet changing conditions, and it changes intent to meet the various situations.

Abraham Maslow describes healthy persons as differing from non-healthy persons in terms of thirteen clinically observed characteristics:

1. Superior perception of reality
2. Increased acceptance of self, of others, and of nature
3. Increased spontaneity
4. Increase in problem-centering
5. Increased detachment and desire for privacy
6. Increased autonomy, and resistance to enculturation
7. Greater freshness of appreciation, and richness of emotional reaction
8. Higher frequency of peak experiences
9. Increased identification with the human species
10. Changed (the clinician would say, improved) interpersonal relations
11. More democratic character structure
12. Greatly increased creativeness
13. Certain changes in the value system[18]

A person who has a healthy personality can function easily and without stress in the many roles he must play. He can be flexible in behavior, and this flexible behavior is highly important as a process of effective communication.

[17] Alfred M. Lee, *Multivalent Man* (New York: George Braziller, 1966).
[18] Maslow, *Toward a Psychology of Being*, pp. 23–24.

Often, we act and react in terms of our perceptions of the roles or behaviors that we *anticipate* will be expected of us. Our perceptions of our own behavior differ from others' perceptions of that same behavior, depending on the time, the place, and the circumstances. We must confront and adjust to this fact as we work with other people.

Communication effectiveness is greatly enhanced by the ability to adjust rapidly to different perceptions and images that we have of others and that others have of us. Effective speech communication requires that we relate to others, and relating to others requires that we understand their perceptions of our images and that we are aware of the possible roles that they can perform and the images that they can create. Any interaction by speech communication, if it is effective, should be consistent with the image conditions, the role expectations, the requirements of the particular setting and of the particular circumstances under which it is taking place. If we do not take these factors into account, regardless of the setting of the speech-communicative event, the chances of success are limited.

In many situations, we project multiple images; and, if we cope successfully in such situations, we play multiple roles. Unless we accept the possibility of multiple roles, we cannot communicate consistently.

A person who cannot cope with the reality of multiple roles and multiple role expectations, experiences anxiety over the problem of which self is really *the self* (as we have noted before, they all are). A person who cannot face this reality often attempts to rationalize in order to hold to one role or to one set of behaviors. If he does not realistically recognize the variety of roles, a dissonance or a struggle is set up between the possible images or roles he actually plays and what he thinks he should do. Unless resolved, this struggle results in communication breakdowns and sometimes even in a personal breakdown. Leon Festinger discusses this struggle as "cognitive dissonance," wherein one set of behaviors is contrary to a set of values. Some adjustment, according to his theory, must be made before the person can behave effectively under these conditions.[19]

Toleration of ambiguity

Human behavior is seldom, if ever, precise or completely predictable. At any instant, any behavior of any human being has many dimensions; it is dynamic, constantly changing. Each of us plays various roles. Each of us constantly operates under conditions in which we know too little about ourselves and too little about those with whom we are trying to communicate. Once we

[19] Leon Festinger, *A Theory of Cognitive Dissonance* (New York: Harper & Row, 1957).

have realized and accepted these facts, we are better able to accept the necessity for toleration of the ambiguity of speech behavior.

Those of us who have been brought up in a culture in which everything was built around the struggle for order and precision (and indeed order was imposed upon us whether it really existed or not) find it exceedingly difficult to tolerate not knowing or not being able to place in clear categories the information that we do have—ambiguity upsets us. But of all the communication systems, speech communication is probably the most ambiguous. In the speech-communication event, we cast out signals and messages toward other people in the hope that something will be received and interpreted. We hope— but we know, or should know, that many of the responses we expect or desire never actually take place.

As a result, we must be realistic enough to accept the fact that we will never really perceive another person because we never can get completely inside the skin of another or inside his world. We must face up to this ambiguity, yet we must keep seeking to understand what is inside the other as well as what is inside us. We must continue our attempts to communicate under any set of circumstances as well as we can, trying always to recognize the kinds of persons to whom we are talking and the kinds of persons who are talking to us. Our adjustments to our co-communicators depend in part on a process called *feedback* (see Chapter 5).

Suppose I should ask you the question: How can I live with my perception of you to your satisfaction? Before you could answer this question, you would need to know the nature of my perception of you. Until you know my perception of you, you don't know whether you can be satisfied with it. If our relationship makes any difference to either of us, we must understand each other's perceptions and, where necessary, must correct them so that we can live with them. Neither of us can live actively and effectively with the perceptions of the other *to the satisfaction of the other* without knowing what those perceptions are.

Summary

Each of us has many different "faces." They are altered by the differences in people with whom we speak; by variations in the time, the place, and the circumstances; and by the purposes of the interactions. Understanding of speech communication depends on realization that these faces are parts of the self. Effective speech communication requires an understanding of others and their perceptions of themselves. We talk to our images of others; and if those images are not consistent with the images they have of themselves, we cannot communicate effectively. New and useful roles can be learned in order to adjust to the images others have of us.

You cannot form any significant or realistic image of me unless I am willing to reveal myself to you. Speech communication is a means of achieving valid images of each other through self-revelation and feedback.

No matter how we view the world or how the world views us, speech communication begins within the self and its relationship to another. Skill in speech communication must be closely associated with a useful and realistic perception of the self as it reaches out to touch another.

For special reading

Sidney M. Jourard, *The Transparent Self* (New York: Van Nostrand Reinhold Co., 1964). Self-disclosure as the basis of our interactions with other people is the theme of this book. The author follows up in some detail our comments in this chapter about revealing ourselves as means of achieving more effective communication. Particularly useful is the questionnaire that starts on page 161. This instrument will help you to develop a rough estimate of your own degree of openness. Try it!

Magdalen D. Vernon, *The Psychology of Perception* (Baltimore: Penguin Books, 1962). Your exploration of your world and the world of the other depends upon some understanding of your ability to perceive. Ms. Vernon has summarized here some of the more pertinent psychological theories on perception.

R. D. Laing, *The Politics of Experience* (New York: Random House, 1967). An English psychoanalyst tells about some of the ways in which we violate ourselves and the consequences of doing so. This book can help you to understand the concepts of your you and my me.

Renato Tagiuri and Luigi Petrullo, *Person Perception and Interpersonal Behavior* (Stanford, Calif.: Stanford University Press, 1958). This is a collection of writings by some of the outstanding psychologists of our time on the problem of figuring out "what another person does, feels, wants, and is about to do." For those who are interested in the more technical literature on the subject, this collection of papers is rich with ideas.

Don E. Hamachek, *Encounters with The Self* (New York: Holt, Rinehart and Winston, 1971). Well written and very useful, this book will supplement and expand on what has been said in this chapter. Such matters as self-understanding, defensive behavior, perception, consistency, and concepts of a healthy self-image are developed clearly and with excellent illustration from Schultz's *Peanuts* cartoons.

Bernice Marshall, ed., *Experiences in Being* (Monterey, Calif.: Brooks/Cole Publishing Co., 1971). Ms. Marshall has a style and an impact of her own that really fit what we are trying to do here. She is "right on" with her idea of learning and her challenge to formal classrooms. Her contributors have caught her spirit, and the collection is very stimulating. Such topics as personal freedom, man within himself, intimacy and death, loneliness, love, encounter, are discussed by some of the real avant-garde people of our time. Don't miss reading the closing essay, "How to Teach a Cow a Damn Good Lesson" by Peter R. Runkel.

John O. Stevens, *Awareness: Exploring, Experimenting, Experiencing* (Lafayette, Calif.: Real People Press, 1971). This useful compendium of exercises and games that help us to know ourselves and others better through expanding awareness grew out of Stevens' work on gestalt therapy. *Caution:* If you use the book and attempt to try the experiment with others, be sure to read the section "To the Group Leader or Teacher" and be very careful about where you use the projects, no matter how much experience and training you have had.

Try this

1   Select a partner in your class group. Sit face to face with each other and, in turn, express your perceptions of your partner and of your own reactions. (1) Describe the other's immediate behavior and appearance. Use no judgmental statements or observations. Simply describe what you see. (2) Verbalize your feelings about the other's appearance and behavior and about the situation in which you now are. Avoid generalities. For example, use "I feel a tight ball in the pit of my stomach" instead of "I think I feel some tension." In other words, be as descriptive and as specific as possible and avoid interpretation as much as you can.

2   On an assigned day bring or wear to class an object or apparel that represents how you perceive yourself. At the class meeting, everyone will be given an opportunity to try to understand others' representations. (A girl who perceived herself as completely transparent wore a dress of cellophane. A student who perceived himself as being covered up with traditional restraints wore many layers of old clothes, including an ancient tuxedo.)

3   In his book *Group Processes: An Introduction to Group Dynamics* (Palo Alto, Calif.: National Press, 1963), and further described in *Of Human Inter-*

action (Palo Alto, Calif.: National Press, 1969), Joseph Luft described what he called the "Johari Window," which represents a person's self-data at any given moment (see figure). The area suggested as having the greatest potential for useful interaction and understanding between people is shown as Block 1 in the figure in which self-knowledge is shared with others. With a partner, discuss how you perceive your selves in terms of the diagram.

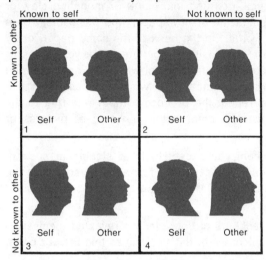

1   What I know about me, you know about me; and what you know about me, I know about me. Our communication is free and open.

2   You know something about me that I don't know. Our communication is not free and open.

3   I know something about me that you don't know and that I keep from you. Here again our communication is restricted.

4   I know nothing about me and nothing about you, and you know nothing about you and nothing about me. Communication between us is impossible.

4   Talk privately with some business manager or supervisor. Try to get him to talk, confidentially, about how he sees himself as a manager and the effect of this perception of himself on the communication within his company.

5   Find out from some administration official of your university or some company what kind of data he (or she) gets about his managerial performance from superiors and subordinates.

6   Arrange time for a confidential interview with a classmate or close friend. Prepare a list of specific questions to ask your partner about your own behaviors, attitudes, appearances, and other aspects of your self as they appear to him. Ask him what about you, in his estimation, makes you different from others. Discuss how these observations coincide or conflict with your own perception of yourself. Repeat this type of interview with several others and compare the various perceptions.

7   Refer to the self-disclosure list on page 53. Think of some person whom you trust and prepare a list of things about yourself you would be willing to reveal to that person. Prepare another list of things you might reveal to a specific person whom you do *not* trust. Prepare a general inventory, listing under each heading of the list on page 53 five personal specific examples that you would be willing to reveal to almost anyone.

8 Stand before your class or group and describe their willingness to accept what you might say, as you perceive that willingness. Allow each member to try to correct or change your perception if he wishes.

9 Draw, diagram, sketch, create a model, or "doodle" a composite picture of how you perceive yourself. You need not be an artist to do this. You may use any medium you wish (pencil, pen and ink, paint) or modeling clay, or you may cut pictures from a magazine or newspaper and paste them on a sheet of paper. Don't use any words. On the back of the same paper, or by creating another model, make a composite of how you think your class or group perceives you. Do not look at the first model while you are preparing the second. When you have finished, compare the two and discuss them with the class. After several weeks, repeat the process without referring to the first effort. After you have finished, compare the two sets of pictures or models.

10 List three persons with whom you expect to have significant speech-communication encounters within the next week. For each person, describe as best you can how he sees his world. How does each vision of the world differ from yours?

11 To what degree have the teachers of your classes revealed themselves to you so that you may communicate with them? Discuss this in your class.

12 To what degree have you revealed yourself to your teachers so they may communicate with you? Discuss this with your teachers and classmates.

Chapter Four

Words, People, and Behavior: Messages and Meanings

Objectives

After studying this chapter, you should be better able to do these things:

- Distinguish between meanings and the symbols and signs that stimulate meanings.

- Know the relationship between experience and meanings.

- Recognize that meanings exist only in people and depend on our ability to perceive, on our conditioning, on our goals, and on the "here and now."

- Perceive how words, objects, persons, and messages are related.

- Identify the degree of availability, the time available, the interinvolvement, and the balance between communicators in various kinds of confrontation events.

- Trace a response from a feeling to a code to organized information or message.

- Use your information to reduce the choices of meaning available to you.

- Recognize the differences among messages, meanings, and information.

- Organize information and messages in terms of the total relationship that exists between you as a speaker and a listener to other people.

- Identify your own needs and feelings that are affecting the order in which you arrange messages received from a speaker.

- Begin to see the unspoken signs and symbols in the communication situation.

Sandra's voice sounded harsh and tense over the telephone as she told her mother, "Mother, this is it! I'm not coming home again. I don't want to be your pawn in your social affairs any longer—"

Her mother interrupted with a rush of words: "You're hiding something! You're sick! You're caught in a phony love affair—it's just your own fantasy! Your father and I have tried so hard to make life good for you! You'll ruin yourself if you go on this way! This will nearly kill your father—he'll never forgive you! You don't realize what you're doing to us!"

What Sandra's mother *meant* was that she loved Sandra so very much that she would never accept or believe that Sandra was rejecting her, that she was hurting terribly—lost—lonesome—and unable to do anything but strike at what seemed to be the source of her pain.

Sandra hung up the phone. Her mother grieved. Sandra grieved. Neither of them knew what the other really meant, and they no longer had any way to find out. The connection between them no longer existed, and actual meanings had not been shared. By Sandra's unilateral choice, they were no longer available to each other. The greatest barrier to communication of all had been erected by her act. With such barriers no one can find his way to another.

Meanings and people

Meanings inside people

Meaning is not inherent in a word or phrase. The word is not the thing it represents. The word "automobile," for example, performs a function of identifying a certain class of object—to persons who have had some experience with vehicles labeled "automobile." Other words, like "pickup," "hardtop," "sports car," "limousine," are more specific. But these words are groups of letters from the alphabet; spoken, they are sounds—no more. *For meanings, we must look inside ourselves* to find the experience that symbols call up or stimulate.

For all of us, the term "automobile" has different referents; that is, it brings different images into our systems of recall. Even the existence of an image does not establish meaning. If someone pointed to a fire-engine red Porsche and said, "automobile," what would it mean to each of us? Would we get the same meaning? We would be looking at the same object, but the meaning of that object to each of us would be highly personal because the meaning of anything is inside the persons who have experienced it. That Porsche may mean luxury to me and speed to you—and to someone else, subconsciously, the power of sexuality.

Donald Snygg and Arthur Combs put it this way: "The meaning of any object or event is the relation which it has to the phenomenal self of the perceiver. It is his perception of its effect upon himself and his efforts and self-maintenance and self-enhancement."[1] The "phenomenal self" refers to you as you see yourself and your world.

[1] Donald Snygg and Arthur W. Combs, *Individual Behavior* (New York: Harper & Row, 1949), p. 212.

Note that Snygg and Combs say nothing about the word or words that are used to describe, relate, identify, or otherwise make reference to the object or event. It is the object or the event that activates a meaning. They point out the difficulties of developing meaning through words are so great that it may be more practical to help others discover the meaning of objects through actual experience. Further, since meanings naturally differ from person to person, the object or event has different potential meaning for different people.[2]

But words are instruments that we must use, and the relationship of the word to the thing or object is of great importance. Julius Laffal, speaking of the psychological nature of language says:

> *Relationships between words and things exist only by virtue of and within the minds of the people who use the words and perform the acts of referring to and of meaning.* The locus of meaning is inescapably within the individual user of language; to picture the relation of word and thing without the user of language is to miss completely the psychological nature of language.[3] [Italics added.]

When we become concerned about words and things, we become involved with trying to find out how such a word as "dog" comes to stand for an object "dog." One way of looking at the matter, Laffal says, is to recognize that there are two things outside the person, the object "dog" and the word "dog." Thus when I wish to refer to the object I may select the word "dog." I become, then, nothing more than a sampler of words and things that seem to have independent existence and relationship.

Laffal warns us that it is much too simple to assume that the word "dog" refers absolutely and always to the object "dog" and is independent of the speaker. At this point, we come to the vagueness of each person as the residence of his own meaning, which is the only meaning he can discover.

The statement that "meaning is the experience people perceive as response to symbols" is thus one of the most significant concepts in all communication theory. When we communicate, we are dealing in the process whereby experiences become meanings; and effective communication requires that we know ourselves and those with whom we speak, in order to develop meanings. If you and I were both present when that "automobile" was pointed out, we both may identify it as "the red Porsche." When we refer to "the red Porsche" in after-the-event communication with each other, each of us would be able to experience through recall the particular object about which we were speak-

[2] Snygg and Combs, p. 213.

[3] Julius Laffal, *Pathological and Normal Language,* pp. 1–2. Reprinted by permission of the publishers, Atherton Press, Inc. Copyright © 1965, Atherton Press, Inc., New York. All rights reserved.

ing. An *"overlapping"* of experiences makes possible a certain level of communication between us. We could not communicate very well without these areas of *overlap* in our experiences and representations of things. *If there were no overlap or commonality of experience with or perception of the referent we would have no basis for understanding each other.*

Experience and meaning are closely related. Meaning *is* experience and is also *derived* from experience. Kenneth Boulding calls the collection of experience an "image."

> *Behavior depends on the image. . . .*
>
> The image is built up as a result of all past experience of the possessor of the image. Part of the image is the history of the image itself. At one stage the image . . . consists of little else than an undifferentiated blur and movement. From the moment of birth, if not before, there is a constant stream of messages entering the organism from the senses. At first, these may merely be undifferentiated lights and noises. As the child grows, however, they gradually become distinguished into people and objects. He begins to perceive himself as an object in the midst of a world of objects. The conscious image has begun. . . . Every time a message reaches him his image is likely to be changed in some degree by it, and as his image is changed his behavior patterns will be changed likewise.
>
> We must distinguish carefully between the image and the messages that reach it. The messages consist of *information* in the sense that they are structured experiences. *The meaning of a message is the change which it produces in the image.*[4]

Thus, we might say that each of us has a storehouse of meanings gathered from his experiences (Boulding's "image"). These meanings are subject to change through addition, alteration, reorganization, and repetition of experiences.

A response to a stimulus represents what we know as an experience. No one else responds to a stimulus exactly as I do; you are unique and so is each response you make. No two persons have the same responses to a given stimulus; therefore, even a "shared experience" is not exactly the same experience for each of the participants. We would expect obvious differences among four men viewing a rural acreage, if one were a real estate salesman, another a highway engineer, a third a priest, and the other a well-driller. The experience of each in response to the view would differ from the experiences of the others.

Let's keep in mind also that when we hear a word we are *experiencing* that word with whatever facility we have for experiencing that particular stimulus.

[4] Kenneth E. Boulding, *The Image* (Ann Arbor: University of Michigan Press, 1956), pp. 6–7.

Human patterns of response to words as well as to other experiences seem to arise from the nature of the verbal stimulation itself; that is, the hierarchy of associations stimulated by a given word; the needs, drives, and perceived self of the person responding; the social-personal demands of the moment; and the degree of intrusion of diverting marginal or irrelevant stimuli.

As pointed out by Julius Laffal, words function to stimulate mental association with actual experience:

> Language does its work by evoking experiential associations which are suggested by pertinent words or, to put it a little differently, by rearranging the relative strengths and likelihoods of occurrence of groups of word-thing responses. The evoked hierarchy of associations, the meaning, reflects a fundamental behavioral and attitudinal shift in the listener in response to the stimulus. Meaning refers to the stimulus side of language, that portion of *la langue* within each speaker which is activated upon the occurrence of a stimulus.[5]

Note that Laffal also recognizes that a new meaning involves a *change* in the already organized collection of experience images.

Meanings between people

If meaning is a private affair, so that my experience in a situation cannot be the same as your experience in that situation, by what magic can we ever get meaning from one to the other of us? *We must accept the disheartening probability that neither of us can ever completely grasp a meaning as the other has experienced it.* However, we can achieve some degree of success in our speech-communication efforts if we create messages and stimuli that relate as much as possible to the nature of the other person's experience and response system. The commonality, however limited, of some experiences provides us with a beginning of understanding. In other words, such things as the phrase "the red Porsche" may be the secret of such success as we have in our communication with each other. When we explore our common experiences, we find bases for agreement to use certain words that will stimulate recall of certain of these common experiences in our response systems.

Genesis of communication

Where and when do we initiate a speech-communicative event? Can we establish a point in time or a place for starting the chain reaction? While

[5] Laffal, *Pathological and Normal Language,* pp. 41–42.

it is almost impossible to isolate a single speech-communicative event and identify its beginning, certain generalities will help us to understand probable origins. The following generalizations or principles will give us the basis for our own personal investigations.

Availability of people to each other

We have already noted that communication between persons cannot occur unless there is some kind of relationship between them. I cannot talk to you unless you and your system of life are, to some degree, available to me. That is, I must have access to some of the characteristics of your world. You cannot talk in response unless some part of my system of life is available to you. A *speech-communication event cannot begin unless persons' systems are available to each other*. Theoretically, the degree of availability is limited only by the content of a given system; however, as a practical matter, few personal systems are totally available to anyone.

Availability, of course, is enhanced to the degree that the persons desire and are willing to communicate by listening and responding, as well as by speaking. Total strangers, passing on the street, may communicate; but before communication can occur, each must become available through his willingness to respond to the other. Even for passing strangers who are willing to respond to the extent of exchanged smiles, no sign or message could be exchanged unless there is some confrontation. No confrontation is possible if these strangers walk different streets at different times. Thus, availability depends also on an event of confrontation. Thus with Sandra. When she terminated the relationship with her mother, she also made herself unavailable for any further confrontation that would allow them to communicate with each other. The situation became even more poignant when Sandra returned her mother's subsequent letters *unopened* and hung up without response when her mother tried to reach her by phone.

Table 1 presents an analysis of several types of speech-communication events in terms of aspects of availability. For each type of event, the table shows the usual (not the exceptional) degree of availability of the involved persons to each other, the time available for the interaction, the depth of interinvolvement of their personality systems, and the relative balance of availability of the systems to each other.

At one end of the scale is the casual encounter on the street where the degree of mutual availability of the personalities is minimal, the time minimal, the interinvolvement practically none, and the balance of the availability about equal. At the other end of the scale are highly communicative interactions that can occur between two close friends or lovers or a man and his wife.

The table includes relatively few examples of the innumerable speech-communication events of our lives, and the data do not hold for all events in any of the categories shown. Each confrontation event is unique; and while events, like persons, may resemble each other, no two are identical. For any confrontation event, availability of the parties to each other, even though minimal and unbalanced, may be adequate for the communication *required by the event*. We don't need extensive mutual availability to buy a newspaper, for example.

The doctor-patient relationship is usually characterized by an uneven

Table 1   Speech-communication events and availability

Type of confrontation event	Degree of availability	Time available	Interinvolvement of personal systems*	Balance of availability
Casual, momentary greeting of strangers	Minimum	12–30 sec.	Almost none	Equal
Buying a newspaper from the newsboy on the corner	Minimum but regular	15–30 sec. daily	Some	Equal
A protocol meeting with a state official of another country, removed from our frame of general reference	Minimum	Variable but limited	Some	Unequal
A visit with a relative who lives far away	Moderate	Variable but finite	Some to considerable	Unequal, depending on who initiates
Radio or TV program, live theatre	Moderate	15 min. to 3 hrs.	Very limited	Unequal
Doctor-patient interaction	High	15 min. to 1 hr.	Maximum	Unequal
Teacher-student interaction				
Elementary	High	4–6 hrs. daily	Maximum	Equal
Secondary	Moderate	1–2 hrs. daily	Moderate	Unequal
Undergraduate	Limited to moderate	3 hrs. weekly	Limited	Unequal
Graduate	Minimum	3–4 hrs. weekly	Moderate	Unequal
Conversations with roommate or close friend	High to maximum	Variable but high	Maximum	Equal
Husband-wife discussion, brother-sister discussion, work-group discussion	Maximum	Relatively unlimited	Maximum	Equal

* Stake each person has in the outcome

balance of availability; and most of us, generally, prefer it so. When we do not feel well, we are interested primarily in our own aches and pains and are not interested in the life systems of anyone else, including the doctor. Moreover, too great an availability of the doctor's life system tends to inhibit the communication required by the doctor-patient confrontation event and to detract from the purpose of the relationship.

Classically, the professor-student confrontation events at most universities and colleges have been as indicated in Table 1: limited-to-moderate degree of availability, time available limited to a few hours each week, limited-to-moderate interinvolvement of personal systems, and an unequal balance of availability. By the mid-sixties, this classic pattern was far from universal in American higher education. Degree of availability between some professors and students became less than "limited." Interinvolvement of personal systems became nonexistent. Balance of availability became, all too frequently, "even"—and null. "Confrontation" acquired connotations of violence. There were many violent confrontations on American campuses during those years, none characterized by significant communication between the parties involved—and none significantly characterized by availability of the parties to each other.

The seventies seem to be different. The availability of faculty to students seems to be increasing under pressure by the students, parents, taxpayers, and other faculty. The balance, however, is quite uneven because of the excessively large numbers of students with whom each teacher must share time and energy. At certain levels and in those schools that are oriented more to the humanities and social life, there seems to be a greater amount of significant communication interaction. However, such interactions do not seem to flow up to the middle and top administration levels. We might predict that the revolution in American education has already begun in the form of a new kind of communication relationship based on availability and mutual concern between student and teacher.[6]

We can justifiably establish the *beginning* of a speech-communication event at that point in time when two or more persons and their personality systems become in some way available to each other. Thereafter, the background of needs, conditions, situations, and the like will come to bear on each person to set the process in motion.

[6] See Neil Postman and Charles Weingartner, *The Soft Revolution: A Student Handbook for Turning Schools Around* (New York: Delacorte Press, 1971). This book is an amazingly practical discussion of ways to change the educational system from the inside by those who are dissatisfied with the ways in which it is conducted and who are searching for ways to change the situation without feeling that all the avenues for nonviolent change have been exhausted. This book, and its wide use in many schools, may be an encouraging sign of the increasing dialogue between students, teachers, administrators, and other functionaries.

Response behaviors

Availability alone cannot account for the origin of a speech-communication event. Among several other essential preconditions for effective communication are response behaviors.

Physical environment determines many of our *response behaviors*. The time, the place, and the physical conditions of the encounter may enhance or inhibit responses essential to a speech-communication event. Most of us are less than enthusiastic about any kind of communicative interaction when awakened from a sound sleep in the middle of the night. Most psychiatrists' offices are quiet, pleasant, with a reassuring atmosphere. No paper mill supervisor would attempt to communicate detailed oral instructions on the main floor of the mill, where the noise level makes unaided speech communication impossible.

All the response-behavior systems, both conditioned and developing, are brought into play in the speech-communication event. These include the physiological systems, the psychological systems, and the environmental systems.[7] In other words, the availability of another person to us allows us to respond to him in terms of our previous conditioning and of our immediate situation.

Our response behavior includes our ability to anticipate the nature of the relationship and the events that might take place because of the interaction. Studies by Leon Festinger and others have indicated that a person whose responses are perceived as deviating from the norms and wishes of his group will be the target of communications designed to influence him toward the group position.[8] When a member of a group takes a position contrary to that held by the majority of the group, he can anticipate that up to a certain point a number of communications will be directed toward him in an attempt to persuade him to change his position.

Goals and directions

Our responses to situations are influenced not only by other persons but also by many elements of our own personal experience that determine our goals and needs. Our goals, wishes, and expectancies result from previous experience, inheritance, and training. Every communication event develops as an attempt by the transmitter to control, modify, or change his perceived environment. His response to the situation, which includes the presence of at least one other person in some perceived state of being and behaving, is

[7] For a careful analysis of stimulus-response systems, see B. F. Skinner, *Science and Human Behavior* (New York: Macmillan Co., 1953).

[8] Leon Festinger, Stanley Schacter, and Kurt Back, *Social Pressures in Informal Groups* (Stanford, Calif.: Stanford University Press, 1963).

usually an attempt to control or alter that environment, including any other persons who may be part of it. This attempt at manipulation immediately extends to all who are involved in the communication event. Each person relates what is happening at any given moment to his own frame of reference and his own experience, and he attempts to control the perceived situation so that it satisfies his own goals and motivations. Whether it be on the public platform, on the stage, behind a microphone, in front of a camera, or within the intimacy of face-to-face discourse, *all participants in a communication event use the communication system to reach their own goals and to deal with their own needs.* It is possible and desirable, however, that a person's own goals will *include* satisfactions of the other's goals and needs. When this happens a greater sharing can take place.

Goals to ideas

We do not consciously perceive all our goals and needs; nevertheless, they influence our behavior and our judgment. Consistent with personal goals, each of us seeks to formulate his responses in a given situation into an idea, which must then be coded into a message before it can be communicated. The process of developing the idea and coding it into a message may be practically instantaneous. Our response, which is determined by the people involved in the situation, by the situation itself, by our goals and our needs and our conditioning, brings us to the formation of an idea. With the idea, the speech-communication event is well on its way to becoming a fact, but this idea must be translated if we are to make some communicative effort related to it.

Messages and information

Feelings are very much the center of our internal world. What happens inside us as a result of what is happening outside us is distinctly different from what is going on in the world external to us. However, our "inside happenings" do have some relationship to the external situation to which we respond. In their book on communication, Gregory Bateson and Jurgen Ruesch deal with this relationship: "While it is impossible for a man to have inside himself a tree corresponding to the external tree that he perceives, it is possible to have internal objects or events so related to each other that their relations reflect relationships between parts of the external tree."[9] *Their analysis suggests three basic methods of codification of the relationships of the external*

[9] Gregory Bateson and Jurgen Ruesch, *Communication: The Social Matrix of Psychiatry* (New York: W. W. Norton & Co., 1951), p. 170.

world into the internal and interpersonal world: counting or "arithmetical relations," analogic mechanisms or models that are recognizable, and classification into categories and subcategories of experience and information. To code an experience we might say, "He talked to me like a headmaster punishing a poor student"; and "He told me the same thing at least three times"; and finally, "This was obviously not a funny joking comment; he appeared to mean it seriously."

To communicate anything about our ideas, which are generated by feelings, we must transmit information about our internal happenings to our co-communicators in the world external to us. Bateson and Ruesch say that "information" has definite characteristics:

> Every piece of information has the characteristic that it makes a positive assertion and at the same time makes a denial of the opposite of that assertion. The very simplest perception that we can imagine, upon which, for example, the tropisms of protozoa are presumably based, must still tell the organism that there is light in that direction and not light in the other direction. Many pieces of information may be more complex than this, but always the elementary unit of information must contain at least this double aspect of asserting one truth and denying some often undefined opposite. From this it follows that when we have two such "bits" of information the gamut of possible external events to which the information may refer is reduced not to a half, but to a quarter, of the original range; similarly three "bits" of information will restrict the possible gamut of external events to an eighth.[10]

If I say, "I have a broken foot," I have eliminated such possibilities as (a) the foot is operating properly, (b) any other part of the body is involved in this statement, (c) someone else had the injury. If the situation requires more specific information, I can eliminate other possibilities. If I say, "I have a broken toe," I have eliminated the other parts of the foot. If I say, "My big toe is broken," I have eliminated the other toes.

Information reduces the number of choices available to a perceiver. In other words, complete information enables a person, through the process of elimination, to reconstruct the message as the transmitter intended. A collection of bits of information arranged in an orderly fashion, showing proper relationships between external events and internal interpretations, showing adequate counting characteristics and adequate classification, and using analogy when necessary may result in a message.

Of great importance to you and me as we attempt to communicate with one another is the necessity for organization and careful selection of our mate-

---

[10] Bateson and Ruesch, p. 175.

rials so that information is provided in a sequence that allows for clear identification. (See Chapter 9, "Barriers and Breakdowns.")

People, organized information, and messages

In spite of what we say or how we say it, some kind of message usually stirs
up experiences and thus meanings in our partner to the communication interaction. Our problem is to arrange our messages for maximum possibility of
getting the *desired* response (that is, calling up the *desired* experience).

Consider these two reports of an incident:

> Carol fell asleep with a cigarette in her hand. She woke with the room
> filled with smoke and on her knees at the bathroom door. She had presence
> of mind enough to pick up the phone and dial the operator and call "fire!"
> The trucks arrived in seven minutes, but by that time she was unconscious.
> At the hospital she was found to have second-degree burns over most of her
> body.

> Carol has second-degree burns over most of her body. She was unconscious
> in her burning apartment when the firemen found her. She had gone to
> sleep with a lighted cigarette in her hand. She woke with the room filled
> with smoke and had presence of mind enough to dial the operator and call
> "fire!" It was seven minutes later when the firemen found her.

Both statements contain the same information; yet they seem to convey
different meanings. The two statements differ in the order of the pieces of information. Which statement would be more useful for a news report? an
anecdote in a short story? a report for an insurance company? for a letter to
Carol's parents? Does the organization of the information have anything to
do with the persons to whom the information is to be given?

Much has been written about outlining and the organization of messages
and information. The usual assumption is that "well-organized" information
and messages or sets of messages will always create more meaning and will
actually convey information more effectively than messages that are not
"organized." The two paragraphs on Carol's fire may help you to see that it
is not so simple as that. A number of factors affect the order or organization
of messages.

If the persons involved in a speech-communication event have similar
perceptions of what is or is not organized and of what good or bad organization may be, it may be possible to develop information in an organized outline
form that is consistent with the joint perceptions. As a test, ask several of

your friends to listen with you to a speech, then outline the speech. Will the several outlines be the same—or even similar? Probably not. Moreover, it is not likely that any of the outlines will correspond significantly with the speaker's outline which he either had in mind or in front of him.

Now, expose the same people to instructions on how to outline a speech. Be sure that all have a similar conception of the method and can perform somewhat equally. Then have the same group listen to and outline a speech made by one of their members who uses the basic outline form they have all learned. You will find much more comparability in the outlines, but you will be astounded at the variations in them. Why is this? Poor instructions? Poor students? These are not the critical factors. The crux of the matter is that each person is a different person with a different set of expectancies, needs, goals, and the like. There is not much you can do about that.

The organization of information and messages is a factor of the relationship between the speaker and the listener. The conditioning, the expectations, the ability of each to relate to the other will determine the manner and the order in which information and messages are transmitted and received and in which other messages are developed from them.

What does this mean with respect to the study of outlining and organization of speech? There are several implications. The first has to do with the setting in which the speech-communication event does take place. In the one-to-one relationship and in the small-group setting, the participants can know enough about each other to adjust dynamically to each other in arranging the order of their message material.

When one person is speaking to a large group, the speaker knows much less about his listeners and is less aware of what is happening to them. He must depend more on some prearranged design of presentation. No matter how complete and detailed a prearranged outline or design may be, it must be flexible; and the speaker must be able to shift his material around when he perceives his audience responding in a way he did not expect. Of course, if a speaker is unable to perceive or to anticipate responses of his audience, a flexible outline won't make much difference.

The study of outlining and organization of ideas is important because it helps us to arrange our messages in a coordinated form and sequence. *But to force a rigid form of organization upon material irrespective of the nature of the listener, the situation, the message material itself, and the dynamics of the interaction is pure folly.*

A listener, as he responds to the messages and develops meaning from them, relates both messages and meanings to his own needs. His priority may be the priority of the sender. The importance of feedback (discussed in Chapter 5) is due to this proclivity of listeners.

Words, signs, and symbols

Words perform an important function in that they provide vehicles by which we can transmit information and create messages. Remember that the words themselves are *not* the information that we are transmitting. Words are representations of things, behaviors, feelings, and the like; they are not things and behaviors, except as we view them specifically as words (for example, when we consider the spelling of a word or the sound of a word or the definition of a word). As we put bits of information together to make a message, so do we put words together to create more complex messages. Words, as media for putting information into messages, also affect the message itself.

Joyce Hertzler shows how a word may become a message:

> Words are constructed by man; each word is a deed, stands for a deed, and makes a deed existential. Viewed operationally and concretely, words are the significant units of connected speech; they are also the smallest units of verbal behavior and the smallest vehicles of meaning. All words have something behind them; they stand for something. As practical devices they are at any given time the rather definite number of means by which reality, as experienced by man . . . is perceived, articulated, labeled and transmitted. . . .

> Words are abbreviated contrivances, products of group living, residues of specific past acts, devised for all these purposes as the members of the group have worked out their schemes of inter-communication and of adjustment to both their tangible and imagined environments. They have been invented and continually perfected through use. Each word is a sort of generalization, which selects and labels a feature, or class of features, from among the welter of irrelevant features. Each *type* of word has its own special function. . . . By means of words properly organized, men are able to identify, objectify, describe, standardize, classify and universalize all their different types of experience.[11]

It follows, then, that the particular selection of words will affect the message. Putting words together is not a casual and random business. The language system includes a logic of arrangement which, when followed, provides a relatively economical and efficient transmission of the messages of men. A person may have a large vocabulary, yet be unable to communicate

[11] Joyce O. Hertzler, *A Sociology of Language* (New York: Random House, 1965), p. 39.

effectively. Words must have some useful relation to the intended information, message, and eventual experience.

Before we can effectively use words as media, we must understand the nature of meaning, the source of messages, the nature of the communicative act, and the systems by which we can produce the maximum in human understanding. Then we may reach out for the mechanics of language, word usage, and word making.

Words, as we use them in language, are symbols. Symbols are not things; they are *representatives* of things. John C. Condon, Jr., asserts that "the ability to symbolize means the ability to call up internal experiences, using only the symbols."[12] Notice that Condon refers to "calling up" rather than "reproducing" or "being."

Signs are not to be confused with symbols. Symbols are representative of things; signs (and signals) serve to inhibit or elicit specific action or response. Signs are not representative; they serve to anticipate an event rather than to represent it. A traffic signal is a sign, not a symbol, as it functions at an intersection. When the light turns green, traffic moves; when it turns red, traffic stops. Our behavioral responses to this type of stimulus are different from our responses to symbols; responses to signs involve conditioning and anticipation of events (specifically for the traffic signal, we have learned that if we run a red light, we may end up in a traffic court or a hospital).

Signs tend to set in motion predisposed or prearranged responses. Response to a symbol is highly personal and is influenced by many aspects of the situation in which the symbol is perceived. Difficulties arise when we attempt to use signs rather than symbols, and visa versa.

Condon suggests a way of distinguishing between signs and symbols:

> The ability to use language means the ability to transfer something of experience into symbols and *through the symbolic medium to share experience.* . . .
>
> Animals can learn to respond to *signs,* but only man can use *symbols.* Susanne Langer expresses the difference by saying that signs announce but symbols remind. That is, animals can emit and receive cries signifying food or sex or danger. But an animal cannot contemplate the nature of food and thereby decide it might be a good idea to go on a diet.
>
> Another distinction between sign and symbol is the difference in number of possible responses. A sign stands in a one-to-one relationship with experience (or object, or the like); a symbol suggests many possible responses.[13]

[12] John C. Condon, Jr., *Semantics and Communication* (New York: Macmillan Co., 1966), p. 12.

[13] Condon, pp. 8–9.

Spoken words and language are not the sole means by which we convey messages in speech. Nor are words essential for signs and symbols. Response is elicited by many signs and symbols that are objects and behavior. A national flag is an object—and a symbol. The jerk of a baseball umpire's thumb is a behavior—and a sign. The bodily movements of a person as he speaks transmit information and messages of both signal and symbolic nature. The tone of voice, the nature of the articulation, tell us a great deal about the person and the moment as well as about the idea or message that he is trying to convey.

Consider the effect of the "wooden Indian" stance of a public speaker on his acceptance by his audience. Frequently the stiff and unresponsive attitudes of his body are inconsistent with the ideas being expressed and tend to send to the audience a conflicting message.

Bateson and Ruesch show how verbal and nonverbal data combine into messages:

> Each individual receives, of course, sense data of the ordinary kind in regard to the other; each sees and hears the other as a physical entity. But in addition each receives verbal and other symbolic matter from the other, and each has, therefore, the opportunity to combine these two types of data into a single more complex stream, enriching the verbal flow with simultaneous observations of bodily movement and the like. . . . The bodily processes of the other person—his postures, tension, flushing, and the like—serve a corresponding function in interpersonal communication. Each person is able to get a multidimensional view of his vis-à-vis, enriching the stream of merely verbal symbols with a recognition of bodily processes in the other, and these are more or less intelligible because of common biological background and cultural conditioning.[14]

Summary

Meanings are in people, not in words. People, being different, will interpret stimuli in different ways, unless there is a common or shared experience that provides an overlap of meaning. The availability or access of persons to each other is essential for meaningful communication. The more available our thoughts, experiences, and feelings are to others, the greater the likelihood that they will understand our messages. The responses that develop in communication events come from the physical environment, the psychological environment, and the physiological environment.

[14] Bateson and Ruesch, *Communication,* p. 207.

Our goals, needs, and expectancies control the nature of the meanings we develop from messages sent to us. Our reactions to stimuli are formed into ideas. Ideas must be coded into information and messages. The coding process involves establishing a relationship between our inner world and the outer world. This is done through classification, counting, and comparison.

Information serves to reduce the number of choices available. The organization of information for effective communication depends upon the expectations of the listener, the nature of the information, and the total relationship between the speaker and listener in the context of the environment in which the communication event takes place. Thus, rigid outline forms are not particularly useful for effective communication.

Words are vehicles for information. They are not the information itself. Messages exist independent of words and can be transmitted by other means. Symbols are representational, and signs are stimulative signals. Both are functional in speech-communication.

Both signs and symbols occur in nonverbal behavior (see Chapter 6) and are interwoven with the spoken word in the creation of messages.

For special reading

Alfred Korzybski, *Science and Sanity: An Introduction to Non-Aristotelian Systems and General Semantics* (Lakewood, Conn.: Institute of General Semantics, 1933). For those who are brave and brilliant! This is pretty rarefied stuff and is difficult reading even for those who profess to know what the man said. On the other hand, this germinal work is the keystone to the whole general semantics movement. While subsequent general semantics work has developed Korzybski's insights, much of the content of this book is still highly relevant to our problems of communication in today's society.

Irving J. Lee, *Language Habits in Human Affairs* (New York: Harper & Row, 1941). The late Irving Lee was a student of Korzybski. This book translates some useful ideas from *Science and Sanity* into more understandable terms. The use of words, the nature of symbols, and our use of them in speech communication in order to stimulate meaning, are central to Lee's book. Lee is lucid and clear, as well as entertaining.

J. J. Bois, *Explorations in Awareness* (New York: Harper & Row, 1957). A clear and brilliant discussion of many of the major problems and solutions relating to our communication with each other. Writing in a direct and vivid style, Bois covers a wide spectrum of the theories of meaning, thinking, and interpersonal communication.

Roger Brown, *Words and Things: An Introduction to Language* (New York: Free Press, 1958). This basic reference in psycholinguistics is not the easiest book in the world to read; but, for those who want to consort with giants, this volume will prove rewarding. Brown digs into the technical aspects of speech and language and their implications to persuasion. His work on meaning is of great importance and supplements our materials quite well.

Hugh Dalziel Duncan, *Symbols in Society* (New York: Oxford University Press, 1968). In this useful book, basic ideas are expressed in a series of propositions or axioms. The function and forms of almost all human communication are related to the propositions developed by the author. The book will be highly useful to you in expanding the ideas of this chapter.

Eugene T. Gendlin, *Experiencing and the Creation of Meaning* (New York: Free Press, 1962). If you want to tackle something difficult and rewarding take this book on. It is a carefully organized philosophical and behavioral analysis of how experience is the meaning and how language can be used to call up the desired experience.

Try this

1   Place a pencil (or pen) in front of you. How many attributes of that pencil can you list in five minutes? (What is it made of? What can it be used for? What persons are related to it? What words can be used to describe it?) Analyze the attributes you have written down. Which could identify *any* pencil? Which would identify that specific pencil and no other? Which could identify an object that is not a pencil?

2   As a class project, list several experiences that have been shared only by members of your class. Assign to each shared experience a vocal symbol, that is, an invented combination of syllables that will mean that experience to all of you. Discuss the experiences using the symbols.

3   Make a list of persons with whom you have spoken in the past week. To what degree is the life system of each available to you? To what degree is your life system available to each of them? Use a percentage scale for rating availability; and remember that no one on your list was 100 percent available nor was anyone 0 percent available. Study these percentages. Do you see any patterns indicating the relation of availability to age, occupation, degree of trust, your needs?

4 Arrange to study the organization of some company in your vicinity. Set up an "availability chart" for all management personnel. Here is one example:

	President	Manager	Foreman
President to		√	—
Manager to	+		+
Foreman to	⊙	+	

+ Immediately available
√ Available with some time loss
— Available only with great effort
⊙ Not available

What does your analysis tell you about communication possibilities in that company?

5 To what degree are your teachers available to you outside of class for discussion of ideas and problems raised by the course? Prepare a summary grid like the one below for your teachers:

	Available at Any Time	Available Most of Time	Appointment Only	Available Infrequently	Never Available
Teacher 1					
Teacher 2					
Teacher 3					

6 Identify the unspoken messages that develop in your classes from the manner in which the instructors deal with the teaching situation.

7 Trace some information through an organized system such as a production plant, the university, a store, the student body of your university. To do this get the cooperation of the principal responsible official, then introduce, at some point in the system, several messages varying in complexity and significance. Arrange to check at various levels of the organization for the following things: (1) time lag from when you introduced message to when it was received, (2) accuracy of the message, and (3) meanings stimulated by the information at various levels.
When you are finished, give a report on what you found.

8 Compare various forms of information in the system analysis above. That is, introduce some information only orally, some only written, and some both written and oral. Which form goes through the system most effectively?

9 Interview the president or general manager of a company regarding the goals and purposes of the company. Now interview one of the workers on the same subject. Are there differences in perception of the goals? Try this with several companies. Can you find a relationship between the degree to which workers and presidents share the same goals and the relative success of the company?

10 Analyze twenty messages you have received in the past twenty-four hours. Set up your analysis sheet with two columns:

Message	Meaning*

* Your experience or a result of the message

As you identify each message, identify the information contained in that message. Identify what each message meant to you.

11 How many symbols and signs can you note during a two-block walk through a shopping district?

12 As a class project, select some inanimate object in the classroom (for example, a desk, a briefcase, a shoe) to serve as a subject for a speech. Each member of the class should outline a one-minute speech on that object. In small groups (three to five members), compare your outlines and discuss common ground and any common development of the subject. In what ways are the outlines similar? In what ways are they different? How do you account for the similarities? For the differences?

13 As a class project, your instructor may ask each member of the class to fill out a Self-Other Perception Scale form for every other member of the class. If so, your instructor will provide you with the forms and instructions. The purpose of this project is to help you get a better perception of others' perceptions of you.

Correcting and Controlling Our Messages: Feedback

Objectives

After studying this chapter, you should be better able to do these things:

- Use feedback habitually in all your interpersonal communication efforts.

- Make nonverbal feedback consistent with verbal feedback.

- Encourage others to respond with feedback relating to the messages you are trying to get across to them.

- Use feedback to develop high confidence and good feeling between you and persons with whom you interact by nonpunitive reactions to others.

- Distinguish between general responses and specific corrective feedback: internal and external, negative and positive, purposive and nonpurposive.

- Avoid overloading your feedback with value judgments, with too much information, and repetition when it has no corrective value.

- Use various forms of feedback including paraphrasing, mirroring, action-testing, replication, feeling reports, pertinent questions, payoff, nonverbal methods, and "perception checks."

They sat face to face on a blanket spread on the sand of a narrow beach by the pounding sea. He had called long-distance just twenty-four hours before to tell her goodbye. He had yielded to her pleas, and now they were meeting for a final confrontation. She wanted to persuade him to reconsider his decision—at least to give some explanation of his reasons for rejecting her. She also wanted to assure him of her continuing love.

Each time she reached to touch him, he withdrew—although she was very attractive and for five years they had been intimate. As she talked to him, he gazed off into the distance and at times seemed to be looking for some particular car along the highway just above. In answer to her questions, he

83

merely shook his head, wordlessly. Finally, in desperation, she asked if he would tell her what he had heard her saying to him.

He replied: "I hear what you're saying but it makes no difference. I really don't know what you mean except you obviously want me to change my mind. I will not. You are very persuasive and I must resist you. You are really wasting my time. I really don't care what you think anymore. Come on, I'm taking you home . . . or you can find your own way if you wish."

Tears filled her eyes as she numbly stumbled into the car. They drove away. Nothing was said during the return trip. They never spoke together again.

Scenes like this occur more and more often these days as the tensions of our time seem to push people apart. How would you have dealt with the situation had you been the young woman? The young man? What means do you have at your disposal to overcome the kind of retreat from communication used by the young man? Your search for these things may be one of the most important things in your whole life, for if you can find some answers for yourself you may one day save a treasured relationship that is in danger of being lost.

Reuel L. Howe has defined communication as a "meeting of meaning between two or more persons."[1] In light of the discussion in Chapter 4, the three words "meeting of meaning" imply a universe of relationships and experiences. In the process of communication, we wish to develop with other persons relationships and experiences that permit what we say to be understood, perceived, and responded to as we intend.

Responses and meanings

As communicators, we seek, through our communications, to create some kind of response in those who receive what we communicate. The simple model of communication discussed in Chapter 1 (Figure 1–1) cannot adequately define what Howe describes as a "meeting of meaning." The term "meeting" implies movement in both directions; that is, both the transmitter and the receiver are sending signals, and these signals meet somewhere. When they coincide, or match up, we may then say that a communication has taken place.

It becomes necessary to complete the "loop" of communication and to provide within the model a process that will allow for the reflection of meaning from the receiver back to the sender. Let us modify our model of communication (Figure 5–1) so that A transmits information C to the in-

---

[1] Reuel L. Howe, *The Miracle of Dialogue* (New York: Seabury Press, 1963), pp. 21–22.

dividual called B, who responds by returning or reflecting back what he receives as C, which we will call C_1; and C_1 is then perceived by A, the original transmitter. In our model, we have now completed the loop of communication and have thus established the basic framework within which we may explore the process called feedback. (See also Chapter 1 for more explicit explanation of models.)

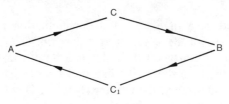

Figure 5–1

We have long been aware of a tremendous need in the process of human communication for some system whereby we may correct misreceptions and faulty responses to what we think we are transmitting in our messages. We need to find ways to *correct our transmission* so that the essential message we try to transmit is actually perceived by the receiver.

When I tell a friend by telephone how to find his way to my house, I cannot know whether my information is being received either accurately or effectively unless my friend repeats the information exactly as he has heard it or paraphrases it back to me—or shows up at my house within a reasonable time, without having had to ask for additional information from other people.

Suppose that your instructor gives the class an assignment, asking each of you to prepare a statement about your "needs in communication." The statements would differ, not only in revealing individual personal character, but also in the interpretations of the word "needs." For such an assignment, the differences in interpretation of a word may be a matter of interest; in speech-communication events, such differences in interpretation can seriously interfere with communication.

When we attempt to transmit any message to anyone, we almost always expect and desire that the message be received adequately and correctly. We should be aware that messages can be mutilated to greater or lesser extent at least at two points in the communication process. The transmission itself may be at fault or the reception may be inadequate for one reason or another —or both. Such faulty transmission and reception are illustrated by the following incident.

One afternoon in late spring, a graduate student finished the last of his examinations—the long grind was over. He phoned his favorite woman, announced that he was ready to "forget this trip" and that he would see her in a couple of hours. Two hours later, aboard his bicycle with a pack on his back, happy in jeans, sweatshirt, and waffle-stompers, he arrived at her home. She appeared—carefully made up, hair à la mode, and dressed for late afternoon and evening dinner and dancing. They stared at each other in speechless fury. His perception was that she had accepted a dinner date with someone else. Her perception was that he had unilaterally changed their plans for the evening.

A message had been mutilated, and the mutilation resulted from two different interpretations of the words "forget this trip." He had meant that he was ready to drive to a nearby lake, indulge in a bit of sunset fishing, enjoy a picnic by a fire on the lake shore. She had understood that they would dine in a good restaurant and spend the evening dancing. Obviously, communication of these two *bypassed* each other.

In their phone conversation, there had been no corrective factors that might have aided adjustment of their widely divergent interpretations of his message: "I want to . . . forget this trip." Had they used corrective measures in their communication, they would have avoided the shock of their confrontation. The conversation could have developed something like the following dialog:

He Hi! It's all over, lover! Now I want to go somewhere and forget this trip. Want to join me?

She Hey! That's neat—you being finished and all. Sounds like you want to get off the head trip, eh?

He Right on! Got any ideas where we might go?

She Hmm. Say—Ramsey Lewis is playing at the Paramount Ballroom—I know I can get a couple of tickets.

He Uh—well—uh—that's kind of a heavy trip. I mean I like jazz and all but I'm not with the crowd and sound right now. I kinda feel I'd like it where it's quiet.

She But it's great music, Baby! And you know you love his style.

He Oh, he's great—but the crowds and the hassle of getting there, and the—

She But it's taking you away from your school thing, isn't it? Isn't that what you want?

He Uh—I'll level with you, Sweetie. I really want to go over to the lake, rent a boat—maybe catch a few fish—then have a campfire on the point—and—

She Cool it, nature boy! It's almost sundown. You couldn't get to the lake by the time the boat dock closes and fishing is over for the day. I dig the nature bit but not right now—it's too late.

He Okay, okay. So what do you think will relax *me*?

She Hey, don't bite me—those vibes don't sound good. I'm just being practical—

He So, you got some—

She Yes!

He Oh, well—I tried—

She You're driving too fast. Listen to what I have to say. The other girls are gone tonight and I've got the apartment to myself, and it's been a long time since I cooked a dinner—

He Wow! Stars and Bars Forever! What shall I bring?

She Yourself, you nut—and plenty of love in your heart—

He Only if we can go fishing tomorrow—

She What am I to do—you're always bargaining with me . . .

He Aww, don't get hassled. How soon?

She How long does it take you to make the distance between us?

He Instantaneously! I'm really there right now!

Notice in the above conversation the degree of correction that each of the communicators made both in the information received and in the information transmitted. In this rough example, a feedback process operating in a communication situation resulted in the correcting and meeting of meanings.

Other factors sometimes operate to prevent messages from getting through and from having the desired effect. A receiver simply may be unable to hear what a sender is saying because of preoccupation with his own thoughts and feelings. In such circumstances, the receiver is simply not available to the sender and thus feedback is impossible. We discussed availability in an earlier chapter, but it is a *first* prerequisite for any feedback of use to *both* parties.

A sender may get feedback in the form of rejection of his overall communication efforts. A receiver may get a message and reject it out-of-hand, without checking to see what the sender meant. In this instance, both will almost certainly misinterpret and misunderstand each other.

What is feedback?

For many years psychologists and researchers in learning have been concerned with how to acquire a *knowledge of the results* of various kinds of educational input. One of the main questions asked by most was "What effect will a knowledge of the results have upon the originator of the transmission?"[2] Likewise, research in the engineering of complex interrelated mechanical and electrical systems has depended a great deal upon the development of what are called servomechanisms. Servomechanisms are machines that are controlled by the *results* of their own function.

Computer technology has made possible extensive applications of cybernetics principles in electromechanical processes. Information about output is fed back into a system; and, on the basis of the feedback, the input and processes of the system are maintained or modified to produce the desired output. We are all familiar with automatic control of heat furnaces, electric blankets, and household appliances. In such devices, information about the output (heat) is fed back into the system, and the energy source (gas, oil, electricity) is modified to maintain the desired temperature.

In radio engineering, "feedback" is the transfer of electronic energy from the output to the input of the same circuit. Many of the special sounds of the electric guitar are created by providing feedback from the loud speaker into the microphone of the same system. The howl or squeal in the speakers of the early days of radio has been harnessed to create "new sounds."

The caveman never heard the term "homeostasis" or realized that his physiology involved feedback processes. Writing in the early days of the computer revolution, W. Ross Ashby[3] and Norbert Wiener[4] discussed the feedback processes of the human physiological system, whereby oxygen, carbon dioxide, salt, hormones, and the like are controlled and maintained by automatic mechanisms that keep the supplies constant in spite of external changes. This system, called homeostasis, works much like the thermostat of a heat furnace.

Human behavior has involved feedback as long as there have been human beings to behave. Only in recent years, however, have we deliberately studied this phenomenon. Dean Barnlund, in reviewing the research on feedback, describes the process as "a requirement of all self-governing, goal-seeking systems whether they are mechanical devices, living organisms, or social groups. To obtain this feedback an autonomous system must be able to observe or scan its own performance, compare intended and actual operation, and use this information to guide future action."[5]

Internal and external

Wendell Johnson talks about both internal and external feedback. Internal feedback is provided by ourselves when we reflect on something we have just

[2] See John Arnett, *Feedback and Human Behavior* (Baltimore: Penguin Books, 1969).
[3] W. Ross Ashby, *Design for a Brain* (New York: John Wiley & Sons, 1952).
[4] Norbert Wiener, *The Human Use of Human Beings,* 2nd ed. (Garden City, N. Y.: Doubleday & Co., 1954), p. 96.
[5] Dean C. Barnlund, *Interpersonal Communication: Survey and Studies* (Boston: Houghton Mifflin Co., 1968), p. 229.

said. External feedback is, according to Johnson, "being sensitive to the re-actions of other people."[6] He points out that when we are getting feedback from others, our *internal* system is also working and that when we are re-flecting on our own conversation we undoubtedly have some image of past and future receivers. This image also affects our process of decision-making. Thus Johnson's two forms are so interwoven that they are almost indistin-guishable. One way of making a separation for our purposes in understanding and growth would be to consider the Johnson concept of internal feedback as part of the process of self-perception.

Johnson's description of internal feedback identifies many of those pri-vate self-critical observations we make about our own behavior. A young lady, dressing for a special occasion, comments on what the mirror tells her about the success of her preparations. In preparing a speech, we may try out phrases or passages to see if they sound right. These are examples of the more obvious self-feedback. Less obvious internal feedback is taking place per-sistently in our communicative relationships with others. Almost at the instant we speak, we get set for responses. The anticipation of the response results from internal feedback that causes us to expect certain behavior. That ex-pectation is triggered by our conception of the moment plus our past ex-periences. We reach a high level of perception if our internal feedback information coincides with the external response. In other words, if we cor-rect what we intend to say before we say it on the basis of what we think will be the response of the listener and the listener actually responds as we an-ticipated, the two systems have moved quite close together.

Reward and punishment

Gerald Miller calls attention to the reward and punishment factors in feed-back. When listeners respond in such a way that their response is perceived as rewarding by the one talking, we consider the response a *positive* one. Those kinds of responses that the speaker perceives as punishing are con-sidered *negative*.[7]

If I get the response I seek in talking to you, Miller would say that was a positive response and thus rewarding. On the other hand, the responses you make that are alien to my purpose I may see as punitive.

Berlo draws an analogy with the system of the control of a furnace in which the thermostat sends out a signal, then reacts to the heat and encodes

[6] Wendell Johnson, *Your Most Enchanted Listener* (New York: Harper & Row, 1956), p. 174.
[7] Gerald R. Miller, *Speech Communication: A Behavioral Approach* (Indianapolis: Bobbs-Merrill Co., 1966), p. 55.

another message.[8] In that system, as in the human system, no control of the operation could exist without the feedback system. Berlo goes on to say:

> The source can use the reaction of the receiver as a check of his own effectiveness and a guide to his own future actions. . . .
>
> *Feedback provides the source with information concerning his success in accomplishing his objective. In doing this, it exerts control over future messages which the source encodes. . . .*
>
> *One consequence of a communication response is that it serves as feedback —to both the source and the receiver. . . .*
>
> Reactions serve as feedback. They allow the source or receiver to check up on himself, to determine how well he is doing in accomplishing his purpose. Feedback also affects subsequent behavior, if the source and receiver are sensitive to it.
>
> When a source receives feedback that is rewarding, he continues to produce the same kind of message. When he gets nonrewarding feedback, he eventually will change his message. In responding to a message, the receiver exerts control over the source. The kind of feedback he provides determines in part the next set of behaviors of the source.[9]

What Miller describes as *positive* feedback results usually in continuation of the sending of similar material while negative feedback may close down a system or result in change of material and approach.

Berlo goes on to develop the idea of feedback at different levels of human communication. He shows that maximum feedback is possible in the close person-to-person situation, while large media systems such as newspapers and television have limited feedback possibilities.

This is not to say that the large media systems have no method of feedback. This whole concept may be understood in relation to our discussion in Chapter 4 of the availability of people to each other. But feedback in large systems presents special kinds of problems. ". . . advertisers facilitate feedback by means of elaborate market research; public relations men obtain feedback by means of public-opinion polls and other devices. . . . newspaper publishers sponsor readership surveys and . . . reader motivation studies. . . . Radio's concern with 'fan mail' and popularity ratings is well known."[10]

[8] From *The Process of Communication* by David K. Berlo, copyright © 1960, Holt, Rinehart and Winston, Inc., p. 111.

[9] Berlo, pp. 111–113.

[10] Bruce H. Westley and Malcolm S. MacLean, Jr., "A Conceptual Model for Communications Research," in James H. Campbell and Hal W. Hepler, eds., *Dimensions in Communication* 2nd ed. (Belmont, Calif.: Wadsworth Publishing Co., 1970), p. 69. This article first appeared in *Journalism Quarterly* (Winter 1957), pp. 31–38.

Feedback as purposive correction

Some social psychologists have suggested that the process of feedback is essentially a system whereby a balance is accomplished in the perceptions of the transmitter and the receiver (called in biology homeostasis; in psychology, equilibrium).

Let us extract from all these studies the minimum idea that essentially *feedback means the perception of the behavior of the receiver by the transmitter in relation to the message that he, the sender, is attempting to send.* Feedback in this context does not require conscious effort by the receiver to communicate back to the transmitter. However, it does require considerable translation *by the sender.* His effective control of his output depends on the accuracy and completeness of his translation of the feedback responses.

However, to make it useful, let's narrow it down even more. Let's define our concept of feedback as essentially *a corrective process.* It may then occur in at least two forms: nonpurposive feedback response and purposive, or direct-check, feedback response. Nonpurposive feedback is widely used in evaluating advertising, for example. If an advertising campaign is followed by a significant increase in sales of the product, we may assume that a certain effectiveness of information transmission has been demonstrated by the sales.

On the other hand, consider the following conversation as a crude example of *purposive,* or direct, feedback.

Transmitter   Feedback is a process of correcting miscommunication.

Receiver   Are you saying that feedback is simply a process of correcting errors?

Transmitter   No. That's not what I mean, entirely, although that is a part of it. I mean that it is a way of being sure that what one person says to another person is adequately perceived by the other.

Receiver   Now you are more complicated than before. How do you know what "adequately perceived" means?

Transmitter   Well, to me, "adequately perceived" means that you get the idea as *I* want you to get it.

Receiver   Oh, then you mean that feedback is a way of checking as to whether or not *I* got the idea as *you* wanted *me* to get it.

Transmitter   Precisely.

Receiver   Have I used feedback effectively?

Transmitter   What do you think?

This basic loop of information can be seen as a way of maintaining a degree of stability of the communication interaction. Once a desirable level of information is established *the whole communication loop becomes a process whereby a stability of interaction can be maintained.*

We can at once see the similarity of mechanical feedback and human-behavior feedback. The concept of feedback is particularly significant as it supports Howe's definition of communication as a "meeting of meaning."

In the broadest sense, feedback in speech communication includes all aspects of response to a given message that are perceived by the sender as indicating effectiveness of transmission. In the narrower sense, which I am arbitrarily using, feedback includes *only* that specific kind of response called corrective, or regulative. *When corrective feedback is operative, the receiver of a message is consciously or unconsciously trying to determine if what he received is what the sender wished to send and the sender is trying to find out from the receiver whether what he sent has been received as he wanted it received.* Communication feedback can be corrective if the *sender perceives* it as such and uses it as such. It can be corrective if the receiver *purposefully attempts* to check his reception of the message. *The most effective utilization of feedback in speech communication may be through the purposeful corrective efforts of both sender and receiver.*

Of course, all responses have some feedback potential. However, *we shall deal with intentionally corrective responses as feedback.* Thus we narrow the functional concept of feedback so that we can focus on some specific behaviors that are useful in speech communication.

Effects of feedback

The effects of feedback on communication are sometimes easy to discern; at other times, they are difficult to isolate. Harold J. Leavitt and Ronald A. H. Mueller tested the assumption that where communication between two persons is the objective, the use of feedback in the form of verbal and expressive language makes for greater effectiveness.

> These findings support the hypothesis that *free feedback* is an aid to accuracy in interpersonal communication. *Free feedback* seems to permit the participants to learn a mutual language, which language once learned may obviate the necessity for further feedback.

> The findings also support the hypothesis that the presence or absence of feedback affects the sender-receiver relationship. *Zero feedback* is ac-

companied by low confidence and hostility; *free feedback* is accompanied by high confidence and amity.[11]

In addition to the research of Leavitt and Mueller, information has been developed through related studies of the process. In his review of the literature on feedback, Barnlund discusses research findings[12] that indicate the validity of a number of insights into the effects and uses of the feedback process:

1 Feedback that is adequate in a given situation may be both positive and negative.

2 Such feedback seems to make a contribution to the improvement of interpersonal relations, to the acquiring of new skills, and the development of insights.

3 Feedback which is in the form of direct reference to an individual's execution of mechanical tasks seems to result in better execution of these tasks than when the feedback is joined with the joint output of both parties or when the performers received feedback only on the performance of others.

4 If there is too much information to be included in the feedback system or the subjects are overloaded with the task of coding and decoding, performance is impaired.

5 Unless feedback is *interpreted* accurately it cannot be used effectively. Unless the receiver deciphers the feedback information with accuracy, receives it with proper relation to the time of the exchange, and has sufficient information from the feedback, it has little value.

Barnlund summarized his findings with this statement: "The timing and amount of feedback, the positive or negative value it carries, and the interpretation made of it—all affect the degree of understanding achieved through communication. The data also suggest that when receivers are encouraged to respond with questions, comments, corrections, or even counter arguments, greater confidence and mutual respect are likely to result."[13]

Feedback response systems

Since many response systems used as feedback increase the possibilities of accuracy in our human speech transmission and decrease the possibilities

[11] Harold J. Leavitt and Ronald A. H. Mueller, "Some Effects of Feedback on Communication," *Human Relations,* Vol. 4 (1951), pp. 401–410.

[12] Barnlund, *Interpersonal,* pp. 229–231.

[13] Barnlund, *Interpersonal,* p. 232.

of error or loss in our communication interaction, we should profit from closer examination of some of them.

Observable physical results

We may observe the responses of people to our orders or directions. *What people do* as a result of what we ask them or tell them to do may, if we choose, be feedback in that it can tell us whether or not they received the essential message and intent that we transmitted. I might tell my son to wash the car today. If the car is washed and polished when I return in the evening, I have a certain feedback that my order or direction was followed. This kind of feedback we might term the observable physical results.

Attempted replication through translation and paraphrase

In the example of the young graduate student and his girl friend, one cause of the breakdown in communication was the failure of either or both to provide adequate checking on what the other one meant. To avoid such breakdowns, we use in human communications a response system that is the elemental aspect of all feedback. In this system, the receiver of a message *replicates* that message or translates (*paraphrases*) that message as he sees it or hears it or perceives it and returns it to the sender to see whether he was correct in what he perceived. This in turn gives the sender an opportunity to discover if what he sent was received adequately. The effectiveness of this response system is shown in the following dialog:

Patient   I haven't slept for the past four nights, Doctor, and I feel that there must be something seriously wrong.

Doctor   You mean that you have had no sleep at all for the last few nights?

Patient   No, I had some sleep, but not as much as I usually have.

Doctor.   How much sleep did you have?

Patient   Well, it's hard to be exact, but I would say that I probably slept about half the time that I usually sleep.

Doctor   You think that this is not good?

Patient   Yes, because I feel tired all the time.

Doctor   Oh, that is a different matter.

Patient   I thought that had something to do with sleep.

Doctor   Not necessarily. You might get more sleep than usual but still feel excessively tired.

Patient Is that so? I guess what I was really saying was that I feel tired and don't seem to be able to get the sleep or whatever it is that I need to relieve the feeling of being tired.

Doctor Now I think that we are getting closer to it.

In the course of this interaction both patient and doctor replicate and paraphrase, in a way, what the other has said in order that their meanings might meet.

In recent years, this response system has been utlilized increasingly by participants in business and academic conferences. The response might be "Now, this is what I think you are saying . . ." If that paraphrase is not accurate, the original communicator then makes the necessary changes. Other phrases often used are "Now, what I heard you say was . . ." and, more commonly, "Do you mean that . . .?" This second type of feedback system in human communications we might call the process of *attempted replication*.

Many of us believe we are fulfilling the feedback need when we ask, "What do you mean?" However, *such questions do not tell the initiator enough for him to make precise corrections;* he may simply repeat what he said before. When we attempt replication in our response (for example, "Do you mean . . .?"), he can pinpoint the errors in perception more quickly and more effectively.

Payoff

The "payoff system" is related to the reward and punishment factors in feedback. Suppose you are shopping for a new car. The salesman has shared with you his enthusiasm about a particular model and has pointed out its many superiorities. He is obviously attempting to persuade you to perform in a certain way. This is not ordering or directing. It is persuading. As you sidestep the decision to buy the car, he modifies his messages to you, correcting to bring about the payoff which comes when (or if) you perform in the way he has attempted to persuade you. In addition, he receives a reward in the form of a commission for having persuaded you to perform in this fashion.

An infant corrects his messages in terms of the payoff system of responses. When his first cries bring pleasant returns in the form of food or warmth or closeness of another warm body, he learns quickly about feedback in the form of payoff. Most parents soon learn to distinguish cries of legitimate distress from those of tyrannical demands for undivided attention and to withhold payoff feedback for the latter. The baby soon learns to correct the form of his vocal output in such a way that it will give him the greatest amount of satisfaction or payoff.

Follow-through

The fourth form of human response that serves as corrective feedback we shall call the "follow-through." The follow-through is some action taken in response to an idea or suggestion that has been made by a transmitter. When a housewife says, "Darling, the grass is getting high," and her husband gets the lawnmower out of the garage, his follow-through feedback indicates that her communication was effective. If he turns the television dial to the baseball game, he may have got the message, but his feedback indicates that he will not act immediately on her suggestion.

Mirroring

Sometimes a special form of replication is valuable in that it allows the sender to perceive himself through the efforts of his receivers to provide an active mirror of behavior and idea. Such mirroring can be quite like mimicry without the malice that mimicry often has. Mirroring a person's physical behavior often provides excellent insight and stimulates corrective actions that make his nonverbal messages more consistent.

Effective use of feedback

Far too little is known about practical applications of feedback in many areas of human communication. There is in everyday life little systematic use of feedback that might enable us to check the effectiveness of our communication to others. Each of us has been frozen into habits of communication that ignore the possibilities and the usefulness of feedback systems. Usually when we try to use the process, our early attempts are self-conscious and appear to be labored and incredibly ponderous. As a result, we may turn away from these attempts before we have learned to use the techniques smoothly and efficiently.

Feedback itself requires that the transmitter be sensitive to the real responses of the receiver, and in turn it requires that the receiver be willing to attempt to test what he has received either by performing or by checking with the transmitter as to meaning, intent, purpose, and function. If there were between persons more actual feedback of the conscious replicating type, we should have generally a higher level of meeting of meanings, which would in turn lead to greater understanding and more effective development of human interaction.

Working on the assumption that all of us must increase our use and skill in feedback systems, let's examine some of the "do and don't" ideas that may be of help to us.

Do make a habit of using some form or forms of feedback whenever you are not really sure what the other person means.

Do use replicative feedback instead of asking a person, "What do you mean?"

Do tell people what you really think they mean so that they can correct your interpretation of their meaning.

Do encourage others to use feedback by using it yourself. Nothing seems to stimulate or encourage the use of feedback more than when people with whom we are talking use it on us.

Do ask others specifically to tell you what they think you said.

Do try feedback as a way of reducing the overabundance of words to a few clear concepts or meanings.

Do seek sufficient feedback from others until you can be satisfied that they have received what you wanted them to receive.

Do recognize that your early attempts will seem obvious and labored but that as you develop habits of giving and receiving feedback your total communication effectiveness will increase.

Do let your body and voice tell the sender how you are responding when it is pertinent.

Do provide positive suggestions whenever you give negative feedback.

Do experiment with ways to provide effective feedback to specific people.

Don't overload feedback by adding your own evaluations of the message. The first job is to get the message; only then can adequate judgments be made about the message. Thus, when my secretary tells me that she can't get to my dictation today because of an extra-heavy load of telephone calls, I need to determine just what she is saying to me before I suggest that she might not be handling her time properly. It may very well be that *I* am the one who is overloading her with telephone duties and that what she is really telling me is that I must decide which is more important to me. Overloading leads to reactions that are often contrary to the messages being given and often results in gross miscommunications.

Don't use feedback to criticize, condemn, or threaten a person. When someone says something that may seem to have negative personal implications, it is usually unwise to reply in a menacing tone, "Are you saying that you don't like what I did?" Such a response often results in blocking of communication, developing or increasing of hostilities—and sometimes in an actual fight. (Criticism, condemnation, threats, and the like are kinds of feedback statements we make as a result of judgments about what is said. In a sense they are forms of overloading. However, they are often used under the guise of feedback to provide the donor an opportunity to retreat quickly from his position of criticism or to avoid being pinned with actually saying what he was implying.)

Don't allow contradictions to appear in feedback through actions, expressions, tone of voice, and other nonverbal factors. If, for example, you are trying to check a meaning with a friend when you have negative feelings about what you thought you heard, you must not allow your feelings about what you thought you heard to come across with your feedback through your facial expressions, tone of voice, or other nonverbal means. This is not to say that feelings and the like are not part of feedback of a certain kind. We have already discussed feedback that gives the sender some idea of the acceptance of his message, which, however, is different from the kind of feedback that serves as a means of developing accurate and useful meeting of meanings between persons. It seems useful to *stick as much as possible to the descriptive and paraphrase type of feedback* as a base until those with whom we are communicating open the door to us for evaluation of their messages.

Don't repeat feedback when it brings no corrective or altered response from the other person. After your attempt to assist in your mutual communication efforts has been rejected, you may not be helping by repeating the feedback. It may first become necessary to establish with the other person a better relationship, which will allow for effective use of feedback. Many people are actually afraid to hear any feedback to what they may be saying. They much prefer to live in a world of fantasy in which they assume that everything they say is perfectly clear to everyone spoken to. To suggest, by feedback, that what such a person is saying may not be understood by the receiver becomes a real threat to the security of the speaker. Until the person is able to deal with the feedback it is unwise to thrust it upon him.

Don't load a feedback statement with more detail and trifles than were present in the original message, unless you have a specific reason for using them to test the nature of the message or its implications. An executive requested reassignment for a secretary who not only repeated his directions practically verbatim but also expanded on details of carrying out his instructions. When those details were of importance, of course the expansion was useful. However, in most cases such expansion and overloading go far beyond the level of usefulness. It is usually better to understate a feedback so that the sender can then provide added information or explanation himself.

Don't give negative feedback to a person in areas or on matters that he cannot correct or change. Too often people pile up corrective feedback data on a person when there is no way the sender can alter or attenuate his messages. The result is a kind of frustration that often debilitates a person and destroys the communicative bond.

Don't try to give feedback of complete nature when time for adjustment is limited or nonexistent.

Summary

In all human communication (written, verbal and nonverbal, sensory, extra-sensory, and subsensory, as well as speech), we seek to improve the manner in which we reach or develop a meeting of meanings. Awareness and use of feedback in communication can be helpful.

Feedback can be most useful in speech communication when it enables us to *correct* and adjust our transmission of messages so that they say what we want them to say and do what we want them to do. While many definitions and concepts of feedback include all responses of the receiver to the message and message situation, our emphasis is on the selective *corrective* aspects of the process, which constitute the heart of the feedback process for maximum interpersonal communication.

Feedback may not be intended as such by the receiver but may be perceived by the transmitter. Feedback may be purposive and intended by the receiver and in the form of attempted replication or paraphrasing may be highly useful and highly corrective. Some feedback becomes evident to the transmitter through observation of behavior of those who are on the receiving end of the communication. The payoff in a persuasive situation may be used as corrective feedback in that it indicates the degree of success of the persuasive efforts. Follow-through on suggestions is feedback. All these represent response forms that can be feedback.

For special reading

Alfred G. Smith, ed., *Communication and Culture* (New York: Holt, Rinehart and Winston, 1966). This book could serve as additional reading for several chapters of Part One. The editor has brought together some excellent studies by leaders in many different disciplines that deal with communication. Of particular interest for this chapter is Chapter VIII, which deals with feedback and control. The chapter contains four articles plus an introduction. The articles range from a technical explanation to reports of experiments.

Heinz Von Foerster, ed., *Cybernetics: Circular Causal and Feedback Mechanisms in Biological and Social Systems;* Proceedings of the Ninth Conference on Cybernetics Sponsored by the Josiah Macy Jr. Foundation (New York, 1953). Wrapped up in this little volume is some of the most advanced thinking about feedback that we have available to us today. The book includes the statements of the principal speakers and the group discussion of presented papers. W. Ross Ashby, for example, discusses homeostasis and is interrupted by Warren S. McCulloch and others, who challenge some of the things he says. If you can get the feeling of the involvement of these scholars, this reading can be very exciting.

Paul Watzlawick, Janet H. Beavin, and Don D. Jackson, *Pragmatics of Human Communication: A Study of Interactional Patterns, Pathologies, and Paradoxes* (New York: W. W. Norton & Co., 1967). Here, again, is a book that is applicable to several chapters of this text, especially to this chapter on feedback and to Chapter 6 on nonverbal communication. The authors deal in a technical way with the nature of information and feedback, then apply their communication principles to an analysis of *Who's Afraid of Virginia Woolf?* The result is a fascinating and provocative set of ideas.

Norbert Wiener, *The Human Use of Human Beings: Cybernetics and Society,* 2nd ed., rev. (Garden City, N.Y.: Anchor Books, Doubleday & Co., 1954). This work opened up the computer age to a wider world. While feedback is inherent in Wiener's approach, the usefulness of his total scheme to contemporary work in communication is obvious. Wiener's chapter "Communication Machines and Their Future" sounds almost prophetic.

Try this

1 Set up a feedback experiment with a friend. Select a subject for discussion. The rules of the game are that each statement made by either of you must be *paraphrased* by the other to demonstrate that he has heard and understood what was intended. Before you continue the discussion, the originator of the statement must be satisfied that the paraphrase expresses what he intended. In paraphrasing, do not repeat the words used by the originator.

2 Make two simple line drawings (geometric designs, sketches of buildings, stick figures, or whatever) approximately the same in complexity. Do not show them to your partner. With your verbal assistance only, he is to try to replicate the drawings. For the first, tell him how to draw it; *he is not to talk to you in any way and you are not to see what he is doing.* For the second drawing, he is not to see your drawing but *he may ask questions* to be sure he understands your instructions, he may use paraphrase or other forms of feedback, and you may see what he is doing and comment (don't touch). When you have finished, compare his drawings with yours. What differences did you note in the rate of accomplishment? In the accuracy of accomplishment? How did you feel as you tried to instruct him in each of the two attempts? How did he feel? Which method of instruction yielded greater satisfaction? In what way?

3   Identify and list the ways available to you to give feedback to your instructors. Do you take advantage of all the opportunities to give feedback to your teachers?

4   Describe a situation in a convocation, church, class, living group, family group, or whatever, in which the conditions were as follows: (1) Feedback was apparent (present) and was ignored by the speaker. What was the result in the behaviors of the speaker and his listeners? (2) Feedback was present and had an effect on the speaker. What was the nature of the behavior of the speaker that resulted from the feedback? Of the listeners?

5   Experiment with nonverbal feedback in responding to speakers in your class group. Try varying your posture, facial response, and gestures to show interest, acceptance, disinterest, nonacceptance, anger, opposition, and the like. Can you measure the effect of this on your speaker? Ask the speaker to tell you what kind of effect your physical responses had upon him. How did he interpret your nonverbal feedback?

6   Try another experiment with a friend. Set up the rules much the same as in the first item above. Without the knowledge of your friend, however, purposely and carefully misinterpret his messages and give him feedback that is *not* what you think he was saying. What kind of reaction do you get? After you have used this method until your partner's patience seems to be almost ended, shift to paraphrasing that identifies as well as you can what you heard your partner say. What differences in behavior do you note in the two situations?

7   In still another two-person experiment, alter the nature of your feedback so that it does two things: (1) paraphrase as accurately as you can what your partner has said, then (2) give your judgments of the *value* of his statement. You might wish to compare, as in the preceding item, feedback which has the nonevaluative paraphrasing and that which has the evaluations added. Can you discern different types of response to the two types of feedback? *Or:* The next time you are involved in an argument say to your antagonist, "What I hear you say is . . ."; then follow with "and what this means to me is . . ." Note carefully the way in which your antagonist responds.

8   Observe the operations of an office group or management staff in some company for at least an hour or more. Identify instances of actual feedback in the speech-communication systems of the office. Note such things as telephone conversations, instructions, orders, problem-solving conferences, information conferences, and the like.

9 Do the same for a staff meeting of the teachers in the department of your major interest.

10 Try talking with a person of another race or culture, using as much feedback as possible. What does it do to your relationship? Report your experiences to your class colleagues. Can the process *you* used or developed be applied elsewhere in order to improve understanding between cultures?

11 Got guts? Sometime when you are stopped (if you ever are) by a policeman try using paraphrase feedback with him. Be careful! Avoid defensiveness; try to understand and help him to understand.

12 After you have given a speech to a group, ask the members of your audience to write, in a short sentence or paragraph, what they consider to be the basic idea you have been developing. What changes would you make in your presentation, design, and development as a result of these bits of information?

13 Set up an experiment involving five or more persons. Select a story or anecdote of rather short length. Have four of the five persons leave the room, tell the story to the one remaining, then bring in one of the four from outside and have the one to whom you gave the story tell it to the second person, then have the second person bring in the third and tell him the story, and so on. Experiment with this chain-type information first without any feedback of any kind, then with feedback at every switching point. Have the rest of the class as observers identify the precise points at which variations in the original message took place. Can you identify why these variations took place?

14 Test the use of feedback in respect to your nonverbal behavior. Ask a friend to describe your behavior (way of walking, talking, moving, gesture, facial expressions, choice of clothing, and the like) without making any interpretations or judgments about it. What effect does his description have upon your inclinations to change your behavior? To continue behaving in this fashion?

Chapter Six

The Eloquence of Action: Nonverbal Communication

Objectives

After studying this chapter, you should be better able to do these things:

- Recognize nonverbal messages that are sent during intrapersonal, interpersonal, intergroup, and intercultural speech-communication events.

- Identify and use more effectively sign, action, and object language.

- Focus on nonverbal messages that are often concealed by verbal messages.

- Identify bodily movements that convey meanings consistent with and contradictory to verbal messages.

- Use bodily activity to send messages without verbal reinforcement.

- Free the body of tensions and restraints so that it may become an effective tool in nonverbal communication and in the reinforcement of verbal communication.

- Use distance or space as a cue in communicating messages.

- Use timing and rhythm as cues that may tell much as part of your total communication effort.

They stood quietly, watching fellow students in their group-process class experience the "trust-fall," in which one person is allowed to fall and be caught by others in the group until he or she can trust the others. No words were being spoken in the room, yet much information was passing among the people who were learning to experience trust in one another.

They had attended the same high school and had taken some classes together at the university. They had a measure of confidence in each other, based on long acquaintance, but they had never dated. As they watched the group enjoy discovering trust, her eyes met his. Across the room, their gaze seemed to lock into a beam. They slowly moved toward each other, eyes still locked on the beam. As they came close, it seemed as if they were suddenly drawn together by a powerful magnet. Their hands met and clasped; then they put their arms around each other—tenderly, quietly, but with a sureness and a trust that words could not have brought about.

In his book *Sense Relaxation,* Bernard Gunther describes nonverbal communication as follows.

Shaking hands
Your posture
Facial expressions
Your appearance
Voice tone
Hair style
Your clothes
The expression in your eyes
Your smile
How close you stand to others
How you listen
Your confidence
Your breathing . . .
The way you move
The way you stand
How you touch other people

These aspects of you
affect your relationship
with other people, often
without you and them
realizing it. . . .

The body talks, its message
is how you really are,

not how you think you are. . . .
There are some girls
who lack support
and are push-overs. Many
in our culture
reach forward from the neck
because they are anxious
to get a-head. Others
hold their necks tight;
afraid to lose their head.
Body language is literal.
To be depressed is, in fact,
to press against yourself.
To be closed off
is to hold your muscles rigid
against the world. Being open
is being soft.
Hardness is being up tight,
cold, separate,
giving yourself and other people
a hard time. Softness
is synonymous with pleasure
warmth, flow, being
alive.[1]

Nonverbal behavior

We have frequently referred to nonverbal factors that influence the communicative interaction between persons. The extent to which these nonverbal behaviors are a part of our communicative effort is, according to many people, deserving of more attention.

Charles Darwin, as early as 1872, wrote an essay, "The Expression of Emotions in Man and Animals."[2] In that essay, he analyzed the expres-

[1] Bernard Gunther, *Sense Relaxation: Below Your Mind* (New York: Collier Books, 1968), pp. 90–91. Copyright © 1968 by Bernard Gunther.

[2] Charles Darwin, *The Expression of Emotions in Man and Animals* (New York: Philosophical Library, 1955).

sions of emotions in man with examples from his own observations and reports and suggested that bodily expression is innate in the species. Since that time, much attention has been devoted to movement but in such isolated conditions that there has been no real coordination of the knowledge and information until the past few years. Now, researchers in many different disciplines are studying nonverbal communication. The current interest seems to center on the intricacies of movement as it accompanies the spoken word and as it appears to be involved in interactions between persons. The effect of eyes upon dominance, anxiety, dependence, affection, and the like, has commanded much attention. Distance of persons from one another during the communication event has attracted a number of researchers, including anthropologists. Such matters as postures, facial expressions, scope and manner of movement, degrees of freedom and restriction of the movements, and muscle tension are subjects of investigation.

The use of various art forms that involve body movement is now becoming functional. Dance artists, mime artists, actors, and singers are becoming centers of interest as people who know how to use movement for communicative purposes. Some of the artists themselves are moving into a special kind of interpersonal work related to therapy. Increasingly, programs in dance therapy, movement therapy, rhythm therapy, and the like, are aimed at aiding individuals to become more effective in their total communicative efforts.

The increasing interest in movement as communication tells us something in itself. For several centuries, we have lived under various social standards that glorified the repression of emotions and the restriction of strong movement except on the athletic field, in the gymnasium, and on the stage and that emphasized highly verbal behavior as the central tool in communication.[3]

Andrew Halpin points his finger at our education system as partially responsible and I tend to agree with him:

> Communication embraces a broader terrain than most of us attribute to it. Since language is, phylogenetically, one of man's most distinctive characteristics, we sometimes slip into the error of thinking that all communication must be *verbal* communication. . . .
>
> Unfortunately, the very nature of higher education forces all of us to place great store by the *word,* whether oral or written. What passes as education often consists of little more than having students regurgitate to the professor the same words that he has given them—untouched in the process by human thought. But the language of words is only a fragment of the

[3] See Martha Davis, *Understanding Body Movement: An Annotated Bibliography* (New York: Arno Press, 1972).

language we use in communicating with each other. We talk with eyes and hands, with gestures, with our posture, with various motions of our body.[4]

Let's take a closer look at the body and its contributions to speech communication. "It has been estimated that in face-to-face communication no more than 35 percent of the social meaning is carried in the verbal message."[5] How, then, is the other 65 percent of the message carried?

Dean C. Barnlund's review of the literature on nonverbal communication led him to the following conclusion:

> Many, and sometimes most, of the critical meanings generated in human encounters are elicited by touch, glance, vocal nuance, gesture, or facial expression with or without the aid of words. From the moment of recognition until the moment of separation, people observe each other with all their senses, hearing pause and intonation, attending to dress and carriage, observing glance and facial tension, as well as noting word choice and syntax. Every harmony or disharmony of signals guides the interpretation of passing mood or enduring attribute. Out of the evaluations of kinetic, vocal, and verbal cues decisions are made to argue or agree, to laugh or blush, to relax or resist, to continue or cut off conversation.[6]

Note that Barnlund finds that "many and sometimes most of the critical meanings" are stimulated by the nonverbal factors. The scope and depth of these nonverbal messages are too frequently overlooked.

Edward T. Hall, in his landmark commentary, *The Silent Language,* starts with the assumption that "What people do is frequently more important than what they say."[7] From this base, he develops a broad theory of interpersonal, intergroup, and intercultural communication. In fact, he takes the position that a culture is its communication.

Hall's thesis is that every human culture is constructed on ten primary message systems. The *interactional system* involves linguistic communication, vocalization, kinesics, and the like. The *organizational system* has to do with the social structure: class, caste, and government. The *economic system* deals with work in maintenance occupations. The biological, social, and cultural relations between male and female fall under the

[4] Andrew W. Halpin, *Theory and Research in Administration* (New York: Macmillan Co., 1966), pp. 253–254.

[5] Randall Harrison, "Nonverbal Communication: Exploration into Time, Space, Action, and Object," in J. H. Campbell and H. W. Hepler, eds., *Dimensions in Communication,* 2nd ed. (Belmont, Calif.: Wadsworth Publishing Co., 1965), p. 258.

[6] Dean C. Barnlund, *Interpersonal Communication: Survey and Studies* (Boston: Houghton Mifflin Co., 1968), pp. 536–537.

[7] Edward T. Hall, *The Silent Language* (Garden City, N. Y.: Doubleday & Co., 1959), p. 15.

sexual message system. The *territorial message system* concerns space, boundaries, formal and informal position relationships, places, property, and the like. Such cultural activities as teaching and learning, enculturation, education, and rearing children are dealt with by the *temporal system.* The *instructional system* deals with teaching and learning. The *recreational primary message system* has to do with participation in the arts and sports, with entertainment, games, and fun. The *protective system* involves the processes of protecting and being protected; formal, informal, and technical defenses; self-defense, and care of health. The *exploitation message system* relates to material systems that allow human contact with the environment and involves the technology of equipment and materials in dealing with property and human behavior.[8] Of all these systems, Hall identifies only the first as directly including verbal or linguistic communication. The others are areas of nonverbal communication.

The coexistence in the United States of diverse subcultures (the "jet set," the WASP middle class, the many ethnic subcultures, the culture of poverty, the various black subcultures, the radical right, the anarchistic left, the youth subcultures—to name but a few) communicates some significant messages about America to those without and to those within. The antagonism—and cooperation—between organized labor and management convey much about our economic system. The overt and covert emphasis on sex in the communications and entertainment media expresses considerable information about American culture. The political divisions of the country (regions, states, counties, urban complexes) and the whole history of public and private domain in the United States are territorial messages. Our free public education system communicates another highly significant message about our temporal culture. Attendance figures for sports contests and for symphony concerts and sales figures for recreational equipment contribute more information about the country.

All these and many more, according to Hall, tell something about us to ourselves and to others. At the same time, they represent areas in which our own communicative efforts are personally involved. Thus, when we become involved in the recreational message system, we can use certain common terms and experiences to interact with each other. For example, we use such terms as "behind the eight ball" (from pool), "four-flusher" and "ace in the hole" (from poker), "Monday-morning quarter-backing" and "carry the ball" (from football), "stalemate" and "gambit" (from chess), "couldn't get to first base" and "threw me a curve" (from baseball). Baseball and football are major spectator sports in the United States; in countries of the British Commonwealth, cricket, soccer, and rugby football

[8] Hall, *Silent Language,* p. 174.

are favored; in Spain and Mexico, bullfighting brings out the crowds—and there was a time in Rome when "everybody" turned out to watch the Christians and the lions. Such national recreational preferences make for differences in the recreational message systems of various countries.

Impossibility of noncommunication

Another assumption is vital to the understanding of nonverbal communication. The authors of *Pragmatics of Human Communication* take the position that it is impossible *not* to communicate.

> There is no such thing as nonbehavior or, to put it even more simply, one cannot *not* behave. Now, if it is accepted that all behavior in an interactional situation has message values, i.e., is communication, it follows that no matter how one may try, one cannot *not* communicate. Activity or inactivity, words or silence all have message value: they influence others and these others, in turn, cannot *not* respond to these communications and are thus themselves communicating. It should be clearly understood that the mere absence of talking or taking notice of each other is no exception to what has just been asserted. The man at a crowded lunch counter who looks straight ahead, or the airplane passenger who sits with his eyes closed, are both communicating that they do not want to speak to anybody or be spoken to, and their neighbors usually "get the message" and respond appropriately by leaving them alone. This, obviously, is just as much an interchange of communication as an animated discussion.
>
> Neither can we say that "communication" only takes place when it is intentional, conscious or successful, that is, when mutual understanding occurs. Whether message sent equals message received is an important but different order of analysis.[9]

So, when the postulates of the impossibility of not communicating are joined with the principles of nonverbal communication, we include a considerable portion of human behavior. It would seem, therefore, that when we deal with the interpersonal communication interaction level, we are dealing with *one of the key building blocks of total human society.*

The speech-communication event involves a continuous many-channeled process of communication. The systems into which it fits are numerous, and it is a constant process. In speech communication, messages are being coded and transmitted through physical movements and attitude; through voice rate, tone, quality; through gesture; through dress and cosmetic

[9] Paul Watzlawick, Janet H. Beavin, and Don D. Jackson, *Pragmatics of Human Communication* (New York: W. W. Norton & Co., 1967), pp. 48–49.

façades; through the use of objects; through the control of space; and through an ordering process in time. In fact, the act of human speech communication is a multimedia process of almost infinite dimensions, many of which are nonverbal.

Classes of nonverbal communication

Jurgen Ruesch, a psychiatrist, and his colleagues have done some interesting research on nonverbal communication. Their studies led them to the conclusion that nonverbal language may be identified as sign language, action language, and object language.[10]

Sign language includes forms of *codification* of written systems into *gestural* systems. For example, the hitchhiker's gesture may be almost "monosyllabic." The tone of voice may serve the function of an exclamation point, a question mark, or a period.

Action language involves those movements that are not used exclusively as signals. Walking, running, sitting, and the like meet personal needs, but they also say something to those who are sensitive to the message of activity. The actual manner of physical movement may carry a considerable load of information.

Object language comprises the *display of material objects* including the human body and its raiment. The arrangement of furniture conveys information about the persons who live with the arrangement. The clothing we choose and the way we wear it tells much about us and may at the same time be a form of message we are sending to others.

Communication about our communication

As we talk with others, we not only speak words to send messages but also provide clues, usually nonverbal, about how the messages are to be taken; that is, we communicate about our communications. The metacommunication aspects of our messages indicate how the receiver should interpret the message proper. Suppose I say to you, "That music is great"; and, as I speak the words, I put my hands over my ears and shake my head. My nonverbal communication says something to you about how you should interpret the message possible from my words. When we are speaking

[10] Jurgen Ruesch, "Nonverbal Language and Therapy," in Alfred G. Smith, ed., *Communication and Culture* (New York: Holt, Rinehart and Winston, 1966), pp. 209–210.

together and I lean forward, look you in the eye, and point a finger at you, I indicate that the verbal message should be interpreted as having some special importance. In both instances my *metacommunication* conveys some instruction as to how you should deal with the verbal message. In effect, I am communicating to you through at least two different channels. One channel may reinforce, emphasize, or contradict what is coming through the other channel. In speech communication, these messages coincide in time; therefore, they must be developed through different channels.

Mixed communication

Nonverbal messages transmitted simultaneously and synchronized properly with verbal messages generally reinforce the spoken communication. "Man, am I glad to see you!" in a given situation might be reinforced by a broad grin; a warm, hearty voice tone; a firm handshake; and an arm thrown across the other's shoulders. In fact, with these nonverbal communications, the words merely sum up an integrated, honest message.

"I hate his guts!" can be honestly said in a tone of loathing, with a curl of the lip, and a hand gesture dismissing the despised individual.

When we are able to communicate honestly, we don't send out mixed communications, that is, nonverbal messages that contradict what we say in words. We sometimes, for whatever reasons, lie in our teeth; and when we do, truth may be revealed through contradictory nonverbal messages simultaneously transmitted or out of synchronization.

Some of the reasons for mixed communication provide comfortable livings for many psychiatrists. A woman said repeatedly to her husband, "I love you," and she believed that she did. But she scorched his breakfast eggs and decorated the living room in green (a color he detested) and overstarched his dress shirts. She was not aware of her deep hostility toward him. Her nonverbal messages contradicted what she said in words.

A handsome young man repeatedly told his fiancée that he loved her deeply and dearly. He had "a dark and a roving eye"; and when she learned of his infidelities, he laughed and refused to discuss the matter. He assured her that he loved her for herself and not for what she could do for him. He used her car freely, never paying for gas, oil, or maintenance. He used her social contacts without hesitation. He frequently borrowed money from her—large sums and small—and never repaid. When she tried to talk with him about the seeming inconsistencies between his behavior and his words, he passed it all off as a joke and avoided discussion of serious and important aspects of their relationship. In this case, we have not only mixed communication but also an example of a kind of power struggle that can destroy close and intimate relationships. His behavior actually imposed upon her, against her will, decisions he had made without reference to her. Now, why she was willing to tolerate the stresses imposed on her by his mixed communication is another "can of worms." Just remember that few of us get through life without episodes of hurt brought on by our own unwillingness to resolve the conflict between verbal and nonverbal messages from others whom we love.

Some mixed communication results from requirements of the social games we play. As we interact with others in social situations, particularly those required by business, political, and community involvements, we use accepted verbal formulas: "Glad to see you," "So glad you could come," "We had a delightful time," "Delighted to meet you," "It's a pleasure"—the list could be nearly endless. We don't always mean what we say; and some of us are occasionally betrayed by simultaneous nonverbal messages: the listless voice, the dead-fish handshake, the deadpan expression, the spineless slump, the deep sigh of bored forbearance.

A small boy says, "Nice doggie—I'm not afraid" and hurriedly crawls into the safety of his father's lap. A student says, "Sure, I understand" and continues to look puzzled. A cat-hating woman says, "Oh, what a lovely kitty!" and shudders slightly. A woman quarreling with her lover says, "I never want to see you again!" and leans slightly toward him.

Albert Mehrabian has reported a study of attitudes revealed through head and bodily movements of persons as they addressed others. The findings indicate that when information communicated through nonverbal channels contradicts information communicated through the verbal channel, the nonverbally communicated information seems to predominate in the interpretation of the person receiving the two sets of information.[11] Such contemporary research merely confirms age-old proverbial wisdom: "Actions speak louder than words."

Mixed communication creates confusion for the receiver. Which message should he respond to, the words he hears or the contradictory nonverbal communication? In many instances, social custom dictates a "proper" verbal response, which may also involve mixed communication. Anyone who must transmit verbal messages that are subject to contradiction by nonverbal messages must be aware of the hazards of mixed communication. Successful politicians and successful hostesses, for example, must often say the "proper" words in the "proper" way, regardless of their own personal feelings; and those who are successful have schooled themselves to avoid betrayal by nonverbal contradictions. In reality these clever ones have learned how to "lie all over."

[11] Albert Mehrabian, "Orientation Behaviors and Nonverbal Attitude Communication," *Journal of Communication,* Vol. 17 (December 1967), p. 331.

Glaringly obvious contradictions between verbal and nonverbal messages are relatively rare; most are obvious only to sensitive observers; some are so subtle that only a lie detector could catch them. People differ markedly in their sensitivity to nonverbal communication. Some take the spoken message at full face value, regardless of nonverbal information. Others can truly say, "What you do speaks so loud, I can't hear a word you say." At the same time research is beginning to make us more aware of mixing. For example, studies in the synchronization of movement with the words have shown that nonsynchronization may indicate some form of illness.

If we are to be effective speech communicators, we must be aware of mixed communication so that we can evaluate feedback consisting of contradictory messages. If we modify to accommodate only verbal feedback, we may be diverted from our purpose, which is that the other person should receive our message as we want him to receive it. We should be alert for nonverbal communication; and when this contradicts the verbal message, we must decide how much we should believe of which message.

The voice as a nonverbal cue or tonal code

Through practice, the voice, which usually reflects some of a speaker's inner reaction and attitude, can be controlled and developed to provide proper reinforcement for verbal messages. The actor, in preparing himself for developing characterizations, learns how to bring his voice into focus as a positive reinforcement of the verbal and physical cues he uses in the performance.

Most of us do not have clear perceptions of how our voices sound to others. Inadvertently, many times, inner feelings that contradict verbal messages are revealed by the voice, thus confusing our speech-communicative efforts. While constructive criticism from friends can be useful as we learn to control the characteristics of our voices, frequent use of a tape recorder is generally more effective.

Pitch

Pitch, of course, is the relative highness or lowness of voice tone, as in musical notes. Few of us, fortunately, consistently speak in monotones; most of us indicate surprise, for example, by a higher pitch of voice tone and disappointment by a lower pitch. But few of us effectively use variety of pitch in speech communication. Varied pitch usually indicates interest in and concern for the listener and can be a valuable reinforcement of the verbal message. A few problems connected with pitch should be noted.

Tenseness of body and particularly of throat will not permit maximum use of the pitch range of which the voice is capable.

Variations in pitch should correspond with meaning; otherwise, the voice tone transmits a message that contradicts the verbal message and serves to block communication.

Too much prestructuring of the pitch changes to be used in a speech-communication situation will tend to destroy spontaneity.

Quality

The physical and emotional state of the speaker affect the quality of the voice. A voice of clarity, resonance, vibrancy, and richness depends on a physical and emotional state of being that allows the speaker to breathe properly, to form words with precision, to open up the passages of the nose and throat to permit maximum resonance, and to avoid unnatural and tense stridencies that contradict the verbal messages.

Volume

Loudness also is a factor in vocal reinforcement of the verbal message. The volume of our verbal productions affects our listeners. Through varying the loudness we can emphasize certain ideas. Through adjusting the volume to the size of the room we can demonstrate that we are willing to accommodate our communication to the listener.

Rate and rhythm

Rate and rhythm are also significant in the system of vocal cues. Relentless rapidity of delivery soon bores an audience and suggests that the speaker is rushing to get through rather than seeking to transmit information.

Changes in the speed of delivery of our speaking reflects changes in our attitudes and orientation toward our listeners. With psychiatric patients, "faster rates, shorter comments, and more frequent pauses have been found to be associated with anger or fear while opposite tendencies indicate grief or depression. Increase in the number or length of pauses may be symptomatic of indecision, tension, or resistance."[12]

Physical activity as a nonverbal cue

Movements of the body provide significant cues either to reinforce verbal messages or to contradict them. Such cue movements may involve the whole body (slumped in dejection, lax in indifference, tensed in apprehen-

[12] Barnlund, *Interpersonal*, p. 529.

sion) or some part of the body (the lift of an eyebrow, the tilt of the head, a clenched fist). Birdwhistell has worked out a system for identifying action in relation to the verbal messages.[13] His concept of kinesics involves the development of representative patterns of action so that they can be analyzed for their message significance. While his contributions to an understanding of the significance of bodily action are great, we are yet a long way from being able to codify behaviors of the body as precisely as some verbal behavior has been identified. However, the movements of the body unquestionably contribute much to the total face-to-face communication process.

Eye contacts alone transmit volumes of meaning between persons. A person who is assured of his position in the interaction may be more inclined to provide direct eye contact with his partner.[14] Anyone who has observed the eyes of others recognizes that much is communicated through their movement. We understand the expression "if looks could kill . . ." because we have sent (and received) such eye messages or at least have observed them. We exchange glances with friends in unspoken commentary on situations.

Movement of the body in communication situations does more than reinforce verbal messages. Most of us are inhibited to greater or lesser degree in terms of bodily movements in communication. If we can use the body to assist in communication, we are rewarded by a release of energy and an increasing freedom of expression that apparently cannot be achieved by any other means.

Freeing the body from the conditioned restraints of bodily activity is one of the greatest problems in developing effective person-to-person speech communication. Our society has generally relegated active physical movement to such places as the gymnasium, the athletic field, or the dance floor and discourages exuberant physical activity in communication situations. Different cultures and subcultures have different standards of physical activity in communication. In some such as the British upper classes, the use of the hands and body to communicate is considered shocking bad form. In others, such as the French, Polynesian, and Italian, there is a great deal more physical activity associated with speech. In few cultures, however, is much attention focused on the body as a communicative instrument.

Mime artists like Marcel Marceau and Francisco Reynders show us the tremendous possibilities of the body as an instrument of communication. The movement of a finger, the bend of the back, the position of a

[13] Roy L. Birdwhistell, "Backgrounds to Kinesics," *ETC.*, Vol. 13 (1955), pp. 10–18.
[14] Georg Simmel, "Sociology of the Senses: Visual Interaction," in Robert E. Park and Ernest W. Burgess, eds., *Introduction to the Science of Sociology* (Chicago: University of Chicago Press, 1921), p. 358.

foot, the tilt of the head, and uncounted movements and positions carry information in various contexts. Communicative interaction that involves free use of bodily movement carries impact, with a high level of accuracy in transmission of the total message.

For generations, speakers have been instructed about how to stand, what positions of the hands should be used to express given emotions and feelings, how the feet should be placed, how to sit, how to rise, and so forth ad nauseum. All these instructions were set down in rules and systems designed to establish rigorous sameness of movement. Now we believe that such standardization is undesirable. *Each person should develop his own mode of physical expression in respect to his intent, the situation, and the context and the nature of the message.*

Physical movement that inadvertently contradicts or intrudes on the message should be avoided. Thus, erratic movement of the hands, shifting of the feet, repetitive and meaningless facial movements and the like will tend to distract the listener from the actual communicative purpose. The body should be used to reinforce rather than to confuse or to inhibit communication.

Further, *bodily movements that serve for nonverbal communication should develop from internal feeling associated with the message being transmitted.* Assuming that primary concern is with reinforcement of the verbal message, we should allow our bodies to reflect the physical components of our messages as freely as possible. Of course, when we intend to send a double message, the body serves as a special instrument. External expression of internal feeling is of great importance in effective communication.

Freeing the body

Freeing the body to allow it to perform effectively as a true instrument of communication is easier said than done. It is not enough to take a course in physical education or athletics. Such training does not necessarily enable you to use your body in the communication setting on an interpersonal level. Oftentimes it makes you more self-conscious and thus more inhibited.

In recent years we have seen a growing interest in growth of the body and in bodily development activities. The interest in Hatha Yoga as a preparation for meditation and a means to increase bodily awareness has drawn many to explore its possibilities. A number of schools now offer courses or seminars in "The Language of Movement," in which students experiment with the whole body as a communication instrument. Much research is being done on possibilities of working out psychosocial problems through getting in touch with your body and working out ways to free it from unnatural restrictions.

Generally, several levels of development in movement are experienced as we seek to free the body to become a useful instrument. The first stage is *awareness*. At the very beginning we must face a social problem of the conditioning that many of us have had. We have been conditioned to think of the body as a necessary evil or as an unclean thing. Our training and conditioning have caused us, too often, to seek to cover up the body because we are afraid of what it is. Part of this comes from the false idea that any awareness of the body leads eventually and totally to sexual sensuality. This is simply not true. Being able to sense the pressures inside you or outside you, knowing immediately when your body begins speaking to you about where it is, recognizing where the threshold of pain is—all these are matters of *sensing,* which some call sensuality. In my new world, I would like for everyone to be totally sensual, that is, able to feel and respond to the magnificent communications that come from all parts of the body, including the sexual communication aspect of the body, which is now recognized as an important part of our total being. However, the sexual is not all there is to bodily awareness.

Close your eyes and stretch out your hand. Curl each finger up tightly and then let it go. Try to put your awareness down into your hand so that you can begin to understand what is happening to your hand when it is up tight and when it is relaxed. Do the same with your feet, legs, torso, head, eyes, mouth, face—the whole works. Tighten these areas up to tension and then relax them. You will find that if you take a little time to do this every day you will begin to discover things about yourself you had never realized before.

Another way to develop awareness of your body is through massage. Massage, properly done, is one of the most therapeutic and stimulating processes. In the hands of a skilled and properly trained physical therapist or masseuse or masseur, you will become aware of how the various parts of your body have been working. You may discover areas of tension that you never knew you had.

One area of study and development in the body arts suggests that because each of us is a total being and because there is no real separation of body, mind, and soul, all hurts, angers, hates, loves, frustrations, and successes are also hooked up to our physical behavior. For years, I have been generally considered feisty and aggressive. Recently, a physiotherapist with whom I was studying called attention to the muscle knots along the back of my neck, along the shoulders, and around the shoulder blades. After some time of massage, the therapist began to add pressure to the stroking and eventually (after several sessions), those knots began to disappear. The therapist did more than just the massage; he talked with me. As those knots were worked away, I was also working—in my mind and by talking with my therapist. In so doing, I was resolving a number of tensions and anxieties I had in my life style. The therapist was working on me as a total being—not just as a brain or as a muscle-bone machine.

The second stage of development comes when we begin to *move freely.* As awareness increases, we are able to detect tensions. When we seek to open up our movement, we can concentrate on certain areas that need help. One of the exercises my students seem to enjoy in this stage is what we call the "Bangies." I have a collection of percussion instruments: drums, tabla, triangles, cymbals, and the like; and when awareness appears to have started to develop, I bring these in and dump them on the floor. Students pick up the instruments and start beating out rhythms. Soon someone is dancing or moving to the rhythm. Before long the whole group may be engaged in a free experimentation with moving in rhythm. After a while we ask one person to stand in the middle of a circle, surrounded by others with instruments. The one in the middle starts to move—just any movement that comes—and the instruments are then struck to catch the basic rhythm of the movement made by the central person. As that person feels his own rhythm being *reinforced,* he begins to let go and to experiment with other rhythms and to broaden and spread the rhythm throughout his body. During these sessions, people who have not expressed their feelings in movement since they were children suddenly find that it is a very exciting, relaxing, and enjoyable experience. More than that, it puts them into a new world of interacting with others.

The third stage of the development comes when we begin to move in an *interaction* with someone else. At this point, outside music or record music is introduced. Blindfolded at first, everyone is allowed to move as he feels in response to the music. Then blindfolds are removed; and the movement or dancing continues, this time with the understanding that, when desired, people may move in relation to each other without touching each other. At first this is a bit tentative; but soon a group begins moving, and the interactions we discover that can be experienced this way are so numerous and so stimulating that we seem to open up totally new dimensions in ourselves and in relation to others.

This is but one of the several processes involved in trying to bring the body to an open, free state so that it can become more a fully functioning part of the interpersonal communication. When it does, it is beautiful!

Space and distance as a cue

Where a person sits or stands during a communicative interaction has message value. There is a difference in the message of an interviewer when he sits behind his desk in comparison to the message he suggests when he comes around his desk and sits closer to you. The physical distance between persons in the communication situation tells a great deal about the nature of their message.

Hall relates space to the vocal message and to the character of the communication in an intriguing scale:

1. *Very close* (3 in. to 6 in.)	Soft whisper; top secret
2. *Close* (8 in. to 12 in.)	Audible whisper; very confidential
3. *Near* (12 in. to 20 in.)	Indoors, soft voice; outdoors, full voice; confidential
4. *Neutral* (20 in. to 36 in.)	Soft voice, low volume; personal subject matter
5. *Neutral* (4½ ft. to 5 ft.)	Full voice; information of nonpersonal matter
6. *Public distance* (5½ ft. to 8 ft.)	Full voice with slight overloudness; public information for others to hear
7. *Across the room* (8 ft. to 20 ft.)	Loud voice, talking to a group
8. *Stretching the limits of distance*	20 ft. to 24 ft. indoors; up to 100 ft. outdoors; hailing distance; departure[15]

While this range is suggestive rather than prescriptive, it does give an interesting perception of the use of space in speech communication.

The space factor is particularly noticeable in small-group meetings. I recently worked with a seminar, the first few meetings of which were in a regular conference room, which was so arranged that members of the group sat at long tables arranged in a hollow square. There was open space in the middle, and a number of unused chairs allowed the group to break down into subgroups separated by empty chairs. While the group was meeting under these conditions, there was a very low level of close personal interaction in the sessions. At the suggestion of one of the members, we moved across the street to a dingy little cellar, less than one third the size of the conference room, in which old end-up cable drums had been arranged closely together in a tight circle. There were just enough stools, and all members could gather around the drums only if they sat close together. Almost immediately after moving to this setting, the tone of the meetings changed from impersonal to a highly personal interactive atmosphere.

[15] Hall, *Silent Language*, pp. 163–164. Copyright © 1959 by Edward T. Hall. Reprinted by permission of Doubleday & Company, Inc.

Time as a cue

Hall said that "space speaks" and "time talks."[16] Time does communicate much. *The rate at which we speak, move, and gesture tells of our inner intensity of feeling.* The cadence of our walking communicates something of our personal feeling and character. Each of us seems to have an inherent basic rhythm that is uniquely his. Our movements also reflect extrinsic rhythms imposed by situation and context. The heavy, slow movement of the ceremonial procession contrasts sharply with the movement on a dance floor.

Those of us who are exactly on time for appointments reveal something about ourselves and our perception of the importance of the situation. Halpin has pointed out some meanings associated with promptness:

> When a meeting is scheduled, whether between two or more people, who waits for whom and for how long says important things about relationships to the people concerned. Most organizations or cultures develop informal tolerance ranges for lateness; to keep a person waiting beyond the tolerance limit is a subtle way of insulting him. However, the handling of promptness and lateness can vary with the subculture and with the functions of the meeting. Thus military officers are likely to arrive a few minutes ahead of the appointed time, whereas professors usually arrive from five to ten minutes after the set time. In the social sphere, only a yokel will arrive at a cocktail party at the stipulated time; whereas good manners require a guest to arrive at a dinner party not more than ten minutes late.[17]

The pause in verbalization is also a factor of timing, as well as of vocalization. A break in the verbal output may provide opportunity for physical reinforcement cues to be made with some strength. A pause is often a method of creating anticipation, as when a speaker, after being introduced, strides to the platform, glances over his notes, looks calmly over the audience as if sizing it up, then stands for a moment looking hard at approximately the center of the audience. By the time he starts to speak, he probably has the attention of the audience; he has sent it the message that he is at ease, in command of the situation, and expects it to respond.

[16] Hall, *Silent Language,* pp. 15ff. and pp. 128ff.
[17] Halpin, *Theory and Research,* pp. 255–256.

Summary

Speech communication involves more than just voice and diction. The body, as an instrument of communication, tells almost as much as and sometimes more that the words we produce through sound and articulation. Some of the more subtle and significant meanings derived from speech communication are developed through the nonverbal systems. It is practically impossible for a human being not to communicate in some way. The channels and cues of nonverbal communication are numerous. Among them are the voice as a tonal code, physical activity as a verbal cue, space and distance as a cue, and time as a cue.

The nonverbal cues of speech are of utmost importance to the total act of speech communication. As we attempt to communicate with others, we should so integrate these many elements to create strong reinforcement for the basic verbal message; or, if we wish to provide a cover-up or protection, we can use nonverbal means to send messages contrary to the verbalization. The old adage "What you are speaks so loud I cannot hear what you say" is indeed consistent with contemporary understanding of human communication.

For special reading

Albert Mehrabian, *Silent Messages* (Belmont, Calif.: Wadsworth Publishing Co., 1971). In a neat little paperback, Mehrabian has brought a lot of the theory and concepts of nonverbal communication. He puts his material in a readable and understanding way. You will find this book one of the more practical and useful in the whole area of nonverbal communication. Read it.

Julius Fast, *Body Language* (New York: M. Evans and Co., 1970). In a popular and very readable way this book discusses the body as a message, territory, handling space as a communication function, touching and its meanings, the nonverbal signs and messages of loving, and the use and abuse of the body as a communication medium. Fast also goes into some aspects of therapy through body language but not enough to confuse the reader or to make the book a technical work on therapy. Have a look at this one.

Alexander Lowen, *Pleasure: A Creative Approach to Life* (New York: Lancer Books, 1970). Lowen, the author of two other important books on the body as a communicator (*The Physical Dynamics of Character Structure* and *The*

Betrayal of the Body) has moved to the frontiers of development in using the body as a beautiful instrument for communication, for becoming aware of yourself and the world around you, and for reaching out to others. His discussions of breathing, muscle tension, feeling and self-awareness, creativity, and rhythm as factors in allowing the body to become free and functional as a means of communicating and thus creating pleasure are outstanding. Lowen's work is basic to a lot of the work being done in bioenergetics at Esalen and other personal growth centers.

Edward T. Hall, *The Silent Language* (New York: Doubleday & Co., 1959). How people talk across cultures and societies as well as within these systems has long been a subject of professional study. But Hall takes on a tough task of examining the nonverbal communication within and between people and cultures. When he says "communication is culture" and "culture is communication" he really means it. The rationale he uses to develop this concept is most provocative as well as stimulating.

Marshall McLuhan, *The Mechanical Bride: Folklore of Industrial Man* (New York: Vanguard Press, 1951). This one will make you hot and cold, mad and glad. McLuhan takes a healthy slug at the manipulation and control of the collective public mind. His book is a collection of advertising gems with his own subtitles and textual analysis of them. Here you will see how the nonverbal works in the areas of the subconscious and the supraconscious.

Jurgen Ruesch and Weldon Kees, *Nonverbal Communication* (Berkeley: University of California Press, 1956). One of the first solid attempts to examine nonverbal communicative behavior in a way that can be understood. If you are at all interested in the nonverbal aspects of communication, you must read this book. While the authors bring their interest in communication from the field of psychotherapy, their analysis and application is outstanding.

Try this

1   Keep track of the nonverbal messages you have responded to during a given day. Identify those that had greatest and least effect on your behavior. Make an entry in your journal covering your observations.

2   Select some classic theme, such as "Good will win and evil will lose" or "Love will overcome all barriers," and either alone or with a small group of your colleagues improvise around it a story without words. Try creating the story line itself without using words to communicate to each other. When the story has been perfected, present it to the rest of the class and see if the message is made clear to them.

3 With a partner, attempt to conduct a conversation by vocal variation or the phonetic alphabet. Sit close to each other with eyes closed. Communicate to each other through varying tone, quality, pitch, rate, and duration of voice. Use only one or two basic vowel sounds, such as "oo," "ah," "ee." Use no words and do not touch each other.

4 With one or more others, enact a situation using only one phrase for all dialog. For example, enact an argument between a taxi driver and a traffic cop, with both parties using only the words "Onions for breakfast."

5 Sit face to face with a friend and let your eyes speak to each other with no verbalization. What messages can you give and receive?

6 Select a partner, then have that person blindfold you. Then without any talking, have your partner guide you around the building, and help you move around and become acquainted with the nature of the space around you. When you have developed a high degree of confidence in your guide, trade places. Notice how long it takes for you to develop confidence in a person when no words are spoken—or did you? What kinds of messages were you able to give and receive during the excursion? Did you get a different perception of the building space in which you have been working?

7 Sit face to face with another partner, across a table. Each of you close your eyes and then find each other's hands. Then explore each other's hands by movement, touch, resistance, and the like. What kinds of messages were you able to transmit and receive by this means? Were there cues about each other that you picked up through your hands which you had not perceived before?

8 Following is a list of emotions. Select from them several which seem difficult for you to express and try to express them nonverbally to the class so that everyone will know which emotion you are showing.

fear—security	sureness—anxiety
hate—love	exhilaration—depression
approval—rejection	success—failure

9 Try to communicate some personal matter to a friend (1) by whispering in his ear, (2) by speaking to him at arm's length, (3) by speaking to him about 6 feet away, (4) by speaking to him across the room, (5) by speaking to him outside at a distance of 25 to 40 feet. What variations and alterations did you make in the nature of your communication in order to convey the message? Now do the same kind of thing for a very impersonal or nonpersonal matter.

10 Using a tom-tom, a small drum, or a set of drums, beat out a rhythm that conveys a message to the other persons in your group. Try to make the message as specific as possible. Use no words or other gestures. Try a "conversation" with another person through rhythms.

11 After conversing with a partner on a commonly agreed topic for a few minutes, describe for your partner the nature of his nonverbal cues and what they have said to you. Tell him what messages you got from specific nonverbal behaviors he exhibited.

12 Turn down the volume on your television set, then, without the sound, try to understand what is being communicated during a newscast, a drama, a documentary, a commercial. What were the nonverbal cues which seemed most useful to you in getting the ideas?

13 Try to get into the production area of some plant or factory where the noise level is quite high (as in a paper mill or saw mill). What nonverbal means of communication are being used? How effective are they?

14 If you are a camera-bug, create a 35mm slide or a super-8 movie film sequence that tells a story without words. If you have the facilities put sound to the sequence with synchronized tape. If a sound-on-film movie camera is available, create a five-minute message without words on some vital issue of today.

15 Take special note of the physical arrangements of the following and comment upon what messages are transmitted to you by the furnishings, the decor, the illumination, and the like. What meaning does such information have for you? (1) a doctor's office, (2) a manager's office, (3) a teacher's office, (4) a restaurant, (5) your classroom, (6) a library, and (7) a supermarket.

16 With a friend over a period of several days or a week, play the game of "What you wear says to me . . ." Each day note what your partner wears, then write down what messages you received about your friend's mood, purpose, feeling, and the like from what is worn. Have your friend do the same with you. Exchange your written notes and talk about why you get the messages you do.

17 Next time you go to the theatre observe what the setting, the costumes, and the lighting tell you about the play. Are these consistent with what the actors say and do?

Chapter Seven

The Focus of Thought, Perception, and Behavior: Attention and Listening

Objectives

After studying this chapter, you should be better able to do these things:

- Live with your perception of the world as your *own* construction from your selection of available information and as consistent with your needs, desires, and predispositions.

- Communicate to the other person's world, which is not yours.

- Develop some control over your selections of things to which you will attend and listen by determining the purposes and intents for which you choose to listen to others.

- Adjust the redundancy, intensity, and other factors of your presentations so that listeners will be more likely to get your intended information.

- Seek out many different stimuli from which you will select information coming to you from another person.

- Cope with those things that command your attention because of their raw power from those you have learned to attend to and those you unconsciously respond to because of prior conditioning.

- Perceive and control marginal stimuli that will distort what appears to be the central message of the person speaking to you.

- Control your reception of the kinds of noise that really distract or disturb you.

- Receive information that you might not expect.

- Follow the thoughts and ideas of someone speaking to you.

"Paul, I hear what you are saying," said Roger to his son after Paul had poured out his hurt and frustration at what seemed to him a rejection of his way of life. Yet, even as Roger spoke, Paul knew that there was no understanding within his father. Paul knew that his father could not know the sinking, hollow feeling in his stomach, the tension in the back of his neck, the choking in his throat, and the utter loneliness that seemed to press on him from all sides. It was obvious that Roger was not hearing or getting the meaning of his son's appeal. Paul did not know about Roger's real hidden fear of looking at his son's problem, which was a strong reminder of an old problem of his own. In his fear, Roger closed down the response system—he would not allow himself to listen. Paul tried another approach. He asked David, a close friend of Roger's, to act as an intermediary, as a mediator, so that he could get his message through to his father. David managed an opportunity to talk privately with Roger. He was able to present Paul's position dispassionately and to help Roger look at his own reactions. Eventually father and son could face each other again, trusting each other enough to open up. They began to listen to each other; and, although they seldom were in complete agreement, they understood and accepted each other much better.

How many times have you sat with a group, tuning in and tuning out the discussion, aware of the general drift but understanding little of what was being said and getting little meaning as a result? If I only hear what you say, I may have only a collection of sounds. If I only see you, I have only visual impressions. Much more is involved in listening than just hearing and seeing.

Listening involves a particular application of the joint verbal-visual stimuli that occur in the speech situation. It is a highly specialized perception process.

Perception and information

We perceive by many means. Our senses all serve as input reception centers through which external stimuli of various kinds may enter our consciousness and unconsciousness. But merely entering our conscious or unconscious "holding tanks" does not guarantee a meaning consistent with the intent of the sender. Raw input stimuli provided by another directed at us may not be sufficient or adequate to stir up in us meaning that is consistent with the intent of the transmitter.

Perception has been defined as a process of extracting information from the world outside us as well as from within ourselves.[1] Information about our environment comes from stimulation of the sense organs by aspects of that environment.

Information permits reduction in the number of alternative choices

[1] R. H. Fergus, *Perception* (New York: McGraw-Hill Book Co., 1966), p. 1.

available to us in any given situation. Suppose we play the familiar game of guessing numbers. I think of a number, and you try to identify that number. As long as you have no information about limits from which you can select the number, your choices ranged from zero to infinity. As a rule of the game, I say that the number may be found between 1 and 100. What I have done, in essence, is to give you information that eliminates all the possibilities below 1 and above 100.

Information about our environment, that is, data that reduce the possibilities of response to our surroundings, comes from an almost infinite number of stimuli which surround us at every minute. Which information we choose to accept, or to allow into our system of knowing, through the jointly operating aural and visual reception centers depends on attention and listening.

We do not know when perception becomes operative in the human system; there are some indications that certain kinds of perceptions occur in the prenatal period. The newborn infant responds, however vaguely and diffusely, to such stimuli as light and noise, thus indicating an ability to perceive, with some degree of information extraction. However, the ability to make selective extraction appears to be limited at birth. As the infant matures, he learns to select from the mass of undifferentiated sounds and lights some that give him pleasure and pain. Eventually, he develops a learned selectivity so that he selects certain information stimuli and leaves much more unexamined. What he learns to select may be determined by the nature of his surroundings in relation to meeting his elemental needs.

Selectivity and perception

The number of possible stimuli available to any person at any moment is almost impossible to determine. Only a part of the total surroundings within range is at once available to all the normal operating senses.

We learn to select from the mass of available stimuli those from which information of importance to us can be extracted. To identify the myriad sights and sounds available at a busy center-city intersection at a given moment would take considerable time—if it were possible to put everything on a "stop-action" or "frozen" basis. At any given moment, it is simply impossible to see and to hear everything that is taking place within range of our perceptions.

What, then, do we see and hear on such a street corner? *From the mass of stimuli, we select those things from which information of importance to us can be extracted.* What determines the degree of importance necessary to prompt the particular selection?

Learned selectivities

We all have learned or habitual selectivities that may block perception of some stimuli and make us more accepting of others. Also, the very nature of some stimuli is modified as the stimuli are received, by the habits or learned reaction systems of the person perceiving them. Such terms as "conditioned reactions," "stereotypes," "attitudes," and "mind pre-sets" have been applied to these habitual selectivities, which are essentially processes of controlling the stimuli that a person will receive.

An Indian guide in the North Woods reads from the conditions around him much information that his party cannot perceive. Thanks to his training and conditioning, he knows the signs of a coming storm or those indicating the recent presence of animals in the area, while party members who do not have his kind of training and experience cannot select those stimuli that provide this information.

The ability of a city fireman to determine the center of a fire and to judge its danger might seem uncanny to most of us. However, through sensory impressions (the sounds, the quality of flame, the intensity of heat, the kind of material burning), he can extract from the situation information that untrained and inexperienced fire fighters could not realize.

This process also has a reverse twist; training and experience can prevent perception. We all have areas in which our training and experience tend to block our ability to select stimuli that give us valid information. Many of us who are black have been conditioned to view anyone who is white as brutal, insensitive, arrogant, hypocritical, possibly dangerous. Many of us who are white have been conditioned to view anyone who is black as stupid, illiterate, shiftless, subservient, possibly dangerous. And we find it difficult, sometimes impossible, to select accurate information from confrontations with persons of the other skin color. Likewise Arabs and Jews seem unable to perceive each other realistically. Our training and experience prevent us from selecting stimuli that would provide information to the contrary.

Complexity of stimuli

Up to a certain point, the more complex a set of stimuli may be, the more attraction it has. Past the point at which the mind or the senses can comprehend the complexity in some ordered system, selectivity falls off; and it becomes very difficult to extract any information. In such situations, we are often unable to perceive information we could readily comprehend in less distressing circumstances. For some of us, math courses and math textbooks present overwhelming complexity. For many of us, the first day of kindergarten and the first exposure to a functioning college campus were of such complexity. The learning period for a new job in a huge industrial complex, a first exposure to a freeway system in rush-hour traffic, entrance into a strange international air terminal are a few obvious examples. Few of us escape occasional disintegration of selectivity due to impact of complexity of stimuli. Frequently, when we face this condition we become suspended in what we know as an ambiguous state and our responses tend to become more primitive and basic.

Intensity of stimuli

Intensity, by its pure force and power, attracts. The intensity of a noise, of an idea, or of a color seems generally to force a high degree of selection of the stimulus. A speaker, whether on the public platform or in face-to-face conversation, who speaks with intensity of feeling and of delivery will attract a greater amount of selection than one without this intensity, other things being equal. Intensity can be subjective, caused by conditions inside the perceiver. For example, I may be very sensitive to high-frequency sounds, while you are less sensitive to them; thus, a single high-frequency sound will seem much more intense to me than to you. Likewise, information about which we feel deeply has more intensity value than that for which we have little feeling.

On the other hand, if we have deep feelings about information and messages we are attempting to transmit through speech, we need to clothe them with linguistic, tonal, physical, and psychic intensity in order to direct the listener to select these ideas from our comments.

Redundancy

Repetition and redundancy make avoidance of a stimulus more difficult. A single stimulus repeated many times has a greater chance of getting into the information system of the receiver than does one of the same significance with less frequent repetition. The use of repeated commercials in radio and television advertising demonstrates the effectiveness of this principle of performance. *In conversation or other speech-communication activity, the person speaking should consciously utilize repetition of those matters he considers of greatest importance.*

Attention and selection

Attention is the process of selecting those stimuli we will use to extract information. That is, it is the process whereby we process only a portion of the information we receive and reject or ignore the rest.[2]

[2] Neville Moray, *Listening and Attention* (Baltimore: Penguin Books, 1969).

Let's go back to our center-city intersection. Our own personal capacities for receiving various kinds of stimuli limit the information we will allow to be available to us. If my hearing is bad, I will not be able to get much from the sounds around me. If my eyesight is poor, I will not be able to make much from the visual stimuli that surround me. Likewise, my sensory conditioning may allow only certain kinds of stimuli to be available to me and will reject others.

The character of the stimuli themselves limits our attention to them. As a rule, the stimuli run a complete range of intensity, depth, closeness, and the like. Some sounds at that center-city intersection are loud, some are hardly perceptible to normal hearing. Some sounds are blatant and almost force us to admit them into our minds. Other sounds are so subtle that unless we are highly familiar with the sounds of the city, we have no perception of them.

If attending is the process of selecting a stimulus and extracting information from it, this process is dependent on the sensory capacities of the individual, the character of the external stimulus, the availability of the stimulus to the senses of an individual, and the past experience of the individual with that particular kind of stimulus.

We should also remember that external stimuli are constantly changing. Their structure, intensity, position, and significance are dynamic. No set of stimuli is ever the same. In spite of what we have said about redundancy and repetition, there is constant change. *No stimulus-response setting in human behavior can ever be reproduced again exactly as it was the first time.* One reason is that the effect of the first experience changes the conditions under which the second experience takes place.

Each of us, in one way or another, regulates the threshold of his perception of various stimuli. As our internal conditioning and needs shift and change, our perception shifts. Thus, the dynamic character of the process is inherent in both the stimulus and the receptor. If you are waiting for the arrival of guests, the sounds of voices approaching may be perceived much more readily than if you were closely watching a television show.

We believe, also, that *arousal* or excitation directed to a given stimulus affects our attention. Thus the drowsy person is not going to get much from his environment.

There is also some evidence to suggest that the degree of mental concentration we direct to a given stimulus affects our ability to grasp it. We also may be more attentive toward things we have *previously chosen* to look for. And, of course, our conditioning to receive certain signals determines a great deal of what we will attend to.[3]

[3] Moray, *Listening and Attention,* pp. 83–84.

Forms of attention

Attention is also a form of perception whereby we select stimuli that permit the extraction of information. Three forms of attention appear to be distinguishable: primary attention, secondary attention, and derived primary attention.

Primary attention

We give primary attention when we select stimuli because of their intrinsic raw form and not because of any learned or expected condition. We focus in spite of ourselves on those stimuli that are unique, bizarre, strong, emphatic, strong in contrast, and the like, simply because they force themselves into our consciousness. Loud noises, vivid contrasts, sudden movements, and unexpected events command attention. We need not exert much effort to attend to these things. Our senses simply give way under the extreme physical and psychic pressures that they create. When we're driving on a highway, the screech of brakes or the wail of a siren commands primary attention. Creators of television commercials strain for effects that force selection by the viewing audience. A fanfare of trumpets, the burst of a roman candle, a seven-foot basketball player surrounded by junior high school students, a unicorn in the garden—such stimuli would be selected by most of us in spite of ourselves.

When a speaker wishes his listener to focus on a certain message, he may develop that message uniquely, as with some linguistic or physical power or with emphasis. He may suddenly shout or whisper or slap the table with open hand. He is thus causing the listener almost involuntarily to select the special information.

Secondary attention

We give secondary attention as a result of selection patterns that we have learned. *We learn to select certain stimuli because they have given us particular information.* Usually the learning process consists of consciously seeking for information from certain types of stimuli. A good listener trains himself to extract information from such aspects as the sound of a speaker's voice, his posture, the way he puts sentences together. From the welter of stimuli at that center-city intersection, the city dweller will give attention to those that give him information he needs. If he is in a hurry to cross the street, he will give attention to traffic signals and the patterns of pedestrian traffic. An out-of-town tourist would not have learned to judge timing of the traffic lights and his chances of crossing the intersection before the light turned red. Poolside spectators often are not aware that a swimmer is in trouble, while a lifeguard is already acting to prevent a drowning. An unmarried aunt visiting a family with young children may not notice that the youngsters in the next room are very quiet—but their mother will; she has learned that silence from children at play indicates mischief of some sort.

Derived primary attention

We give derived primary attention when secondary attention requires little if any conscious effort. We learn to select certain stimuli because they provide useful information; and, after we have repeatedly attended to these stimuli, *selection of them becomes habitual, almost automatic.* A good typist is often not fully aware that she has heard the ping of the carriage-return warning bell, but she automatically responds to it by finishing a word or a syllable and returning the carriage. The experienced driver almost automatically and unconsciously attends to stop signs, road conditions, traffic conditions, and the like. A traditionally trained speech teacher unconsciously notes such things as a speaker's voice and platform behavior and the content organization of the speech. A good speaker who has had considerable experience unconsciously watches for signs of acceptance or nonacceptance of his ideas.

Experiments have shown that we are able to exercise considerable control over what we will attend to. Our criteria of selection seem to relate to location of source, frequency of transmission, loudness, semantic continuity (or logical relevance to reality), rhythm, expectancies determined by other signals, and the like.[4]

Listening

Listening is a complex and unique function of perception and attention that involves both auditory and visual capacities of the listener. Listening is a selective process in that we pick out from the many stimuli surrounding us those most fitted to our needs and purposes. The process of selecting stimuli that have the most *expected* meaning and significance is also highly important to effective listening behavior; we shall speak of this later. Selectivity includes the bringing of some particular stimulus or set of stimuli into the central focus of the listener's perception. Like attention, listening develops at three levels. We listen to some stimuli that cause a listener to focus upon them because of their suddenness, intensity, or contrast. There are also stimuli that we have trained ourselves to listen to or force ourselves to focus upon. There are those sounds and ideas that we listen to automatically.

[4] Moray, p. 88.

A constantly shifting process

Listening is a constantly shifting process. We do not focus upon one stimulus for more than a few seconds at most. Like the sweeping search of the radar antenna, our senses constantly scan the incoming stimuli to find those that carry information of importance to us at a given moment. The shifting is usually not random. We tend to follow things that are related to each other. In the quiet of a late evening as I sit reading, I listen as my son returns home. I hear him open the garage door, then the engine of the car as he drives into the garage, the closing of the door, his footsteps as he comes into the house. During that sequence, I may not be aware of other sounds that are being received by my ears.

Even when we are following some organized series of stimuli, as in a speech or a television program, there may be interruptions caused by intrusions of other stimuli that have more connection to our needs or that have such intensity as to force us away from the center of our focus.

Effects of motivations, feelings, and purpose

The process of listening is highly affected by the motivations and feelings that surround any given moment. When we are listening, however effectively, to someone talk, our motives and needs are operating with great power. The *purpose* of listening to someone talk is of great significance. We listen more effectively when we apply the principles of secondary attention; that is, when we consciously select, from what we are hearing, information that we need or want. We get more value from a speech, for example, if we determine beforehand what information we want from the speech; we can then listen on the secondary level.

It is quite as important to *want* to know what another thinks as it is to know that he thinks as we do. *The desire to listen to another person exerts a powerful control over our listening behavior.* The desire to listen, however, comes as a result of expected satisfaction of a hierarchy of needs, purposes, and intents that are wrapped up in our decision to focus on what another person is saying. When we are unable to focus upon something, we may be responding to some hidden feeling or motive that is rejecting the stimulus.

The desire to listen does not come easily for most of us. Too often we want to hear only certain kinds of information, and we tend not to listen to contrary information. Too often, too many of us hear only what we want to hear. It takes a disciplined mind to be aware of one's own desires and expectancies and to take them into account in seeking information that is not consonant with them.

A student who was bucking for an A in a course made many opportunities to talk with the teacher—always asking "How am I doing?" Every time, the teacher responded, "You're going to make it." The student thought he heard that he was getting his A. The teacher, however, was reassuring him about passing the course. To the student's shocked surprise, he "made it" with a C.

In such situations, feedback works very effectively with the process of attention. As speakers, we can check frequently to be sure that our listeners are really listening to what we are trying to communicate. Deliberate use of feedback for correction is one way in which listening can be focused.

Relationship of stimuli to other experiences

The selectivity that we exert in listening to others is determined in part by the similarity or relationship of the stimulus and its information to other immediate experience or to removed experiences that have occurred with some intensity and are well remembered. As we listen, we make connections with the past. If the past experience has been pleasant, rewarding, and enhancing, we are likely to attend to similar stimuli readily. If, on the other hand, the past experience has been traumatic, unhappy, or destructive, we may either attend to similar information in order to avoid repeating the unpleasant experience or we may simply not attend. The avoidance patterns of the students in the Black Bag case[5] at Oregon State University a few years ago is a classic example.

In that situation, the class group at first ignored the presence of the Black Bag simply because the members could not deal with it and had no frame of reference in which to place its existence. Later, when the press moved in with cameras, microphones, and hot lights, most of the class got up and left rather than confront the situation. A majority of the class members believed that the press would report the matter unrealistically and to their disadvantage.

Likewise, in the heat of the student rebellions on university campuses or the demonstrations against our involvement in Vietnam, many people focus their attention on the external aspects of the rebellion rather than on the underlying discontents and injustices actually present in the systems. Many members of the faculties and administrations feel severely threatened by demands that they confront their own inadequacies and oversights; therefore, their attention focuses on the superficial aspects of the dissent and avoids the deeper issues. Likewise many government officials operate under constant threat conditions.

The immediate closeness of the stimulus is also likely to affect our listening behavior. A person who moves very close to you to speak and who directs his remarks immediately to you commands much, sometimes all, of your attention and thus increases the probability that you will listen to him.

[5] See Appendix (pp. 270–274) for a summary of the Black Bag incident.

Information and noise

Listening is affected by the ability to separate the desired information-bearing sounds from noise. "Noise" we shall define as stimuli that are contrary to and distracting from the essential information intended or desired in any given stimulus. Surrounding us in almost any situation in which we attempt speech communication, there will be much distracting material. When this distracting material causes changes in the nature of the basic message and thus affects the development of the meaning in the communicators, we can say that the noise is interfering. Most listening is susceptible to such interference.

When a stray or marginal stimulus carries information that is quite similar to the intended message of a central source, it is more likely to create distortion of the intended message than if it were quite different. Stray stimuli that are quite different from the intended message system may also distort the message if they are particularly strong or intense. Up to a certain point of strength or intensity, a honking horn outside the building will do less damage to the message of a lecturer in the class than will "side-bar" conversations going on in the class itself. Many of us have learned to study with some form of music, from radio or phonograph, blasting the air around us. That we are not distracted entirely from our studies indicates that noise by and of itself is not necessarily distracting but that the condition and the relation of the noise to the message of the transmitter determine the degree of distraction.

A listener can increase his effectiveness in listening when there is some unrelated noise. The very presence of this unrelated noise may stimulate the listener to concentrate more carefully on the central material.

Expectations and receptions

What one expects to hear may affect what he actually hears. For example, a listener who expects a person to be angry when he speaks most likely will interpret whatever the speaker says as being angry talk. The effect of such pre-sets on listening behavior is highly significant. We can learn the mechanical skills of listening, but as long as we are hampered by pre-sets, we cannot adequately receive the essential messages that are sent to us through speech. It is not always easy to identify our own pre-sets; it is even less easy to eradicate them. To increase our effectiveness as communicators, we should attempt to identify our pre-sets sufficiently that we can at least consider their possible significance to our development of meaning from a given set of stimuli.

During the period when members of the Black Student Union were beginning to present "non-negotiable demands" to college administrations and when the Black Panthers were demanding, a few miles from the campus of the University of California at Berkeley, "Free Huey Newton!" a student from a northwestern liberal arts college attended a series of meetings in Berkeley.

A number of Black Power advocates spoke at these meetings. In planning to attend, the student decided that he wanted to be able to learn, as best he could, why they felt as they did. In preparation for effective listening, he talked with several black members of his university community about various concepts and expressions of Black Power. He identified some of his pre-sets; he realized that he expected bitter, irrational denunciation of such things as "whitey," "the Establishment," and "police brutality." His black friends helped him to realize, also, that there were deeper and more significant problems involving education, poverty, freedom, and personal commitment which the usual inflammatory talk did not reveal. He learned also that many of the bitter and irrational outbursts had origins in real frustrations of black people who had been unable to acquire what they perceived as their rights. So, when he attended the meetings, he tried to look beneath the surface for the potent reality. He did not completely eradicate his pre-sets, but he was better able to evaluate their influence on the meanings he developed within himself as he listened. He was able thus to hear more of what the speakers were saying and less of what he expected to hear.

Practice and reception

In listening, we sometimes find ourselves in situations similar to those in which stimuli are so complex that selectivity is numbed; we find ourselves attempting to listen to an essential message presented in a dialect or a vocabulary strange to us or in an unfamiliar subject area. A computer programmer trainee cannot at first listen effectively to shop talk in "computerese" about bits and bytes, "loaded and looping," input and output. An unfamiliar dialect of a known language is at first hard to listen to; a Middle Westerner may not be able to listen effectively when he first hears messages given in a genuine Down East accent with its flat a's or in the slow drawl of a Deep South accent. After some practice in listening to a particular kind of talk, we usually can listen more effectively to similar varieties of talk. A person who has often discussed philosophy can listen to philosophic discussion more effectively than one who has had no such practice. Likewise, one who has listened to many messages in cockney dialect can listen to what a cockney says more readily than one who has not had such experience. This seems obvious, but the clinker in the pit is the possibility that the experience will establish a set of expectancies that do not match what is going on at a given time. In effect, this experience has value and danger to it.

Screens of needs, habits, attitudes, and pre-sets

We can learn to listen to and for certain kinds of stimuli. However, our needs may condition us to listen only for what will meet those needs, and we may extract only information that will serve our immediate personal self needs.

Our habits, our attitudes, and our pre-sets may create screens that will block certain kinds of stimuli and prevent reception of the information that these stimuli might provide. We all have these screens, and we should be able to recognize them and their significance so that we can circumvent them when necessary.

Familiarity with a subject or with a kind of stimulus can cause us to develop an instant awareness of its presence. Repeated exposure to the stimuli we want to attend to will increase the probability that we can maintain our attention on these items.

Our wishes, too, can affect the perceived intensity of the stimuli we pick up from listening. In other words, a stimulus related to information we wish to avoid may not seem so strong as one that carries information we very much wish to hear.

Developing listening effectiveness

We cannot establish a set of rules or guidelines for successful listening because a rule that is effective for one person may not work at all for another. However, there are some general considerations that may help each of us to construct his own set of rules for increasing his listening effectiveness.

We can develop habits of seeking beyond what we expect a situation to produce. We should keep testing our expected or anticipated impressions against what we actually find in a given statement by another person. For example, I know a banker who reminds me of a fundamentalist preacher. Everytime I hear him speak, I expect him to say something relating to religion or church matters or sin, hellfire, and damnation. I must seek in myself other views of this banker so that I can listen effectively when he talks about interest rates and home-improvement loans and overdrawn checking accounts.

We can develop habits of focusing attention on the speech of others. At times it seems absolutely impossible for us to listen to a speaker. When we are confronted with this common barrier that prevents reception of information, we might examine the clarity of our motives. If we really do not want to hear what he says, we are not likely to gather much information from his presentation. "But," you say, "I don't want information—I want a grade in the course." Aha! Thus motives and purposes foul up the listening process. Whatever our motives, if we do not focus our attention on what another is saying, we cannot listen effectively.

We can prepare to listen. Casual or chance listening to talk from which we should get considerable information is not effective. Before we start a particularly significant listening task, we should get ready for it. How? We can determine our anticipations beforehand; and, as we listen, we can look for variations from what we expected. Sometimes, we need to convince ourselves beforehand that there are things of importance to us to be heard in a given situation or from a specific person.

We can check our own role and purpose in any given communication situation. We need to examine ourselves in terms of our purpose and function so that we can perceive the information that does develop in terms of the context of our actual situation.

We can examine the role and purpose of the speaker (whether formal or informal). When his purpose is to submit information that relates to our purpose to get information, we are more likely to get the message. It is not always possible to determine the speaker's purpose, but even the effort to do so aids effective listening.

We can determine how we wish to relate to the speaker. Our relationship with the speaker is an important function in the listening process. If we perceive the speaker as one who has much influence on our getting the things we want, we probably will not need to exert much effort to respond and to listen to him. However, if we are listening to someone whom we do not perceive to be closely associated with our needs and goals, we may need to concentrate more carefully on what he is saying.

We can identify the style and language of the speaker. The sooner we become consciously aware of his idiosyncracies, the sooner we can focus our listening on what he is saying and can avoid being distracted by noise.

We can, to whatever degree possible, determine how the speaker sees the world and follow his thought in the context of his world.

We can look for information that may be new to us or contrary to the ideas we hold. We should identify these and use them for comparison with our own images and conceptions.

We can determine the relevancy of bits of information to our own needs and purposes. To determine the relevancy, we should know what our needs and purposes are and we should be sure that we know what the information itself is.

We can test the reliability of the information we get from a speaker. Its validity and reliability should not be assumed because it deals only with our personal selves. We must consistently test the ideas that a person transmits to us to see if they are reliable enough for us to use for our own needs.

We can deliberately attempt to perceive the relevant stimuli of the speaking situation from as many different viewpoints as possible.

Listening is a selective process; therefore, we should try to select from what a speaker is saying and doing those messages that carry for us the greatest amount of meaning.

External influences on listening

The dynamic society of our age is full of rapidly changing complexities. I visited the famous Fillmore and Carousel Auditoriums in San Francisco. The changing patterns of music that were presented there are a testimony to the complexity of tastes and perceptions in our society at that time. The "light shows" and the great sweeping complexity of them challenge the imagination. In all of this crashing barrage of complex sound and sight, one must seek some central idea or thought to select from the experience or he will become so disorganized as to become helpless and exhausted.

The highly integrated and useful person who is sufficiently mature to cope with this dynamic society has been called by Alfred M. Lee the "multivalent man": ". . . multivalent is our being of 'many kinds.' It is our succeeding in being 'many things to many people.' We say things to a friend such as 'Do you want me to speak to you as a teacher, a fellow student, a counselor, a fellow employee, or a personal friend?' "[6]

This multivalency allows us to see more of the possibilities of interaction with those around us. Attention, therefore, can be dispersed among a wide variety of signals and symbols occurring at any given moment. As the attention shifts rapidly among these, it is multidirected and allows more possibilities of choice.

If the direction is uncoordinated and purposeless, confusion will result in our lives. *There needs to be an integrating factor that provides us with the basis for selecting certain stimuli from what people say.* This integrating factor may be of the greatest importance to our role as listeners in any given situation and to our ability to recognize this role. That which integrates our listening and our perception is compounded of our purpose, our goals, our needs, and our functions in a given situation. It is determined by "where we are" at any given moment. When one serves as a counselor he attends to and listens for a different set of meanings than he would if he were a judge, an advocate, a student, or a teacher. As we strive for maturation of our personal skills in human speech, we may learn to listen to any given set of messages from several

[6] Alfred M. Lee, *Multivalent Man* (New York: George Braziller, 1966), p. 79.

positions—as long as they do not destroy each other or create noise that cannot be overcome.

Summary

Perception is the process of information extraction from the many stimuli surrounding us. Selectivity is a key condition of perception in that it provides for the choosing of those stimuli from which we will extract information. Selectivity is affected by the complexity, the intensity, and the redundancy of the stimuli.

Attention is the process of selecting those stimuli we will use as sources of information. Our sensory capacities at a given moment limit the number of stimuli we may be able to select. The character and availability of stimuli themselves also limit our ability to select them. Our past experience with various kinds of stimuli also affects our ability to use them effectively.

The stimuli around us are constantly changing in structure, timing, and other aspects. Our changing needs and conditioning are also involved in the selection of the information stimuli.

Three forms of attention are distinguishable: primary attention, secondary attention, and derived primary attention. Primary attention involves unlearned selections of stimuli. Secondary attention is a condition of learned selection patterns. Derived primary attention is given after learned patterns of secondary attention become automatic.

Listening is an essential part of the speech-communication process. It is as important as the transmission act of speech. Without either of these behaviors, speech communication does not occur.

Listening is a complex function of perception and attention that involves the auditory and visual capacities of an individual. We are conditioned to listen to or to extract information that satisfies our need systems. We all have developed such personal attributes as habits, attitudes, and wishes that may screen out many information-bearing stimuli.

Listening, like attention and perception, is a constantly shifting process. It is affected, as are the other processes, by the feelings, goals, and arousal systems of an individual. The desire to listen to another person exerts a powerful control over our listening behavior. Our listening is also affected by the relationship of what we hear to other experiences; to the closeness of association with previous experiences; to the absence of noise and distortion; to our expectations, needs, and attitudes; and to the intensity of the stimuli.

Effectiveness in listening begins with conscious effort to seek beyond what we expect. We need to identify our own motives in the situation and to relate the information we receive to our needs. We must prepare to listen if we are to listen well, and the preparation requires us to examine our relationship with the speaker and with the information involved.

Our society and its systems provide many external forces that tend to prevent us from listening to each other efficiently. To be most responsive to this complex world is to be the "multivalent" person with an integrating purpose and direction.

For special reading

Argyle Publishing Corporation, *Principles of Selective Listening* (New York: Argyle, 1968). This is a programmed course and has some value in developing your understanding of listening behavior.

Paul Bakan, ed., *Attention: An Enduring Problem in Psychology* (New York: Van Nostrand Reinhold Co., 1966). Gathered together in this small paperback are some of the outstanding theories about attention and human behavior that have developed over several generations. Attention is related to perception, learning, personality development, and other aspects of behavior.

Ralph G. Nichols and Leonard A. Stevens, *Are You Listening?* (New York: McGraw-Hill Book Co., 1957). In speech communication, this is the pioneer work on listening. Nichols is the leading specialist on listening behavior, and this book covers many areas of listening skill and processes. Anyone interested in studying listening or in developing greater skill in listening would do well to start with this work.

Daniel J. Weintraub and Edward L. Walker, *Perception* (Monterey, Calif.: Brooks/Cole Publishing Co., 1966). In a neat and short paperback, the authors have compressed the major theories of perception and perceptual development. This book will be good background reading for further study of listening.

Larry L. Barker, *Listening Behavior* (Englewood Cliffs, N. J.: Prentice-Hall, 1971). Here is a concise and comprehensive little book on the nature of listening and "how to" listen. Barker discusses several kinds of listening and gives good hints on things to do to improve your listening behavior. He is clearly on the same "wave length" as this text and has written a good supporting work.

Neville Moray, *Listening and Attention* (Baltimore: Penguin Books, 1969). This is a paperback summary of some of the research on listening and attention in psychology and physiology. It is a good source for you who want to dig deeper into this subject.

Try this

1   As you listen to a friend talk to you, try to get what he is saying so that you can tell it back to him to his own satisfaction.

2   Make a list of things, people, ideas against which you are prejudiced. Do you think you "tune out" when you hear these words? Most people do, or some barrier to effective listening exists. Try to figure out what caused these prejudices so you can understand your responses. Hopefully, this will help you to avoid "tuning out" or distorting information when you hear these words.

3   Construct a short story containing several "loaded" words that might activate prejudices of a given group. Read the story to the group members. Then have three or four of the group leave the room, returning one at a time to tell the story. Compare the various versions. Did people listen effectively?

4   In anticipation of a lecture or sermon or other kind of public speech, try to identify the things you think will be said. As you listen, check these off. After the speech, jot down things you heard that you had not expected.

Things I expect	Were said	Things I did not expect that I heard

5   In your journal put a list of ideas to which you are *most* likely to listen regardless of their source. Add another list of ideas which you are *not* likely to hear or perceive no matter where they originate.

6   As you prepare a speech, try to identify what your listeners will expect you to say. Then line these ideas up against what you want to say. How will you hook up the two sets of ideas?

7   In class ask a speaker to prepare a short sentence or paragraph summarizing the substance of what he gives in a speech. Have him keep this until you have heard the speech and have written a short sentence or paragraph summarizing what you heard. When you have finished, compare the two statements.

8 In your journal, list the people in your class whom you are most likely to listen to and those you are most likely not to listen to. Then comment on what factors seem to be working to cause you to make these selections.

9 In your journal, list some of the important things that have attracted your attention today. Identify them as to how they came to your attention: through primary means, secondary means, or derived primary.

10 With a tape recorder (battery operated), place yourself in the commons or on a street corner or off somewhere in a park or at the shore or just anywhere—even in your own room. Now let your attention wander and dictate into the recorder everything that you observe during a five-minute period. In the same place, play the tape back, while you check to see what you missed. Can you detect any pattern to your original free wheeling of attention? What do you think determined that pattern, if there was a pattern?

11 Experiment with different kinds of music while you study. Which type aids your studying the most?

12 Place an orange in front of you. Now list all the possible topics that can emanate from your inspection of that orange. Remember, there is no limit to the directions you can take.

13 For a special evaluation of your classrooms (past or present), read the following descriptions of the two kinds of environments; then decide which of your classes offers the greatest opportunity for thinking, perceiving, listening.

The Open Classroom This classroom is characterized by the following conditions: (1) Students in the open classroom are engaged in many speech-communication events. (2) Students feel free to talk with the teacher, and the teacher feels free to talk with the students within the classroom time. (3) Students and teacher share active responsibility and share in the excitement of learning—the teacher learns as well as the student. (4) Students move forward on their own. They assume independent responsibility for their own learning. They do not wait for the teacher to tell them what to do or how to do it. They constantly seek ways and answers for themselves. (5) There is a minimum of teacher authority actually exercised. The fundamental authority or fundamental responsibility for learning rests with the student, and he recognizes it as such. (6) Differences of opinion between teacher and student are aired freely and openly. (7) In the open classroom, the student feels the teacher has a personal interest in his achievement. (8) In the open classroom, the central thrust is learning and growth.

The Closed Classroom In contrast to the open classroom, the closed classroom operates for a somewhat different purpose. Here are characteristics of this kind of classroom: (1) The students mainly listen to the teacher lecture. (2) The teacher is always in full command of every event. (3) Students are in awe or in horror of the teacher. (4) The students assume no responsibility for developing subject matter and depend wholly upon the teacher to tell them what to do. (5) No differences of opinion from that of the teacher are advisable because they may endanger the grade. (6) Students feel the teacher has little or no interest in their personal success in the course. (7) Everything always goes on the teacher's prearranged schedule, and no changes can be made because of student needs. (8) Students do not become personally involved in the subject matter. (9) Grades are paramount.

Chapter Eight

Decision-Making, Commitment, and Problem-Solving

Objectives

After studying this chapter, you should be better able to do these things:

- Identify problems more effectively.

- Make decisions and solve problems.

- Make commitments as decisions.

- Work out your personal decisions and agreements with others.

- Distinguish between valid and phony agreements.

- Make your decisions knowing how they are determined by your goals, needs, group pressures, rationalizations, and authority.

- Resist group pressures to agree when agreement is contrary to your own personal decisions.

- Test the credibility of "authorities" who seek to persuade you to accept their decisions as your own.

- Separate the elements of a problem in order to deal with it more effectively.

- Identify your goals and the obstacles you face in achieving them.

- Move toward solving your problems from the point of encounter.

- Distinguish between problems and solutions.

- Set up clear criteria for the solution to a problem.

- Create and deal with alternative solutions for consideration when trying to solve a problem.

Sam wanted to go to graduate school. Until now, however, it had been a wish somewhat divorced from reality. But the summer following his undergraduate graduation was almost over and his summer job would end in three days. What then? Seated in front of a warm campfire this night Sam finally encountered his problem. Staring into the flames, he began to take stock of himself, what he wanted, where he wanted to be, what was in his way, and how he might get where he wanted. He began to make some decisions about his life that would set him on a committed path of action for some time to come. The realization of the significance of this moment caused him to shudder a bit as he began to fit things together. "Now," said Sam to himself, "I must decide what I want to do when I leave school. Can I face up to what I really want to be and do?" Big decisions were immediately ahead and problems were to be solved.

We are constantly in process of making decisions. What we really do, as we make a decision, is to make a commitment. A commitment is a personal resolution. It is a resolve to do or to cease from doing some act, to adopt or reject some attitude, to anticipate doing an act, to adopt or reject some objective.

Can you identify the decisions that you have made in the past twenty-four hours? Try it! What kinds of behavior have you called or identified as decisions? How many decisions have you made within the past ten minutes?

Decision-making and commitment

A unique characteristic of a decision is that no such commitment existed until that moment when the decision was made. Any decision can be similar to a past commitment that no longer exists; but, because of time and space, each decision, and thus each commitment, is a unique event.

Often, after we have sat for a time to study or to type, we become uncomfortable and find it helpful to stand up, stretch, walk around the room several times. The decision to perform the act of standing up, stretching, and walking around the room is a commitment to perform certain behavior on a simple level of responding to the discomfort of sitting in a chair for a long time.

In collective bargaining negotiations with representatives of labor and management, a mediator, because of his position, must assume an impartial attitude toward the arguments of the participants in the negotiations. In one series of negotiations, it became necessary to reach an understanding of the meaning of certain phrases in the old contract. As mediator, I asked the labor representative to present his definition of the term, which he did. I then asked the management representative to present his definition of the term, and he refused to speak. After a time, I asked the question in another way in an attempt to get a definition. After five unsuccessful attempts to get his definition, I decided to stop trying. I had committed myself, after observing the behavior of the representative, *not* to pursue my inquiry further. At the same time, I decided that thereafter I would present any inquiries to this person in private, with only the two of us present. In so deciding, *I anticipated doing a certain kind of act.*

Attitudes and decisions

An attitude is a complex organization of commitments to behave in a certain way sometime in the future. (Some call this organization of commitments a predisposition, but the term is neither useful nor adequate for our purposes.) These commitments may have been arrived at through many means. The attitude itself represents a kind of commitment or decision. An attitude that is prevalent in the business world in spite of the Women's Liberation Movement is the resistance to women in managerial and executive positions customarily held by men. While this attitude is undergoing modification in response to enforcement of federal law, the cultural commitment to oppose selection of women for traditionally male jobs will probably continue to be strong in our industrial society for some time. (See Chapter 10, pages 200–201 for further discussion of attitudes.)

Throughout the complexity of our problems with civil and political disorders, there are numerous commitments to act in certain ways; and many of these attitudes not only conflict with each other but also result in overt and sometimes violent conflict when people who hold them confront each other. Such conflicts between attitudes have occurred on college campuses, on the streets of urban ghettoes, and in international conferences on Vietnam, Korea, and the Middle East. They occur, as they have throughout history, between man and woman; between parents and children; between law enforcement officers and criminals; between factions in schools, politics, and religions.

Most of these commitments that make up attitudes develop unconsciously. Many factors in our environment contribute to their existence. We might say that the needs, plus environment, plus the conditioning of a person lead him to make certain types of commitments we call attitudes.

Decisions to act

The resolve to perform an act or to reject some objective is a decision. How did you decide which school, college, or university to attend? Do you remember the kind of commitment that began to develop toward that decision?

A person's commitments are often internal and sometimes hard to perceive until the commitment appears in the form of action. Like the visible portion of an iceberg, the overt and obvious commitments are only a small part of the total commitment structure that governs a person's life. We see only the very upper portions of the total commitment structure that determines the life functions of any individual.

Decisions and agreements

A commitment is not an agreement. *Agreements between persons can be constructed from commitments that have already been accomplished.* They may be actually nothing more than reinforcement of a commitment already made, or they may be a creative new set of commitments that has not existed in any form before.

As a mediator at the collective bargaining table, I always find it exciting to watch development of agreement between representatives of labor and management, whose commitments are markedly antagonistic to each other. The union representative comes to the table with demands or requests that his membership has instructed him to present to management. He is expected not only to present these to management but also to return with management's acceptance of them. The management representatives, on the other hand, may have demands to make to the union, or they may be soundly and firmly committed to *not* granting any of the union demands. Commitments are not permanent and they change with the changing pressures and conditions that surround the individual. So, the representatives at a collective bargaining table begin to assess how far they can really go toward realizing their originally stated objectives. In the course of negotiations, they begin to readjust their commitments under various pressures. When their objectives (or commitments as to what they will accept) are readjusted to the point where there is a meeting ground, an agreement may result.

In a typical contract negotiation, a union committee came to the bargaining table asking for an increase of 75 cents per hour in wages over a three-year period. The company offered an 8-cent increase in each of the three years. After weeks of bargaining, the union modified its demand down to 55 cents. The company increased its offer up to 15 cents for each of the three years. At this point, apparent stalemate was reached and no agreement was achieved until a few hours before expiration of the old contract. Under the pressure of a potential strike, both parties shifted their commitments and came to agreement. The company offered 20 cents the first year, 15 cents for each of the two remaining years; the acceptance by the union representatives was ratified by vote of the union membership.

Phony agreements

Phony agreements are those that a person appears to make but does not actually make; that is, they are commitments that he has no intention of fulfilling. Agreements in which no real commitment is made have plagued mankind from earliest times. Wars have been fought because agreements called treaties proved phony. Every civilization in the history of man has developed laws providing penalties for phoniness in agreements known as contracts.

When an agreement is imposed upon a group through a forced consensus, there is no real commitment on the part of some members of the group. Many groups, such as juries and small committees, are required to reach unanimous decisions before taking action. Often, in such groups, all agree on a course of action except one person. In order to maintain the "integrity" of the group, that one person many times gives up and agrees to go along with the others. The chances are that the dissident who yields and agrees, at least on the surface, to accept the other point of view, never really accepts it, never has any genuine commitment to it. Likewise, agreements made under duress or extreme pressure tend to be phony agreements.

Sources of decisions

The total structure of commitments that a person makes actually represents his particular and unique system of behavior. Thus, the conscious and unconscious decisions that we have made throughout our lives and are constantly making represent and reveal the nature of our personalities.

Various conditions are connected with the process of making commitments or decisions. One condition, which we have recognized for many centuries, is that *decisions arise as the result of judgments or some form of reasoning to a final conclusion.* Notice that I said "some form of reasoning" and that I did not say "valid and reliable reasoning." Reasoning, whether reliable or unreliable, valid or invalid, fallible or infallible, good, bad, or indifferent, still serves as a basis for decisions made by people. We like to think that reliability, validity, and infallibility of reasoning are factors that affect the eventual decisions that we make. Yet, if we cannot detect the difference between fallible and infallible reasoning, reliable and unreliable reasoning, or valid and invalid reasoning, we are not likely to be influenced by those differences. Since almost any form of reasoning may lead to a decision, everyone should have some sensitivity to the process of reasoning and should be able to distinguish between the good and the not so good. Most of us still believe that commitments made from sound reasoning will probably be more effective and more useful than those made from unreliable reasoning.

Decisions may arise also from the whole hierarchy of our internal motives and need systems. All these are involved in our decision-making. *Our needs strongly affect the decisions we make.*

Group pressure and decisions

Pressures brought upon us from groups to which we belong also affect our decisions. Obviously, throughout our lives, our families have exerted pressures upon us that have led us to commit ourselves to behaviors of certain kinds.

One of the most significant and serious problems for our society is the effect of group pressure on individuals and the degree to which individuals are controlled, against their will, in their decision-making and their commitments by pressures of the group. One might argue that there is nothing wrong with making a decision or committing self because of group pressure when we wish to be acceptable to the group; in such instance, we are making a decision in terms of our basic wishes. This avoids the point of the argument, however. Basic wishes may not be consistent with the eventual decisions that are being made. In fact, reasoning may not be consistent with the eventual decision, which is too often made from fear or because of pressures that supersede the needs and demands of the individual. Too many of us have been so conditioned into behaving as does the group that we respond to the group pressure in much the same way that Pavlov's dogs responded to the bell. This is not to say that intelligent and thorough group decision-making is not a valuable system. It is to say that any group may easily impose its will upon any individual in that group, against the wishes and needs of that individual, in which case, the individual is in trouble because his real freedom is abridged.

Many times in our national history, the group-pressure effect has been demonstrated at political conventions. Every four years, a number of partisan activists of both major parties give lip service to platform planks they do not personally accept and close ranks to support candidates they personally detest—all in response to group pressures based on "party unity" and "success at the polls."

Many a good student has lost his academic standing because his living group, fraternity, or social group refused to allow him the opportunity to pursue his academic work without social ostracism.

Likewise many of the "flower children" among the hippies, whose philosophy and principles were significant in American culture and showed promise of maturing into a significant movement, were smothered and absorbed by a powerful subgroup of narcotics users and pushers who took advantage of the free thought and action culture to destroy it; and the "Jesus Freaks" seem often to be smothering the free and open expression of true religious feeling by imposing certain criteria and behaviors on their group.

Some of the most significant discoveries concerning the effect of groups upon decision-making were made by Musafer Sherif[1] and Solomon Asch,[2] who found that groups influenced the judgments of individuals regardless of the "facts" that were present. That is, individuals tend to conform to group judgments even when their own evaluation of the facts leads them to different conclusions. Conformity of this kind is a highly important factor in our interpersonal interactions.

[1] Musafer Sherif, *The Psychology of Social Norms* (New York: Harper & Row, 1936).
[2] Solomon Asch, *Social Psychology* (Englewood Cliffs, N. J.: Prentice-Hall, 1952).

Decisions and authority

Decisions also come from the pressure of authority. From our earliest days, most of us have been taught, often by punishment for transgressions, to make decisions that are consistent with our parents' wishes. For most of us, the strongest parental influences have been exerted by the mother. It was the mother who gave us substance as a result of our first cries. It was the mother who first stroked us in response to our cries. This gave satisfaction and conditioned us to please the source of these satisfactions. We learned early to respond to authority figures, that is, persons who could punish or reward us in various ways. This response then became generalized to include all those whom we perceive as having authority. Thus, *many times our decisions are strongly influenced by the person with authority who suggests or demands that we make a particular decision.*

Often, men or women deeply in love with another will, because of that love, allow the other almost complete power over themselves. When the love is not reciprocated this can be a cruel, destructive, and hurtful experience to the one who loves. Too often people forget that *a relationship is greater than the people involved.* Thus the power to impose decisions exists only so long as the recipient (or one who loves) will actually follow the other's demands.

Much too frequently, students in our universities respond to their teachers with nearly total subservience (the system of grades, of course, does not prevent this reaction). When students have been asked to determine their own grades and the method of arriving at grades, they have shown singular unwillingness to assume the responsibility offered. The opinions of teachers are too often accepted by students as ultimate truth rather than as expressions of individual points of view. This is not to say that many teachers do not abuse their authority role, for they do.

Credibility of the source is a factor in the acceptance of any information. This is particularly true in dyadic relations, such as man and wife, boyfriend-girlfriend, lovers, in which one or both partners get caught up in dishonesty or lying. When this happens they lose touch with the reality of each other because neither can rely on the other's statements or messages.

Essentially the same principle operates in the influence of authority on decision-making. We tend to assume that persons in positions of authority have high credibility to those who perceive their authority. Any of us, of course, can see the fallacy of this particular concept. It should be obvious that *the power to reward or punish does not necessarily include those factors that contribute to credibility.* Nevertheless, the position or status of another person can affect our commitments. A strongly religious person is likely to be influenced by his pastor or priest in terms of many decision areas as well as in religious commitment.

In the classroom, the authority of the teacher often induces students to make commitments that, left alone, they would not make. This is not to say that such commitments are wrong. I am not making a moral judgment on the commitments; I am merely describing the function itself.

Speech communication and decision-making

Speech communication involves a wide spectrum of decision-making. For purposes of clarity, we shall divide these processes into intrapersonal and interpersonal decisions.

Intrapersonal decisions

Intrapersonal decisions involve those commitments we make that are not shared by anyone else. Some decisions, such as what we are going to say at any given moment, the choice of person to talk with, or the purpose of our talking, we make all by ourselves, without direct reference to anyone else.

In speech communication, one of the most significant areas of intrapersonal decision-making is related to feedback. In feedback, we receive many different signals from which we select those that are most useful. Then we must decide on the meaning of the signals we have selected. Indeed, *the creation of meaning by an individual is an intrapersonal process of decision-making.* The adjustments that we decide to make as a result of the feedback are commitments to perform certain kinds of acts.

The young man in the black bag[3] made a number of highly significant intrapersonal decisions in connection with his choice to appear at all sessions of a speech class with his identity concealed. Having decided to appear in that fashion, he later made the decision to continue in his black bag throughout the term. It was his own private decision, also, that caused him not to reveal himself during the entire period. (It is believed that there are classmates from that group who never learned his identity.)

Our choice of whom we individually will follow, our choice of leadership or partnership, involves intrapersonal decisions. Intrapersonal decisions of this type are also involved in decisions about whom we should try to lead. We have no desire to influence some people through our leadership; we very much want some others to follow our directions. As we relate to others, we are constantly making intrapersonal decisions about following and leading.

Individual decisions, particularly intrapersonal decisions, are often made

---

[3] For a summary of the Black Bag incident, see Appendix, pp. 270–274.

quite rapidly. Within a short span of time, seconds or even fractions of seconds, a large number of conscious and unconscious decisions may be made.

Interpersonal decisions

Interpersonal decisions are those that involve other people more directly in the decision making. Suppose that you and I become involved in deciding what we should talk about. We then make some kind of commitment as to how we are going to relate to each other.

When we become involved with another person or with a group, whether it is a staff group, a class group, an informal group, a family group, or any group of any kind, one of the decisions that we unconsciously make has to do with the amount of claim or control we will allow others to have on our actions; that is, how much effect we are going to allow others to have upon our own decision-making. We are seldom aware of the process of making this decision; but each time we associate with another person we must resolve a question in relation to that other person: *To what degree are we going to allow that other person to control our behavior?*

This decision to allow others "in" to our life-space as co-decision-makers is the key to interpersonal relationships. If we are willing for another to have some influence upon our decisions, we are then relating at an interpersonal level. If we refuse to grant another any influence (consciously or unconsciously) upon our decisions, we are staying closed up within our intrapersonal selves. However, the selection of a leader by a group becomes an interpersonal matter when you and I allow others to have equal voice (or vote) in that decision.

Group decision-making

Group decision-making is more complex and more involved than the interpersonal and the intrapersonal decision-making. *A group decision is a collection of common individual commitments.* It involves intrapersonal and interpersonal decisions. When several of us agree to perform a common act or to accept a common anticipation of action (that is, an attitude) through joint discussion, we are making a group decision. A unanimous, or consensus, decision occurs when all members of a group make the same commitment and proceed to perform similar behaviors.

Majority decisions represent something less than total group commitment in any given matter. In many groups, there are always some people who are not committed to any action that the majority of the group will follow. When unanimous, or consensus, procedure is used, no decision or commitment is made that is not followed by everyone in the group. Both types of group commitment have values and weaknesses, depending upon the demands of a given situation.

Interactions of the members of the group itself represent various kinds of commitment to each other. Each person responds to another person in a manner different from that of anyone else. In any group, each member chooses among the others those whom he likes and dislikes and those with whom he will and will not do certain things; and his pattern of choices usually will be different from the choices made by anyone else in the group. *The interpersonal interactions that are apparent in any group are the result of a type of decision or commitment of the individual members with relation to each other.*

True full commitment of a group to a common action, a common objective, or a common attitude is practically impossible in a complete sense because each one of the group members, as we have so often mentioned, sees the world differently. You and I may stand at the bottom of the steps of the east entrance of the United States capitol in Washington, D. C., and by concurrent agreement we may decide to walk up those steps. Now, that is a simple decision, a simple commitment; but the decision *I* make to walk up those steps is not the same as the decision *you* make to walk up the steps. While we both have decided to walk up those steps, we may each be doing it for a different purpose. Neither of us can walk up exactly in the same way or in the same place as the other.

A personal crisis service group decided that each member of the group would persuade five persons to come to the next meeting. This decision was unanimous and everyone left the meeting expressing conviction that things were really going to happen. Now, I don't know about the others, but in my own mind I'd accepted the *idea* of getting five people, although I knew I couldn't really *get* five people. My own private decision was that I would probably try for five and there were three prospects I would definitely approach. However, I was none too sure that I could persuade any of them to attend the meeting. My decision really was different from the group decision, and I'm sure that the decision of each individual in that group differed from our joint decision—and from the individual decision of every other member.

At a certain level of abstraction, a group may reach a joint commitment. *The more abstract the proposition under consideration, the greater the possibilities of joint agreement; and the more concrete the proposition under consideration, the less the opportunity for full agreement.* In the monthly meeting of a union local, there will be genuine full agreement about the highly abstract proposition that "in union there is strength"; but concrete details of planning the local's annual picnic will be determined by bare-majority vote. The level at which agreement can be reached must be sought by a group. Collective bargaining between labor and management or between any other groups presents a classic example of how the parties to a disagreement seek the level at which they might reach agreement.

In one typical instance, contract negotiations bogged down over a clause about hiring part-time employees. Before this clause could be acceptable to both parties, the term "part-time employee" had to be defined to mutual satisfaction. One proposed definition was "a part-time employee is one who works less than forty hours a week, on irregular schedules, and is not subject to the benefits of regular employees." Another was "anyone who works less than forty hours per week." Obviously, the latter definition would cover more people than would the first definition; it not only would cover more people but also would permit a wider range of interpretation. The union wanted a very specific definition so that it would include all part-time employees as dues-paying members of the union. The company wanted the broad definition so that it could, at its own discretion, decide on those persons who would secure the full benefits of the employment. In order to reach agreement, it was necessary for both parties to accept a definition more abstract than either wanted: "Part-time employees are all those employees who are not regular employees." Only on this could they agree. Application was left open, depending on circumstances of future specific cases.

The effectiveness of decision-making in groups depends largely on the degree of appropriateness of the alternatives that are available to a group. Suppose we are a committee on student discipline in a large university. One of the rules of the university is that no member of the university community shall interfere with the orderly conduct of classes and administrative business. We are called upon to decide upon the discipline of students who, during the course of a demonstration, caused disruption of classes and of the university administration.

If the regulations restrict us by spelling out in detail the choices we have and the conditions of each choice, we would be limited in the decisions we can make. Suppose we have only two alternatives: expulsion with denial of readmission or a one-semester suspension with readmission subject to review. There would be an immediate division within our group. But suppose instead of two possibilities, we have eight, ranging from a nonpunitive warning to summary expulsion. There would be six other alternatives between these two extremes; our decision-making would have greater possibility of common agreement. *The more limited the alternatives, the greater the possibility that strong differences will arise.* The appropriateness and inappropriateness of the alternatives that are available to the group will depend in part on the variety or range of choices available.

Appropriateness may also be related to the degree to which the choices available fit the particular situations. In this case, if we had no policy or precedent and were free to make the decision, the number of alternatives would be almost infinite at the beginning of our deliberations. Alternatives for consideration would then arise from each of us present as we submitted our ideas. This is one reason why such decision-making groups should have wider latitude in the alternatives available.

Problem-solving

We have said that decision-making and problem-solving are different processes. So they are; however, the two are closely related. Certainly, decisions are involved in the solving of problems. The existence of problems requires the making of decisions, and problem-solving activity is essential to human life. The distinguishing difference between the two processes lies in the manner in which problem-solving organizes the decisions. *Problem-solving is a system of arranging and organizing our decisions so that they will have the greatest usefulness or value.*

Effective problem-solving permits a person to cope with the conditions around him through an organized and rational system of related decisions. Some of the ways in which decisions are organized to solve problems are familiar to all of us.

We may let someone else tell us how to act to solve the problem. (Note that this is a decision.)

We may use an organized, rational procedure of studying and analyzing a problem and acting on our conclusions.

We may let the problem "incubate" in the unconscious until a solution occurs to us on which we can make a decision.

We may suddenly have a flash of insight that will reveal a solution to a problem on which we can act.

We may solicit the aid of others in a joint discussion of the problem and seek to get a joint decision.

We may act on the basis of intuition or some hidden, unidentified feeling which seems to direct our action.

In all these approaches, decisions play an integral part in the total process; but in problem-solving the decisions are fitted together in a particular manner.

Problems

All problems have certain elements. In any problem, there must be a goal, obstacles to achievement of that goal, and the point of encounter at which we become aware of the obstacles. Notice the identification of the following problems: I want an album recorded by a new jazz quartet (*goal*). I am in a record shop (*point of encounter*) and find that the record costs more than I have with me in cash (*obstacle*). In coping with the problem, I must deal with factors from all three of these aspects. The goal may be strong or weak; I may very much want the record right now or I may be only mildly interested in adding it to my collection. The degree of intensity of my desire to reach my goal will influence my attempts to solve the problem. The nature of the obstacle, my financial situation, is important; the cash in my pocket might be all I have till payday or I might have a checkbook and credit cards. If the record shop is a "cash only" establishment, the solution of my problem may be more difficult to find than if the management will accept a check or a credit card.

Practically all our human problems can be placed in the goal-obstacle-encounter context, which allows us to examine problems closely and provides an opportunity for us to find effective solutions.

Goals   First, no problem exists unless there is essentially some goal or target or desire that we strive to accomplish or reach. Our goals are simple and complex, rational and irrational, conscious and unconscious. Some are inherent in our physiological nature. The seeking for food, for elimination, and for maintaining the equilibrium or balance of our biological systems are almost purely physical in nature. Each of us also has psychological goals that serve to sustain and enhance our selves. Our social and cultural conditioning sets up other goals of behavior which we are expected to follow. (The sociocultural goals are often interrelated with the physical and psychological goals.) Acceptance by others around us is a psychological goal related to the eventual self-realization objectives. Acquiring economic substance or becoming a leader are social goals.

In addition, goals may arise from a particular situation. In almost every situation in which we find ourselves, goals or objectives affect our behavior in that situation. When we start out in the morning, we have goals or objectives for the day. Some are not so clearly perceived, while others are very obvious; some are inherent in our bio-social-psychological existence, while others are developed from the situation facing us.

Likewise, goals may be developed jointly, to be shared by several persons. Persons who decide that they wish to form a corporation to produce lumber products have a common goal. In the venture, each person in the group also has specific goals of his own, but these are related to the group goal.

Our goals may have a quality of generality or specificity. A member of the track team may be trying to run a four-minute mile. In one sense, that would be a specific goal; but, in order to accomplish that four-minute mile, a number of more specific objectives must be met. He must be in condition; he must have a plan for the amount of time to be expended for each quarter of the mile. Thus, if he plans to run the first quarter in 53 seconds, the second in 60 seconds, the third in 67 seconds, and the last in 60 seconds, he is setting intermediate, or more specific, goals to accomplish. *To accomplish a major objective, we must reach certain subordinate or contributing objectives.* The more specific, intermediate, contributing goals to any of our objectives we are able to determine and allow to occur, the more likely we are to understand and develop ways to reach the larger target. My yoga teacher impressed upon me that I must not try to achieve an *asana* (position) until my body was ready. He kept saying, "Do what your body will allow you to do without pain or trauma. Your body will tell you when it will complete the *asana.*" I became much more conscious of the importance of the intermediate stages of goal seeking when I became overdesirous of achieving a headstand and forced myself to a point where I hurt my neck—almost seriously. Determining specific goals has very significant implications to all of our behavior.

A student entering a university often has some general idea of purpose or goal of his education. The student who decides, for example, to become a lawyer soon discovers that there are some intermediate objectives that he will have to meet such as pre-law undergraduate courses, law school, and bar examination. Any student whose larger target is a degree must achieve many subordinate goals and must plan the intermediate steps for each year of his work. Certain school requirements must be met, required or desired courses have prerequisites that must be successfully met, and so forth (sometimes ad nauseam). On the other hand, more and more students are coming to the university with a desire to become better human beings. Their goal is vague and abstract; but when they allow themselves to explore their interests and their personal inclinations at their own speed without undue pressure to "become human" or to gain a vocation overnight, they often find a rich rewarding experience in the process of "becoming." These people are willing to allow the subordinate goals to come to be before forcing the final step. Too many students come to school today feeling that society, economics, and parents demand vocational or professional competence in four years or less and thereby lose sight of some important intermediate goals that are prerequisite to a truly competent human being.

Obstacles   The second characteristic of a problem is that the goals are blocked, hindered, inhibited, resisted, opposed, obstructed, or restrained by some thing, person, idea, or combination. These barriers we call obstacles. Without obstacles, there are no real problems; were the goals reached with no form of obstacle, there would be no problem. *The existence of the obstacle to achievement of a goal creates the condition that we identify as a problem.*

Attainment of a college degree of itself presents no problem. However, between a high school senior and that degree there are many barriers; and these barriers create problems. There are entrance requirements. Classes may not be available when he needs them. He may have inadequate high school background in some subject areas. Funds may not be adequate for expenses. In four years or so, any student encounters a host of major and minor barriers; the route to a degree is beset by problems.

Point of encounter   The third characteristic of a problem is the point of encounter, when one becomes aware of obstacles between him and his goal. *The circumstances of time and place surrounding the point of encounter are important aspects of the problem itself.* A street blocade is certainly an obstacle for a driver who wishes to use that street. If he is on an errand that has no particular time restrictions and permits alternative routes, the point of encounter will not present him with a serious problem. If, however, he has selected the street as a shortcut to the airport where he must catch a plane to keep a vitally important appointment in another city, at the point of encounter he will become aware of problems of great moment to him.

If we can perceive and define our problems in terms of the goal-obstacle-encounter triad, we have taken the first rational step in the process of problem-solving. However, this first step is often quite difficult. *Many times we perceive problems in terms of symptoms,* and these do not necessarily relate to the nature of the goals we may have. The race riots that began in 1965 in Watts and the campus confrontations that started about the same time were symptoms of some very serious and very basic problems of our society, as were the prison riots of 1971 and 1972. Few people calmly and carefully examined the nature of the goals of the people involved and the obstacles to these goals that existed in the affected communities. Nor did many examine the goals of the overall society to determine what obstacles became apparent at the points of encounter of the various civil disorders.

Actual differences in and conflict of goals may cause us to stalemate at this first step. Here decision-making becomes a part of problem-solving. *Clear decisions must be made about what goals are to be sought as an essential aspect of the initial step of problem-solving.*

Once the goals have been perceived or decided upon, it is reasonable to identify and to examine both the obstacles and the nature of the encounter. This process requires systematic investigation of these factors so that we may understand what they are and their relation to the eventual realization of our basic and total objectives. In the process of this examination, we often change our objectives (decisions again) or become more intense in our desire to reach the goals.

Criteria   During this examination we may discover certain conditions that must be met if we are to reach our ultimate objective. These conditions can be identified as the *criteria by which we will judge any possible solution to the problem.* We are not ready to explore possible solutions until these criteria have been established. The criteria help us to select (by decision again) the type of solutions that may be useful.

Alternatives and solutions   The examination of possible solutions is of extreme importance. At the outset, there usually are several alternative possibilities available for the solution of a problem. The more alternatives, the greater the possibility of finding good solutions. Solution possibilities should include as wide a range of possible methods as we can create or discover. Of course, all the possible solutions must be in terms of the established criteria.

Having identified several solutions, our next step is to test each one. The testing is a rational process of making decisions as to the degree to which each of the possibilities does or does not satisfy the established criteria. For example, I am thinking of purchasing a new car. My examination of the obstacles and the encounter lead to the following:

Goal: New car.
Obstacles: Not enough money, resistance of wife.
Encounter: Service man reports, after attempting to tune engine, that major repairs on old car are essential.

So, in developing criteria for the solution, I find at least the following: (1) must satisfy wife, (2) must be able to finance without excess costs, and (3) must meet my needs for transportation.

With this sketchy analysis of the problem, I may then visit a number of car dealers (examination of possible solutions). With each one I review the criteria that have come out of my encounter with the problem. As I go from one to another, I may now and again reexamine my whole problem. My criteria may be modified; for example, I might add that I want a new car that will be consistent with my perceived status in the community. Eventually, I may make a decision about which new car I shall purchase. (Remember that the first decision was the result of an alternative issue that arose in the encounter; namely, whether I should buy a new car or repair the old one.)

The rational recognition that this decision may lead me to the goal does not necessarily mean that the problem is solved. The decision to act does not necessarily include the decision on *what* action should eventually be taken or exactly *how* that action should come about. I may decide to buy a new car offered by one dealer; but immediately the means of financing, the time of delivery, and the like become problems. These, in turn, are subject to problem-solving treatment.

Further, *the decision to act must emerge from the total "need-emotion-rational" condition that prevails when the decision must be made.* In other words, the decision on a solution is still not the action. After I have decided on the new car, I still must sign a contract, clear out the trunk and glove compartment of the old car, turn over its keys, and take delivery on the new one. The act itself requires additional pressure, which, in this case, the salesman will provide—with suave alacrity.

We often reach general decisions about large or small problems, then find that decisions to perform specific acts required by that general decision are not so readily made. A general decision to lose weight in order to solve the problem of clothes that no longer fit does not assure consistent rejection of desserts. A decision to make better grades as a solution to the problem of a condition does not guarantee the act of studying day after day. The decisions to perform specific acts may not follow from the decisions of general nature.

The use of problem-solving

An organized approach to problems is not necessarily an inherent process; it can be learned. The approach can become an effective instrument with which to deal with personal problems as well as with group and social problems. First and foremost, each of us needs to understand himself and his goals. Further, we must be able to reveal ourselves so that others can help us to understand our problems.

Problem-solving is not a singular decision process, as we have seen. Such decisions as which goals are desirable, which obstacles are significant, which criteria should be used, which solutions are applicable are critical to the process. Throughout, a multitude of smaller decisions are made in relation to eventual behavior and action.

The process, as an organized method, can be applied by groups in dealing with their problems. Administrative staffs, organizations, work teams, committees, and other combinations of people on a less formal basis, such as the family, may find the use of an organized approach such as we have described most useful in dealing with problems or with tasks that become problems.

Summary

Decision-making and problem-solving are separate but related functions. Decision-making is the process of making commitments. Problem-solving has a larger scope and encompasses a wider range of behaviors, including many decisions or commitments in solving a single problem. The process of reaching a commitment is not always a rational process. Much of it comes from our need systems, conditioning, past experiences, our here and now, and our hopes for the future.

Problem-solving, on the other hand, is a process of organizing decisions around our goals and the obstacles to those goals, so that we can accomplish our objectives. A problem consists of a goal or several goals, obstacles to the goals, and a point of encounter. By developing our decisions around

these factors we may reach solutions. It is not an inherent or automatic system that we humans normally follow. It must be learned and developed as a
particular skill.

A decision to act is only one kind of decision. Attitudes are kinds of
decisions. Agreements between persons are constructed from decisions
arranged in reference to another person or persons. Some "agreements"
are really not agreements at all; forced consensus, for example, is one such
agreement in which there is no real commitment. Our decisions come from
judgments, reasoning, motives, need systems, group pressures, authority
pressures, intuition, and so on. Decisions *not* shared with other persons are
*intra*personal; *inter*personal decisions involve two or more persons.

Group decision-making is a more complex process. It involves a collection of individual decisions around a central point. For any group, joint
commitments about specific matters are more difficult than joint agreement
about abstract matters.

Our total speech-communication activity is a type of decision-making
with ourselves and with those around us.

For special reading

J. P. Guilford, Moana Hendricks, and Ralph Hoeptner, "Solving Social Problems Creatively," *Journal of Creative Behavior,* Vol. 12 (1968), pp. 155ff. For
those of you who are interested in research, this concise article outlines some
of the testing instruments used in examining a form of problem-solving behavior. The article summarizes a series of research projects seeking to find
a way to measure the presence of creative ability in problem-solving.

J. P. Guilford, *The Nature of Human Intelligence* (New York: McGraw-Hill
Book Co., 1967). If you want to dig this matter of problem-solving in depth, a
prerequisite is this work by Guilford. This book is a comprehensive survey of
the factors of intelligence, not the least of which is problem-solving. Chapter
14, in particular, deals with problem-solving in a specific way.

John Dewey, *Logic: The Theory of Inquiry* (New York: Holt, Rinehart and
Winston, 1938). Do you feel like taking on a tough task? Try studying this
book to get some of the mass of information from it. Here is a logical and
philosophical analysis of the basic theory of problem-solving in great detail.
This work has probably had more influence on the theory of problem-solving
current in American education than any other source.

Try this

1 Outline a personal problem in terms of goals, obstacles, and point of encounter. Try to identify the alternatives at each point and how you arrived at the various decisions.

2 List all the decisions you can remember making during the past 24 hours. Group them into the following categories:

1. Decisions about goals
2. Decisions about procedures (i.e., how you're going to accomplish some goal)
3. Decisions about specific actions
4. Decisions relating to the here and now
5. Decisions relating to the future
6. Decisions that were pleasant
7. Decisions that were unpleasant
8. Other

3 Identify five major decisions you have made in your life. Try to determine what kinds of source or sources influenced each of these decisions.

4 The next time you go to someone for help on a personal problem, tell him first the following things about your problem:

1. Your goal or goals
2. What's obstructing your reaching these goals
3. When, why, where, and how you became aware of the problem

5 Describe some behavior of yours that comes from attitudes (patterns of decisions, remember). Set up your analysis in the following pattern for the sake of clarity:

My behavior (describe the behavior and when it happened):

Seems to come from the following predecisions:

6 Listen to a group discussion. Try to identify the contributions made by members of the group in the following categories:

1. Goal-involved statements
2. Obstacle-involved statements
3. Point-of-encounter statements
4. Solution statements
5. Decision statements

7   Arrange a group discussion around some topic. Try to guide the discussion to follow the problem-solving process.

8   In your journal identify the situations during the past few weeks when you have made decisions to go along with group-decisions as a result of group pressure.

9   Douglas McGregor says, in *The Human Side of Enterprise* (New York: McGraw-Hill Book Co., 1960, p. 33), "Behind every managerial decision or action are assumptions about human nature and human behavior."

> The extremes he calls Theory X and Theory Y. Theory X assumes that the average human being has an inherent dislike of work; will avoid work if he can; must be coerced, controlled, directed, threatened with punishment to put forth adequate effort; wishes to avoid responsibility; has relatively little ambition; and wants security above all.
>
> Theory Y, in contrast, assumes that the average person does not inherently dislike work; will exercise self-direction and self-control; learns to accept responsibility, and even to seek it; has the capacity for imagination, ingenuity, and creativity in solving organizational problems; but, under the conditions of modern industrial life, only partially utilizes his potentialities.

Observe as many different managerial situations as you can. Try to classify them as to which assumptions underlie the behavior of the managers. Do the same for teachers, for elected officials.

10   Grid A is adapted from Robert Blake and Jane S. Mouton, "The Managerial Grid in Three Dimensions," *Training and Development Journal,* Vol. 21 (January 1967), p. 255. Locate the section of the grid in which each of your several classes exists.

Grid A

High concern for teacher status and popularity Low concern for student growth and development	High concern for teacher status and popularity High concern for student growth and development
Low concern for teacher status and popularity Low concern for student growth and development	High concern for student growth and development Low concern for teacher status and popularity

Teacher status and popularity (vertical axis)

Student growth and development

Below are two other sets of contrasting concerns that can be cast into similar grids. Locate where each of your classes exists in these sets by drawing a line under the parallel set that best describes your class.

For *facts*	*vs.*	For *student welfare*
High		Low
Low		High
Low		Low
High		High

For *recall of data*	*vs.*	For *problem-solving and decision-making*
High		Low
Low		High
Low		Low
High		High

Chapter Nine

Danger Signals and Booby Traps: Barriers and Breakdowns

Objectives

After studying this chapter, you should be better able to do these things:

- Avoid barriers and breakdowns in speech communication.

- Provide enough intensity and variety to your voice to maintain the attention and interest of your listeners but avoid excessive intensity and loudness.

- Select the right time to say the things you want to say and avoid saying things out of context and out of time.

- Avoid wandering away from the interest of your listener and from your purpose when you are speaking.

- Evaluate your own predispositions or attitudes so that you can set them aside in order to hear what others may be saying to you.

- Avoid screening out ideas that seem to contradict newly acquired opinions.

- Seek out reasons why you should or should not respect or accept the ideas of a person speaking to you. Avoid accepting ideas merely because the speaker seems to be credible.

- Avoid showing hostility to a speaker or to a listener, even when you feel it, unless he understands and accepts such show of feeling.

- Withdraw from the communication situation only as a last resort in order to protect your own integrity.

- Avoid being excessively conscious of your self as you try to communicate with others.

- Be wary of drawing too much meaning from one example, either as a listener or a speaker.

- Avoid the either-or type of judgment. Always seek for shades of difference and a range of possibilities.

- Avoid interrupting the communication taking place between others when what you may have to say is irrelevant to *their* concern or subject.

- Be wary of trying to put too much information across in a short time or under extreme pressure.

- Get your response to a speaker back to him as soon as possible after you have received his message.

The speech-communication process provides innumerable opportunities for mistakes and errors. In every interaction between persons, there are possibilities of miscommunication. Most communicative obstacles fall into two categories. *Barriers* explicitly inhibit or block effective communication. *Breakdowns* are failures of the human communication system. An inhibiting factor that exists before the communicative attempt may be considered a barrier. A fault or failure in the attempt itself may be considered a breakdown.

We shall not deal extensively, at this point, with the broad societal-cultural factors that affect the communication interaction, although many barriers and breakdowns originate in a surrounding social atmosphere larger than the immediate event.

You will not find in this chapter prescriptions for definite methods by which all of those problems can be overcome. The search for methods, for procedures, and for techniques by which you may overcome these obstacles must be done by you as you explore your own speech behavior in relation to others. The particular methods that you use to overcome the obstacles must be of your own creation. You must be the one to deal with you in surmounting barriers and in preventing breakdowns to effective communication.

What follows, therefore, is an attempt to help you increase your sensitivity and understanding of some of the barriers and breakdowns that may exist in your own speech-communication efforts.

Within the speaker

Many barriers and breakdowns to effective speech communication originate with the speaker or transmitter. Essentially, most of these speaker-related difficulties exist because he is unable to relate to his listeners.

Excessive intensity

Excessive behavioral intensity used in presentation of a communication message may destroy the message. It may cause the listener to be diverted from the subject matter of the essential message while focusing primarily on the overt behavioral manifestations of the intensity and thus to lose much if not all of what is said. The receiver simply does not perceive much of the information transmitted with too much intensity by the speaker.

During the 1960s, and particularly after the Free Speech Movement on the campus of the University of California, Berkeley, the fabric of American society was repeatedly rent by what some have called riots and others have called civil disorders. Many of these events were characterized by excessive behavioral intensity: names were called, utilizing a vocabulary reproduced by euphemism or dashes in most newspapers; arrests were invited, sometimes re-sisted, sometimes made with excessive force; property, from windows to computer installations, was wantonly destroyed; individuals, including some young children, were killed in exchanges of gunfire; one young man burned himself to death on the steps of the Pentagon.

These violent demonstrations were for the most part founded on griev-ances that seemed legitimate not only to the protesters but also to many in the larger society. Certainly, the riots got attention; but, for most people, the excessive intensity of the protests destroyed the essential messages. The gen-eral public, many of whom were basically inclined to hear the grievances and to support remedial action, were alienated by the presentation; they focused on the violence, which they could not condone, and never adequately perceived the grievances. This public reaction manifested itself in response to the violence on campuses and to violence in race relations. In 1972 at the Olympic games in Munich, the action of the Arab guerillas set in motion alienation far in excess of the real issues at stake.

Too loud

In an intense communication situation, a speaker often increases the actual volume with which he speaks, in order to emphasize his idea. The resulting response is similar to that in the excessive intensity situation.

We cannot communicate when we shout at each other. The sheer assault on the eardrums may cause the listener to focus on the volume and thus to lose the message. However, we all have a tendency, when we are not certain of our ground or of the validity of our arguments, to increase the decibel force of our voices. A message that did not get through to the listener when offered in a normal conversational tone will not penetrate any better if repeated verbatim in a louder voice—but some of us keep trying.

One of my friends has a most deflating argument, if it could be so called, when we become involved in a minor disagreement—a quiet "Why are you shouting?" At that point, I have lost the argument.

Inadequate intensity

Many communications are lost because the communicator seems to have no feeling or emotion about his speaking. We run into this low-intensity phenom-enon when we are trapped in lecture halls and in social situations from which we cannot readily escape; a speaker goes on and on with no seeming basic energy or real interest in what he is saying. Such a speaker usually is so gen-erally low-intensity that he doesn't even follow through on La Rochefoucauld's maxim: "We frequently forgive those who bore us, but cannot forgive those whom we bore"—he is not even aware of our boredom.

Too early and too late

Effective timing of communication is important in every kind of human relationship. Our sensitivity to the probable reception of a comment by a listener should—but too often does not—determine when we speak or remain silent. Too often we speak before people are ready to listen or when what we have to say is no longer relevant.

During a cafeteria bull session on campus politics, one student who was not actively participating in the discussion suddenly blurted, "Any of you got any idea what he's going to ask on the poli sci test this afternoon?" No one really heard him. The conversation went on as if he had not spoken. Ten minutes later, when campus politics had begun to pall as a topic, he tried again, "Doesn't anybody have any idea what he's going to ask on the poli sci test this afternoon?" He got the focused attention of the group—all members of the political science class. One coed groaned, "Oh, Lord! *This* afternoon? Why didn't someone tell us?" He had tried to tell them but before they were ready to listen.

One evening a group of us at a party started swapping limericks. As limerick after limerick brought the house down, I struggled to remember even one or to invent one so that I could contribute my addition to the evening. So, I pondered and tried to concoct one and lost track of what was going on. After some minutes I completed my limerick and happily blurted it out. After a short, rather awful silence in which no one laughed, one of my fellow guests said, "That's not a bad limerick, but what does it have to do with the election tomorrow?" During my creative period, the conversation had changed course a couple of times.

Timing is often essential to effective communication. The moment for the perfect squelch or other retort is right then, not five hours or two days later—which is when most of us finally think of one. The time for the angry retort is probably *never!*

Inappropriateness

The appropriateness of a communication in interpersonal interaction is governed by many things. Propriety may be a matter of the form of language or subject matter or manner of presentation, and it is dependent on cultural conditioning of the listeners. A funny story about a recently deceased person is highly appropriate at an Irish wake and highly inappropriate during a funeral. A bawdy ballad appropriate for a beer bust would be inappropriate for a Wednesday evening prayer meeting. If the purpose is to communicate, it is not appropriate to use profanity or obscenity during interpersonal interaction with persons who are offended by four-letter words—the shock value of some terms has been somewhat dissipated by profligate overuse in the recent past, but they do offend still.

Inappropriateness often creates a barrier founded in the embarrassment of the listeners, who respond by simply tuning the speaker out. Or, they may interpret what they hear in quite the wrong way.

Signal-to-noise factor

The difficulties we have discussed are closely related to what engineers in the communications field call the signal-to-noise ratio. George von Békésy has described this phenomenon:

> Any amplifier generates noise and . . . the noise limits the usefulness of a transmission system. The important thing in a communication network is not the output level obtained but the signal-to-noise ratio, for it is this ratio that determines our ability to recognize the signal as distinct from the noise. In the nervous system . . . "noise" is always present, in the form of a general background of spontaneous activity.[1]

Von Békésy describes the measurement of loss of information as "the number of bits lost when the information is passed through a system divided by the number of bits introduced at the input."[2] We shall discuss noise later in this chapter.

Inability to use feedback for corrective purposes

Sometimes the most sensitive of us cannot adequately pick up feedback in a communication situation; that is, we cannot tell, no matter how keenly aware we are of verbal and nonverbal responses, if our essential message is getting through to our listeners. In some social situations, courtesy demands that a listener give evidence of absorbed interest even if he is disinterested to the point of boredom. It is not politic for a junior executive to display any impatience or disinterest when the chairman of the board holds forth at interminable length about corporate policy. Most of us learn as children that on some occasions in relations with our parents a pokerface and no feedback best serve our needs of the moment. In such feedback situations, a speaker must be psychic (and few of us are) to sense the true response in his listener.

However, some of us carry with us as speakers more or less serious barriers to communication in that we cannot use feedback for correction of our transmission of messages. We do not modify what we say or how we say it even when we have feedback indicating misunderstanding or lack of comprehension or overreaction to messages. On the other hand, some receivers close down any kind of feedback as a means of terminating the engagement.

[1] George von Békésy, *Sensory Inhibition* (Princeton, N. J.: Princeton University Press, 1967), pp. 6–7.
[2] Von Békésy, p. 8.

Few of us, fortunately, are as unaware of feedback as is a professor with whom I rode home from an out-of-town evening meeting. The meeting ended a long, hard day; and when I crawled into the passenger seat, I was quite tired. He, however, was enthusiastic about some idea (for the life of me I could never remember what it was) and, as he drove, was expounding on it. About 10:30 P.M., the headlights were probing the darkness, the tires were singing on the pavement, the engine was purring, and his voice rose and fell. That's the last I remember till we pulled up in front of my house 45 minutes later. He was still talking about his idea. The best I could do was to stumble out of the car and thank him for the ride. I am not sure that he didn't continue talking to himself all the way home.

Now, there was feedback that this man could have picked up and used to correct his communication. Total lack of verbal response could have clued some people. But even he should have picked up, on that occasion, the heavy breathing that accompanies sleep. From what I have been told, my breathing when I sleep is not merely heavy—it would be audible over a buzz saw. But then, perhaps he was not really interested in interpersonal communication.

Much communication is lost or thwarted by the inability of speakers to use feedback. It is essential not only to perceive feedback but also to use it to correct messages and adjust them to the person to whom one is speaking so that they can be accepted.

Rambling

Free association of ideas can be useful on some occasions; but, in the modified form that we call rambling, it becomes a barrier to communication. There are social occasions in which the purpose of speech communication is less transmission of information than interchange of stroking behaviors, a sharing of being alive and being together; in such communication events, rambling is acceptable and presents no barriers. But a speaker's tendency to ramble—that is, to wander from his essential message, to be diverted into detours, to verbalize about associated notions that may or may not be relevant—can seriously impede communication. During our school years, most of us are exposed to at least one rambling teacher, and from such a teacher we do not learn much about the official subject that he is supposed to teach.

Too fast or too much

Generally speaking, we can listen effectively to spoken words produced at about three times the normal speech rate. Quite frequently, however, in conversation or other situations, we move so rapidly from one point to another, from one stage to another, from one aspect of an idea to another that our listener becomes lost along the verbal highway; or his "receiving apparatus" gets "jammed" by too many messages for which he does not have meaning.

Human speech apparatus is such that no one can enunciate words at such a rate that they cannot be heard and understood as words by normal human hearing apparatus. When we say that speech is "too fast," we are referring, not to actual pronunciation and delivery of the words, but to the content of speech; and we mean that the movement from one idea to another is too rapid. Such rapid movement inevitably results in inadequate transmittals of information.

Even with familiar subjects, our hearing apparatus is capable of receiving words at a faster rate than we can find meaning for them. With unfamiliar subjects, with unfamiliar vocabulary, with new information of any complexity, we need more time to settle on meanings of the sounds we hear. The phrase "let the news soak in" is a colloquialism, but it expresses the need in each of us as a listener for time to absorb information we receive. If bits of information flow in too fast, we can assign meanings for only fragments or perhaps for none. As speakers desiring to communicate information, we should take care to give our listeners opportunity to absorb our messages. Generally, complex ideas should be repeated in different words and when feasible should be presented from two or more different points of view before moving along to the next idea.

Some professors spew forth pertinent information too fast for students to absorb. Such lecturers usually know a great deal about their subject and feel compelled to present as much as possible of their knowledge for the benefit of their students. In their eagerness to teach the subject they defeat their purpose—they do not teach the students. A brilliant young mathematician conducts courses in advanced mathematics. His mind is agile, he perceives things quickly, he knows his subject matter thoroughly, and he even has a sense of humor; but it is almost impossible to follow his lectures. He starts his lecture as the bell rings and begins to fill the board with formulas and numbers, to illustrate what he says. He moves from one formula to another with remarkable clarity of presentation but usually so fast that few if any of his students can keep up with him. His speaking rate is actually a bit slower than normal; and he delivers the complex ideas precisely and clearly, but fails to provide supporting examples or to give his students breathing spaces in which to discover the meaning of each stage as he goes along. One math major, who not only needed the course credit but also wanted the information presented, tape-recorded the lectures, copied everything from the board, and thought about it all later when he could stop the action and ponder.

Too slow or not enough

A speaker creates obstacles to communication when he fails to provide enough information for the listener to grasp what is being said. Sometimes, when given too little information, listeners attempt to find out and, if they are really curious, try to push the speaker to a deeper and more thorough statement. More often, however, listeners simply lose the thread of the presentation and are not sufficiently interested to try to find it again. When a speaker does not provide enough expository and explanatory material to flesh out his ideas, the very ideas are often lost in transit. Once a listener has lost a few ideas, he may tune the speaker out, simply because he does not understand what is being said.

Within the listener

We have dwelt on the problems created for listeners by speakers. We shall now talk about those things which the listener has or creates that provide obstacles to or cause breakdowns in the full reception of an adequate message.

Contrary attitudes

My grandfather was barely tolerant of Democrats and was convinced that any Socialist was not only misguided (almost certainly by the Devil himself) but also absolutely wrong about everything. I've often wondered how my mother was able to persuade her father to hear Norman Thomas speak at a political rally. When he returned from the speech, I asked Grandfather what Thomas had said. "The same old poppycock. That man is out to destroy the American way of life." Grandfather grumbled on for several minutes, but what he said revealed that he had been unable to hear a thing that the speaker discussed. His attitudes were so contrary to the things for which Norman Thomas stood that no amount of argument, no line of logic, and no amount of persuasion could bring my grandfather to have any rapport with or to listen to the Socialist candidate for president. To him Thomas was "that radical," and "radical" to Grandfather meant "unredeemably bad." As a matter of fact, Grandfather, like Thomas, was a reasonable human being, and some of the less controversial statements made by the Socialist were essentially the same as he himself had made on occasion. But he could not hear even these when Thomas spoke them.

Contrary attitudes in listeners prevent adequate perception of a speaker's message and thus create barriers to effective communication. Political candidates often must cope with more or less hostile audiences. In some Southern communities, pastors who spoke out for civil rights could not penetrate the predispositions of their congregations and lost their churches. The "generation gap" is always in part a communication problem caused by predisposition barriers on both sides of the gap.

We all have prejudices, attitudes, and pre-sets; and, once in a while, we find ourselves in communication interaction with speakers whose positions are contrary to our own. To overcome these barriers, a high level of tolerance, understanding, and personal poise is required of every listener. A listener must evaluate his own attitudes carefully and try to set them aside if he would truly hear and understand what someone on the other side of an idea might have to say.

Newly acquired contrary opinions

Attitudes of long standing are less effective as barriers to contrary ideas than are newly acquired opinions. For example, a graduate student who has just been convinced that the life of a college professor is best for him will not be a good prospect for a recruiter from General Motors. After a couple of years on a college faculty, he may be even more firmly convinced; but he will be better able to hear the contrary arguments of an industry recruiter. The proximity of the acquisition of a new opinion affects the rigidity with which the opinion is held; time may cause an opinion to become more vulnerable. This does not mean that a person holds an opinion with any less firmness after a passage of time, but the longer he has held an opinion, the greater the chance that he will listen to contrary ideas. Don't waste your time proselytizing among recent converts to another creed.

Jumping to conclusions

Listeners are less likely to get the full message when they decide what is to be said before it is said. In a student senate meeting, a young man rose to speak against an appropriation for a special student activity, with which he was closely associated. His affiliation with the activity was well known and as soon as he rose to speak, everyone assumed (jumped to the conclusion) that he would speak in favor of the appropriation. Few of his listeners really understood what he said; in fact, when he presented facts to show that the appropriation was not needed, many felt he was arguing for the appropriation.

The effect of jumping to conclusions is much the same as that of contrary attitudes—the listener is unable to hear what is actually said. But, as Irving Lee has pointed out, we tend to get agreement when it is possible to make factual statements about a situation, and we can expect disagreement when only inferential statements can be made about a situation.[3] Thus, if the listener is unable to hear or to review the facts and only makes judgments about what is being said, he is less likely to get the basic message. All of us, too often, rush to decision before we know enough of the facts to make such a judgment. This tendency creates serious barriers to good communication.

[3] Irving Lee and Laura L. Lee, *Handling Barriers in Communication* (New York: Harper & Row, 1956), pp. 1–23.

Suspicion or lack of acceptance
of the speaker

One of the more obvious obstacles, and yet one of the most subtle, is related to personal acceptance of the speaker. The forms of suspicion and lack of confidence are many and varied and often are hidden from perception by the listener. A statement attributed to a source of low credibility is usually perceived as much more biased and unfair than an identical statement issued from a source of high credibility. If the listener, therefore, is suspicious of the speaker, does not feel him to be reliable, opposes him, is hostile to him, or feels that the message may be prejudiced, that listener is not very likely to hear what is being said.

The effect of source credibility was tested in a campus information program on health and medical care. To one group, the speaker was introduced as an M.D. and research specialist in the field of medicine and human affairs. The same person in another setting with a similar group was introduced simply as a fellow student. There was a lower degree of acceptance of information presented by a fellow student than of that offered by a "medical specialist." Exactly the same speech was delivered to both groups.

A research professor of psychology described for a group of mediation specialists in labor relations a series of experiments on resolution of conflict between groups of people. Although this subject matter is the essence of the labor mediation work in which all his listeners were constantly engaged, many simply tuned the academic speaker out. Acceptance of the speaker was low and little of his information got through the barrier. At a later session, a member of the group who had studied the same area spoke on conflict between groups, duplicating much of the information presented by the professor. Acceptance of the later speaker was high, and the information was closely attended and understood. There is still in our American society a profound mutual suspicion and distrust between town and gown, between those who work in business and industry and those who work as faculty members. This lack of acceptance creates some serious handicaps to communication between groups.

The barrier caused by suspicion or lack of acceptance is basic and presents a very critical problem. We are more likely to follow or perceive messages from those people whom we accept and trust and whom we do not suspect than those from people who, for whatever reason, we feel are not qualified to speak or have intentions threatening to us. We often are unable to perceive the actual facts of qualification.

Within either speaker or listener
or both

Some types of communications barriers and breakdowns can occur in the speaker or the listener, or in both simultaneously.

Hostility

One of the most serious obstacles to the transmission of information between two persons is the degree to which they fail to accept or actively reject each other. When the degree of rejection moves beyond the simple level of doubt or hesitation to a level of outright hostility, the communication barrier and breakdown are great.

There are many levels of hostility. Some are so subtle, so buried in the subconscious, that the hostile person himself is unaware of them. Others exist in the consciousness but are carefully guarded to prevent overt manifestation. Whenever you attempt communication in the face of conscious or unconscious hostility in the other or in yourself, you are confronted by a more or less serious barrier to communication. Overtly displayed hostility by the listener erects such a barrier to communication that few, if any, speakers can get to him.

Sweet reason cannot penetrate to potential receivers who are snatching up rocks to hurl at a speaker and at any windows within throwing range. A straightforward bullhorn-amplified speech by a police lieutenant will communicate little to a mob that is screaming epithets of extreme hostility at policemen. A black drop-out who is consciously and overtly hostile to school, the system, and all whites, is not going to listen to a white male social worker in a well-cut suit. Status-threatened whites who are banding together to prevent a black family from moving into their neighborhood are not prepared to hear anyone present arguments in favor of integration and open housing.

Hostility *within the speaker* toward the listener may so affect the manner in which he transmits the message that he does, in fact, turn his listener away or short-circuit the receiving apparatus. At one of the teach-ins of the period of the Berkeley Free Speech Movement, the first speaker erroneously assumed that everyone in the audience was opposed to his position. He may have harbored much diffused hostility anyway, but he took a belligerent attitude toward his audience and salted his comments with antagonistic and highly emotional negative language. Much of his message was valid and should have been meaningful to his listeners, but his hostility so affected the audience that hardly a bit of what he said was ever heard. All that most members of that audience could remember were the hostile comments directed at them. Hostility begets hostility. When we become aware in another person of hostility directed at us, most of us respond with at least potential hostility; we instinctively become alert, prepared to take self-defensive action in response to threat. Hostility in any participator in an interpersonal interaction is almost immediately compounded by the response to it. Whenever it appears, hostility works in both directions to block and even to destroy communication.

Withdrawal

The quiet ones in a group who sit back and take little active part in the discussion or the communication interaction may be participating in their own way; they may be listening carefully and reacting internally. This behavior is not full-scale withdrawal and may not interfere with communication.

However, when a person "turns off his listening apparatus" and does not hear what is going on, he is withdrawing from the interaction; and his withdrawal may cause a breakdown in communication.

Breakdown is almost inevitable in dyadic, or two-person, communication when one member of the dyad actually ceases to participate either in listening or in speaking. I once asked a student to stop by for a minute after class to discuss a project that he was working on. As he stood by the desk, the girl he sat next to in class waited for him at the door. I started our dyadic communication event by asking a question about the nature of his project. He blinked at me, gulped, and just stood mute. I repeated the question; his only answer was "Would you mind—I have to go now—could we talk about this another time?" I decided, as I watched him hasten to the door, that I really couldn't blame him; all things considered, in the spring of the year, the girl was more deserving of a young man's fancy than a speech project. But his withdrawal made communication with me impossible.

Other forms of withdrawal that often inhibit communication are hidden in the psychological pathologies. Psychological disturbances in perception, evaluation, expression, action, ability to cooperate, social orientation, and the inner experiences of an individual may cause various kinds of withdrawal. Whether voluntary or pathologically involuntary, any withdrawing prevents another person from breaking through the shell to the inner thinking and action of the person.

Self-centered behavior

We are all essentially self-centered, and most of us at least occasionally exhibit self-centered behavior, which is more extreme at some times than at others. Self-centered behavior may, in part, be related to the psychological concept of narcissism, or self-love. A person who is so self-centered that he is unable to relate to any other person or to see any part of another person's world maintains a serious barrier to the transmission of messages.

A speaker, both in formal and informal situations, may often use speaking as a way to enhance himself rather than as a method of communication. (I do not imply that they are not related, but I refer here to the overemphasis on self-enhancement.) I know at least one professor who takes himself as a lecturer most seriously. He has worked hard and practiced long hours to create the image that he wants to project, which is of a handsome, virile, erudite superexpert with a beautiful voice. When he speaks to a class or other audience, he pours out carefully constructed phrases studded with esoteric terms—all in precise articulation and an obviously forced deep bass voice. He is rather fun to watch—but he communicates very little.

I am not suggesting that self-enhancement is not a vital factor in any personality. It may be a valuable motivating factor. But when overly conscious concern for *self* becomes apparent, the communication process with *others* may break down.

Noninvolvement, nonparticipation, and nonresponsiveness

We have spoken of the quiet ones who apparently are not involved in a discussion but still take part by listening. In a sense, their noninvolvement is a type of withdrawal and can contribute to breakdown in communication. In fact, persons who understand communication interactions can use such withdrawal to hurt their partners. It is a very cruel system when used purposely. Likewise, many administrators in business and academic organizations refuse to reply to efforts from underlings to communicate upward. This brings a great deal of unrest and dissatisfaction on the job. A noninvolved person may be receiving all that is going on, but he is not reacting to it in an open way so that there is any visible or discernible feedback to the transmitter.

The involvement of all those who are participating in the communication event must be active, and it must include the sending and receiving of messages by all parties to the event. The nature of audience involvement is, of course, not evident to a mass-media communicator, who speaks into a microphone, which gives him no feedback so that he can correct his communication as he goes along. He must create, in his own mind, an image of his listening audience and speak to that image. Of course, this is what we all do anyway, whether the audience is present or not, but the radio or television communicator has a greater problem in this respect because his perception of his listener is much more generic and vague than the perception I may have of you if we are talking face to face.

Several faculty members were assigned by the administration to serve as a special committee to prepare a report on a very critical campus problem. The service was not voluntary, and all members of the committee appeared at the meetings. With one exception, the members took active part in the discussion. Their level of involvement was high; that is, each felt a responsibility for contributing, for listening to others, and for helping to think through the problem. One person sat in silence. He made no contributions. He stared out the window a good part of the time. Efforts to involve him in the conversation were ignored. Even direct questions from the chairman brought nothing but "I don't know." It would not have been politic for him to duck the meetings, so he was present—and that was all. For all practical purposes, he was worse than useless to the group; his unresponsiveness cast a pall about the deliberations that made everyone feel uneasy as long as he was inactive.

Involvement, participation, and responsiveness are essential conditions to good communication. When, for any reason, they are absent, we can expect communication difficulties to arise.

Allness

One of the most common forms of communication breakdown results from the assumption that all things are included in a single statement. Irving Lee calls this the disease of the details being left out.[4] For example, a friend of mine has an English bulldog. Now, my only previous contact with English bulldogs involved one that bit me when I was a child. For years, without really thinking about it, I assumed that all English bulldogs are ferocious, and I acted on this assumption by avoiding them. With my friend's dog, I have had to focus on my allness assumption. That dog loves everybody—even me.

The process of allness, or the breakdown that we call allness, results from overgeneralizing from one example to all those things of a given classification. I once asked a Middle Westerner what the people in his home state were like. His response was "They're all bullheaded reactionaries." Whatever he meant by that imprecise term, every person in that state is not a "bullheaded reactionary." He did not include himself in that category and he maintains his voting residence there. "Bullheaded reactionaries," whatever precisely they may be, do not vote for Democrats; and in the previous presidential election, the Democrats had carried that state by a narrow margin. The use of such a single, all-inclusive description contributes to communication breakdown.

Only words

In communicating with each other, a number of unrealized assumptions underlying our use of language present us with serious, if unrealized, prob-

---

[4] Lee and Lee, pp. 21ff.

lems. One is that words themselves have meanings. Another is that the words are like boxes and carry things in them that have meaning. Still another is that another person who speaks or listens to us speak uses words in the same way we do.

We have suggested before that one of the foundations of the development of symbols in communication is that meanings do not reside in the inanimate character or physical characteristics of the symbol; *meanings exist only inside people*—in their feelings, ideas, and emotions. Each person has a different set of meanings for any given word. Therefore, if we listen only for the words that people speak and assume that each word used means to the speaker exactly what it means to us, we may—indeed, often do—end up with a great deal of misunderstanding.

Not too long ago, there was much reference to the "hip generation." To some, the term meant bearded, barefoot, oddly dressed people who rebelled against everything possible. To others, this meant a way of thinking that represented an honest questioning and rebellion against actual evils in our society. To still others, it meant a lunatic fringe of people, mostly artists of one kind or another, who tried to startle and attract attention through their bizarre behavior. To others, it meant a strange unfathomable generation of people who never found their place in society.

The essential differences of the meaning for each person is obvious. This very difference of meaning within each person requires that we be sure to explore meanings with each other as a basic condition of effective communication.

Disease, trauma, and malfunctions

Individuals with specific diseases or malfunctions of the communication apparatus or with emotional disturbances carry within them formidable barriers to communication. At one time or another, all of us suffer at least minor forms of malfunctions and trauma that upset our communication ability.

Obviously, the person who is hard of hearing will have difficulties in communication unless some adjustment is made. Persons with articulatory disorders, with neural disorders that affect speech, and the like, present particular problems of communication. Helen Keller's struggle to communicate demonstrates the effect of physical handicaps on communication.

Many people have more or less severe problems of psychic trauma or shock that create breakdowns in their communicative relationship with others. As an extreme example, one man within the space of two days lost his parents, his family of three children and wife, and his brother in four separate auto accidents. He suffered such shock and trauma that for months he was unable to speak at all.

Inadequate perception of symbols and situations

We discussed words, signs, and symbols in Chapter 4. When we fail to perceive any of these adequately, when the meaning in us is not that intended by the use of a word or a sign or a symbol, we may experience discomfort resulting from faulty communication.

Inadequate perception of situations can cause communication problems. It is not always simple to evaluate a situation adequately or accurately. If you heard the shouts of boys playing touch football in the yard, then a crash of glass, then found the picture window broken and a football on the floor, your perception of the situation would probably be reasonably complete and accurate. If a young man nearly knocked you over as he stormed out of the house and you found his fiancée in the living room in furious tears, you would probably be safe in perceiving the situation as a lovers' quarrel.

Adequate communication often requires adequate perception of the context, and the best of us are often unable to understand some situations in their true meaning, because of factors beyond our control.

Shortly after the close of World War II, four persons shared a closed compartment of a train en route from Rome to Paris. One was a dowdy Latin teacher from Iowa who had a Victorian outlook on life. One was a young actress of obvious blond beauty, somewhat younger than the teacher and not a bit Victorian. Opposite the two women sat a colonel and a sergeant from the same unit in the United States Air Force.

As they were traveling through the mountain areas in the North of Italy, the conductor popped his head in the door to announce that the train would shortly be going through a rather long tunnel, that the lighting system of the coach was inoperative, and that there would be a period of darkness. He assured the group, however, that everything was under control and wished them not to be disturbed.

Shortly after the train entered the tunnel and the coach became quite dark, there was the sound of a kiss, followed by a resounding slap, then silence, which remained unbroken. When the train emerged from the tunnel a few minutes later and the compartment was again full of light, the four passengers, in the reserved way of strangers on a train, gave no outward sign that anything untoward had occurred. However, each had an evaluation of the situation.

On the face of the colonel was a great red welt that carried the imprint of a hand.

The schoolteacher felt considerably heartened by what she saw. She assumed that the colonel had tried to kiss the actress and the actress had slapped him for his effort. This made her feel warm toward the actress and much more secure in the presence of the two men.

The actress was quite amused by what she saw and could hardly hide her enjoyment of the situation. She assumed that the colonel had tried to kiss her, had made a mistake, and had instead kissed the schoolteacher and was rewarded with the stinging slap.

The colonel was angry. He assumed that the sergeant had tried to kiss the actress and that the actress had tried to slap him off and had missed and hit the colonel instead.

The sergeant stared out the window with apparent disinterest. He did not need to speculate. When the compartment became dark, he had kissed the back of his hand, then pasted the colonel as hard as he could. He had long yearned to slug that "fancy bird" colonel who commanded his outfit!

Inadequate sensitivity

A person who is not capable of perceiving or sensing accurately what the other may feel or think or do is encountering a serious barrier to effective communication. On the other hand, a person may also be overly sensitive and inclined to overweigh or overevaluate nonverbal and verbal expressions, thus giving them more importance than they actually contain. This, too, creates communication difficulty.

Most of the time, we do not need psychic powers to determine whether another person is happy or sad or worried or harassed or relaxed; we need to be only somewhat interested and observant. We can usually tell from verbal and nonverbal feedback—if we perceive the feedback—whether our communication efforts are acceptable or may become offensive. Some people are cursed with psychic rhinoceros hides; since they cannot be easily offended, they cannot sense that others might be. But most of us do project our own sensitivities and tend to follow the Golden Rule: we do not say or do to others what would upset us if said or done to us.

A nice balance of sensitivity—neither too much nor too little—contributes much to effective communication. A person who is himself exceptionally sensitive may have difficulties in communicating with those who are less sensitive. Being himself aware of subtleties in the responses of others, he may project his sensitivity on others and unconsciously expect them to pick up nuances and subtle nonverbal messages that they are not capable of perceiving. An exceptionally insensitive person cannot communicate very effectively. He cannot adequately evaluate situations or tune in on the receptivity of his listeners or perceive much feedback (let alone use it). He goes through life constantly saying the wrong things in the wrong way to the wrong people at the wrong times.

Either-or behavior

Anyone who views the world on the either-or basis is a constant center of communication inhibition. To such a person what is not white is black, and there are no shades of grays; what is not good is bad; what is not right is wrong. In terms of logic, this represents what is called a disjunction, which artificially separates all units of a given type into only two categories. Most human behaviors, most meanings, most factors involved in human communications are subject to many shades of meaning and interpretation. Thus, to assume that a matter is either one or the other of two possibilities is to leave out a number of other possibilities that might actually exist.

At the first of a series of contract negotiation meetings, management offered a proposal of wages and fringe benefits. Upon presenting the proposal, the company representative said flatly that the union could either accept the proposal or reject it, but that there was no other alternative. The union representative retorted that if that was the way it was going to be, the proposal was rejected as of that moment. Such a collision between two either-or attitudes is not unusual in early stages of contract negotiations, but the either-or attitude is often a problem in various kinds of negotiations. In this case, instead of "Take it or leave it" countered by "We leave it," both parties should have been reaching for other possibilities that could be achieved and would be acceptable to both parties.

An erroneously rigid interpretation of parliamentary procedure dictates that a motion must be either passed or defeated. There are many alternatives to this either-or resolution, although there is a tendency in many groups to force a motion through to this decision rather than permit amendment or deferral of action on it. Too little use is made of the adjustment procedures in parliamentary operations.

Everything is just like this

Relatives do it to children: "He's just like his grandfather" and "She's just like Cousin Ermatrude." Sometimes we are conscious of our evaluation ("She's just like a teacher I had in seventh grade"); in other situations we do not realize that we like, or loathe, a person because we subconsciously feel that he is "just like" someone we've known before. Our communication problems start when we proceed to deal with that person as we would with the one with whom we have compared him. We all tend to do it, not only with people, but with things, problems, situations, events, and the like. This tendency, which presents a serious handicap to communication, is based on the faulty assumption that anything is "just like" anything else. As far as we know, there are no "just alikes" in any realm of human knowledge.

Several years ago, I conducted a training program for stewards of a large union local. The stewards were assigned to various small groups for the course. The first group of trainees was somewhat slow in learning and was not particularly interested in the program; it took a great deal of effort to get interest aroused and to get them involved. When the second group started the course, I assumed that it was just like the first group and used the same approach that I had eventually developed for the first. I had hardly started when an older fellow in the audience asked for a rest break, which I immediately granted. He then came to me and said something like this, "Look, Professor, you don't need to convince us that we need this. We wouldn't be here if we weren't convinced. Why don't you skip this opening stuff and get down to the bread-and-butter business that we're after?"

Inability to distinguish fact from opinion

Opinions can be of great value, as long as we identify them as such and do not accept them as facts. Many written and spoken statements are presented in declarative form, as if they were facts. We all write and speak in this way; we just do not start every statement with "I think that" or "It is my opinion that." Most of the statements that we use and hear and read are actually opinions. A person who cannot distinguish between fact and opinion often misjudges the nature of information he receives; and his misjudgment can be a significant barrier to effective communication.

All of us are repeatedly trapped by the fact-opinion problem. My son reported to his sister one day that the "old man" was willing for them to stay out until 1:00 A.M. I was not thus willing. Now, my son was not lying; he was not deceiving his sister, but he made the mistake of giving his *opinion* of what I would feel as a *fact* of what I had said. I had said, "There are several things to be considered. I'll let you know as soon as your mother and I have talked it over." My son had used his opinion of the outcome of the parental discussion as representing a fact. Problems followed.

Barriers external to the speaker and the listener

External barriers are similar to many problems and obstacles found within individuals, but they exist outside the speaker-listener interaction itself.

Low credibility of the source

In our communication interaction, we incorporate information in messages that we transmit, and we receive information in messages from others. Much of the information transmitted is not self-evident in the communication situation nor does it originate with the speaker; it comes from some source, which may or may not have credibility. If a gypsy fortune-teller at a carnival tells you that you are about to inherit a million dollars, you may feel a wild surge of hope (depending on your evaluation of fortune-telling); but the gypsy has less credibility than the lawyer, with your great-uncle's will in hand, who might give you the same information. A specialist in any area will generally have more credibility as a source of information about that area than does a layman. Identical information about the effects of air pollution on public health will be more credible if the source is the United States Surgeon General than if it is a medical student. The *New York Times* has more credibility as a source of information about national and international events than does the local *Shopping News*.

All too often, we produce and receive—and act on—information from sources with very low credibility. This creates particular havoc when a participant in the communication interaction is aware of the low credibility of the source. The information may be valid, but the result of such awareness is often an immediate blocking of the essential message. But even more important, our use of low-credibility sources for message data endangers the actual quality of messages.

Distance from the source

One of the most common problems of the mass media is that the source of the message is far removed from the receiver of the message. When the message is transmitted to the whole world (via Telstar), the problem involves both physical and psychological distance. Communication becomes less effective as distance prohibits immediate and accurate feedback so that the sender can correct his message.

A corporate executive in New York City can communicate with the manager of the Bombay branch office by telephone, with much helpful feedback in both directions. Communication between the two coasts of the United States is much more effective than in the time of the 1849 California gold rush, when the only medium was letters and at least six weeks elapsed between transmission of a message and arrival of feedback. We are now able to communicate with relatively immediate feedback all over the world and out into space.

The advent of highly sophisticated telecommunication systems will span the physical distance, but the psychic distance is another matter. In a classroom or an office, as well as in international affairs, we can observe psychic distance between two persons that prevents them from communicating with each other.

Large number of station transfers

The parlor game of "Gossip" used to be popular at parties. With players in a circle, one person whispers a statement to the person on his right who, in turn, whispers what he thinks he heard to the person on his right, and so around the circle. The last person announces to the group what he thinks he heard and the originator announces what he whispered. The two statements seldom bear any remote resemblance to each other. "Gossip" is only a game, but its basic principle is a fact of everyday life.

Let's consider each person who receives and then retransmits the message as a transfer station. Then let's note that at each transfer station there may be some loss in the message or some reshaping of the basic idea. We can then see that the more station stops there are for the transmission of any given message, the more likelihood there is of the message being garbled at the end.

Let's translate this to human organizations. Many large corporations and institutions in our country have organization charts whose vertical dimensions may run through eight, ten, twelve, and fifteen levels. In corporate communications that involve verbal transmission down through the chain of command, each transfer station inevitably leaves its mark on the essential message. The board of directors meets for two days to develop a new corporate policy. The president then meets with all the vice-presidents for half a day to brief them on the new policy. Each vice-president transmits something of the policy to his staff and so on down the line to foremen to crew chiefs to nonsupervisory employees. When a large organization relies solely on one-way verbal transmission of messages, communication breakdowns attributable to transfer stations create chaos.

There is a growing awareness that the number of stations through which a message must go, particularly when we're talking about human stations, may have a great deal to do with the breakdown of human communications in many fields of work.

Interruptions

Any interruption of the flow of messages and feedback in a speech-communication interaction causes a breakdown, however minor it may be, in communication. If a dog chased a cat across the platform during a formal address, the interruption would interfere for the moment with communication; however, if no other interruption occurred and depending on developments and how the situation was handled, the essential message of the speaker would probably not be significantly blocked. In the business world, executives routinely instruct their secretaries to block visitors and incoming calls while they are engaged in face-to-face communication with others, and a caller hears a pleasant but firm "I'm sorry, Mr. Roth is in conference. Could I have him call you later?" An executive's time is valuable, and it often is important to him to receive and to give information as completely as possible in the time available—and interruptions prevent effective communication.

Constant nonrelevant interruptions from sources external to the flow of information between two persons tend to destroy the communication if for no other reason than that they use up the time necessary for the full communication to transpire.

Size of group

Theoretically, communication with one other person is easier to accomplish than communication with many others. Obviously, if you and a friend were talking, with ample feedback and interaction between you, your communication would probably be at least reasonably effective. Let's keep adding people to the situation until you are talking to a hundred people in a room. To communicate with any effectiveness under such circumstances, you would have to change your speaking method from that used for one-to-one interaction. Each one of those hundred persons may have a different reaction, a different set of symbols, and the things that you say may mean different things to each person in the group. There is not enough time for each person in the group to provide you with ample feedback so that you may correct, for each one individually, all the misconceptions he may have of the information that you are trying to develop. The larger the group in a speaking situation, the greater the loss in full understanding and the more nonpersonal the structure of the communication becomes. The public speaker, in order to deal with this, uses many more repetitions and other devices in order to compensate for the problem.

Related to all areas

There are some barriers that cause trouble from both within and without the speaker and the listener. These monsters create havoc in the total efforts of any and all involved in trying to communicate through speech.

Noise

In an early section of this chapter, we mentioned the signal-to-noise ratio. We have all experienced bad telephone connections, in which hums and buzzes and static and echoes of other conversations prevent us from hearing clearly or making ourselves heard. We've also experienced similar extraneous interferences with radio and television reception. These are familiar instances of noise within the technical communication channels. Let's translate that principle of "noise in the channel" to the relationships between persons. There may be noise or distracting screens that make communication between persons difficult. I refer not to actual sound, but to physiological and psychological conditioning, attitudes, and the like, which tend to create conditions comparable to noise in the telephone channel. The result is that the message is usually at least garbled. Many obstacles and breakdowns are "noise-type" phenomena, insofar as their effect on our communication is concerned.

Amount of information within the channel

We have been for some years in the midst of what is called the knowledge explosion, which is causing problems in many areas of our existence. Specifically in communication, we have the problem of channels jammed with more information, much of it pertinent, than any human being can absorb. No doctor or scientist can begin to keep up with developments in his own field of specialization as published in medical and professional journals. In many organizations, pertinent and important communications are channeled to various persons according to distribution lists. Many recipients hastily initial the items (without reading them) and pass them along to the next person on the list; others hope to find time eventually to read and therefore hold items till the "In" basket overflows or someone else demands a particular memo or publication. Duplicating machines and computer printouts have compounded the problem, and executives are inundated by paper.

You may have five minutes in which to explain the function of an intricate machine to a person who knows nothing about it. You feed in all the information you can during the five minutes, but it is impossible for the listener to get all the information and make it hang together. There is just too much of it. The amount of information we transmit must depend on the ability of the person receiving it to understand and use it. When he cannot handle all of the information, the channel becomes jammed and excessive loss occurs.

Ken Macrorie detailed aspects of the problem of jammed channels in our general culture:

> Too many messages. . . . My world stuffed with messages. They hurtle at my door and pile up on the stoop, swirling out with a gust of wind to litter the entrance. The entrances of my mind are littered, with bad and with good. Every message that comes in lessens the chance of every other message. . . .
>
> Neither [businessmen nor intellectuals] have seen clearly the state of the message-drowned world. Its critical characteristic is not the dearth of high-quality messages—or even the profusion of second-rate messages—but

simply the profusion of all kinds of messages. Not only do they increasingly distract us from firsthand experience, but they scatter our brains.[5]

Consistency of information flowing through the channels

Communication is disrupted when contradictory material appears in relation to any given idea. For example, in an engineering firm, daily announcements made over the public address system gave pertinent information about status of contracts of the firm and those responsible for work under such contracts. On three successive days, three different men were named as heading the project under one contract. The personnel situation in the firm was unfortunately such that the inconsistency of information created an uproar, compounded of professional jealousies, insecurity of employees, and confusion about channels of authority. Before the situation was clarified, several staff members threatened termination and at least one resigned. The surface inconsistency itself created considerable noise and disturbance among those who were receiving the information.

Time lag

In speaking, one of the most serious problems with which we have to deal is the elapsed time between transmission of a message and completion of the communication loop. Time may be a factor of distance. Today, with tape recorders, videotape recorders, film, and the like, we have many ways of preserving at least some of the external characteristics of a speaking performance; yet, there still is difficulty because of the differences in time and immediacy.

What you and I might say on a tape-recorded conversation within the next few minutes might mean little if anything to us two days from now. A recorded interchange, heard later out of context of the conditions existing when the words were spoken in our communication situation, might lose significantly in meaning.

The passage of time, particularly after the impact of the interpersonal speech-communication situation, eats away the substance and meaning of a message. We speak as a result of certain conditions and feelings and responses that are current at the moment and of such multiplicity that we can never recapture them in exactly the same intensity or in the same extent or degree.

Communication interactions once experienced will never be experienced again. All that exists of them is a memory; and, as time passes, that memory is eroded. Thus, the farther away in time the message is from its origin, the greater the likelihood of that message losing more and more of its meaning.

[5] Ken Macrorie, "Too Many Messages: The Popular Arts," *Reporter Magazine* (July 20, 1961), p. 39.

This is not to imply that meaning does not lie within the person. It means simply that the set of symbols that come out in the form of sounds and physical behaviors simply do not strike upon the same set of conditions that existed before. Now, this doesn't mean that a different message for the same set of symbols might not be construed after the passage of time. In the world of written language, for example, it is commonly understood that after the moment of writing, a given message may be interpreted in many different ways depending on the nature of the person who reads it. And, since meanings are in persons, each person who reads it has a different meaning. Essentially the same phenomenon occurs in spoken language, although the system itself is in quite a different context and within a different set of symbolic forms.

Summary

Our basic purpose is to improve our speech communication with each other. Our next task is to identify, at least in part, the obstacles, or barriers, and the breakdowns that appear to destroy or at least to inhibit the full realization of effective speech communication. For the sake of clarity and organization, we have divided our discussion of these communication problems into several units.

We first looked at those difficulties that exist primarily within and about the speaker; that is, those kinds of internal behaviors, conditions, and situations that cause a speaker trouble in his communicative efforts.

Our second category concerned those problems that exist within the listener. Since speech communication is essentially an interaction between at least two persons, we should realize that some of the barriers and breakdowns in the communicative effort may exist inside those who are at the receiving end of a communicative interaction.

In our third category of difficulties are the inhibitors of speech communication that occur within both the speaker and the listener either jointly or separately. These inhibitors are closely related to the interaction process that is taking place.

The fourth area we identify as those difficulties external to the speaker and the listener; that is, factors surrounding the interaction of the speaker and the listener themselves and over which they may or may not have some immediate control.

In the last category of problems we discussed some types of obstacles and breakdowns that are related generally to the overall speech-communication situation.

We have listed here a large number of possible obstacles or barriers and breakdowns of effective communication, many of them overlapping. It is, as it were, like a tapestry or a complex set of wires woven together to create a screen through which human beings try to communicate with each other. Each one of the barriers or breakdowns alone may not result in too great a hazard. But, in combination with other barriers, they may almost completely destroy human mutual understanding. On the other hand, a single barrier or breakdown existing in great degree or intensity may have such impact as to destroy the communication.

Certainly, not all the obstacles have been identified. Some have been identified more effectively than others. They are not all the same type or kind, but they all represent barriers to human understanding.

Our next step should be the exploration of ways in which we can overcome these barriers. And that is precisely what the whole business of speech-communication studies is attempting to do. Each of us must attempt to find ways to prevent development of or to overcome these and other barriers that may exist in our communication efforts.

Our own individual creativity and ingeniousness must be used in devising ways to overcome the barriers. So now the question is put to you straight: Which of these difficulties affect your communication and how will you overcome these difficulties?

Only you can create the "miracle of speech" for yourself.

For special reading

Irving J. Lee and Laura L. Lee, *Handling Barriers in Communication* (New York: Harper & Row, 1956). The late Irving Lee was one of the most exciting and effective teachers I have known. This handbook grew out of his work with several companies in helping them to improve their speech-communication effectiveness. After Dr. Lee died, his wife brought these materials together into book form. You will find this clear, useful, and thought-provoking.

Irving J. Lee, *Customs and Crises in Communication* (New York: Harper & Row, 1954). Here is an excellent collection of cases for the study of barriers and breakdowns in communication. Lee selects from classic works, from the statements of people contemporary to his day, and from many different sources and levels of activity. There is rich material here for your personal study or for class discussion.

Wendell Johnson, *People in Quandaries* (New York: Harper & Row, 1946). Here is one of the most provocative books about the problems people have in communicating with each other. Johnson hits to the heart of the misunderstanding and miscommunication that occurs between people. You will find him stimulating and full of ideas.

Jack R. Gibb, "Defensive Communications," *ETC.,* Vol. 22 (June 1965), p. 222. Here is a short and pointed report of the way in which defensiveness prevents a listener from concentrating upon the message, causes a communicator to send off multiple-valued cues, with the communication event ending in a circle of responses which becomes increasingly destructive of the people and the communication efforts.

Elwood Murray, "What Are the Problems of Communication in Human Relations?" *Journal of Communication,* Vol. 1 (May 1951), pp. 23–26. Murray, one of the leaders in the general semantics movement, points out that communication problems are essentially problems of human relations and vice versa. In this short article, he identifies three kinds of problems: physical disorders, psychological and semantic disorders, and one-way communication.

Carl R. Rogers and F. J. Roethlisberger, "Barriers and Gateways to Communication," *Harvard Business Review* (July–August 1952); reprinted in *How Successful Executives Handle People: Studies on Communication and Management Skills,* No. 12 (Cambridge, Mass.: Harvard College, 1948–1954), pp. 28–34. Here is a clear-cut, concise statement by two leading communication specialists. Rogers presents the problem from the point of view of human behavior and Roethlisberger from the context of industrial relations. This article was one of the early commentaries on communication barriers and still is useful today.

Try this

1   In your journal, identify as many incidents as you can recall of speech-communication barriers and breakdowns that have occurred in your interpersonal interactions during the past week. Now, in retrospect, write out procedures that might have prevented or avoided these difficulties.

2   In your school, a number of student activities are under the supervision of faculty and staff. Seek out some event on your campus where an interpretation of rules and regulations has caused some furor. Try to trace the origin of the regulation and the various stages through which the regulatory information passed before it was received by the students involved in the incident.

3   Identify as many examples as you can of the "allness" type of statement in radio or television advertising.

4 In his book *Communication: Patterns and Incidents* (Homewood, Ill.: Richard D. Irwin, 1960), William V. Haney has collected an unusual number of incidents demonstrating various communication errors. Select two incidents that you feel to be most dramatic and significant and make an analysis of them in the following aspects: (1) the nature of the error or errors; (2) the extent to which these errors are common to your experience; (3) procedures you would use to avoid, eliminate, or otherwise correct the errors described in the incident.

5 Prepare a demonstration in which you dramatize some critical barrier or breakdown. Then "replay" the dramatization with a corrective system that will avoid the difficulty.

6 Arrange a special conference of students-faculty-administration of your university for the avowed purpose of examining the barriers and breakdowns in communication on your campus.

7 Cross-cultural communication is one of the most serious problems of our time. Find as much as you can about the barriers and breakdowns, other than differences in language, relating to our speech communication with the following: (1) disadvantaged to/from the affluent; (2) black to/from white; (3) United States to/from Latin America, Russia, China, North Vietnam, South Vietnam, India, Pakistan, Cuba, South Africa, Japan, Korea.

Chapter Ten

Changing Behavior: Persuasion

Objectives

After studying this chapter, you should be better able to do these things:

- Use speech communication persuasively.

- Cope with your desire to change the behavior of people by understanding the nature and the extent of changes that can be brought about by persuasion and considering the wants of others.

- Use the wants, needs, and wishes of yourself and others in changing beliefs.

- Examine the influence of attitudes on your own and others' behavior.

- Use the hierarchy of needs affecting human behavior to change yourself and others.

- Use the tension in the physical-emotional system to remove disequilibrium.

- Function as a persuader in bringing about an equilibrium in another's need system while providing you with the ends you seek.

- Arouse energy in others that moves them toward action.

- Know your own goal in terms of specific behavior of the persuadees.

- Relate your goals as a persuader to the goals of your persuadee.

- Use the most effective material at any particular stage of persuasion.

- Cope with deprivation, threat, and conformity as they affect the persuasive possibilities in any given situation.

- Keep the total physical effort of delivery consistent with your purposes as a persuader.

- Develop a unique style of persuasion that fits your needs, your personality, and your situation.

- Defend yourself from efforts to change you to a direction or action you do not want.

You are about to confront, at your request, a young man or woman you have loved deeply for a long time. In recent months, however, you have been alienated from each other through your own responding anger and hurt at the other's behavior. Your loved one has pulled away from you because of fear of what you may do, of desire to find other relationships to test the love, and because of an inner turmoil of guilt because of the nature of your previous relationship. You want very much to reinstitute your relationship and to move it on to a higher level of trust, love, and closeness than either of you has ever experienced.

What will you say to your former love? What will you do? What will you *not* say and do? Are you able to change your loved one to reach the goals you seek? How will you proceed to deal with your partner? When you can perform, in a situation such as this, to bring about change to reach *your* goals and *also* the goals of your partner, you are operating on a highly effective level of persuasion.

Through speech communication people have been induced to part with worldly goods, even life itself; to change attitudes and beliefs; to alter systems of behavior; and to make decisions that affected their whole lives. From ancient times, speech communication has been recognized as a powerful tool in controlling and directing the decisions and actions of human beings.

Persuasion in society

Properly used, speech persuasion can be a force for inducing people to perform in a manner that will bring good to themselves and to their society. Improperly used, it can bring evil and destruction. Whether it is used for good or evil depends primarily on the nature of the person using it rather than on the process itself.

It is not our province to delve into the ethics of those who would use speech communication for persuasion. That is a matter for the privacy of individual conscience. It is important, however, that we recognize the significance of the tool as a force in human society. Like many tools, *speech-communication persuasion has no inherent good or evil and can be used by both good and evil men.* Persuasion is like a surgical scalpel, which may be used by the surgeon to save a life and, in the hands of a murderer, may be used to destroy life. Whether persuasion is used to advance the cause of humankind or to destroy man depends on those who use it and on those who are the targets of its force.

When improperly executed or poorly used, the tools of persuasive communication may work to our disadvantage. A scalpel improperly sterilized and inadequately sharpened may be an instrument of death, even in the hands of a surgeon. Persuasive communication, likewise, when poorly conceived and inadequately applied, may yield undesirable results. *If we feel justified in using the techniques of persuasion to manipulate our fellow human beings, we should also feel obligated to use these techniques with mature responsibility.*

We all have needed and have developed some measure of skill in persuasion since we were very young children. We have persuaded parents to modify edicts; we have persuaded peers to join us in specific activities; we have, all of us, used persuasion all our lives—some of us with greater success than others. Persuasion skills are essential in many occupations: sales, of course; law, especially in the courtroom; mediation; public relations and advertising; teaching; any supervisory work—to name but a few.

There have been con men ever since there were little old ladies and gullible, greedy fools with coin of the realm. Demagogues have contributed to the shaping of history since there were masses to be swayed by speech-communication persuasion to more or less violent action. We are bombarded in our contemporary culture with persuasion, used and abused. We have our demagogues; we have our con men—the breeds are not new in the history of man. *If we know something of the techniques used by persuaders, we are forewarned and can avoid being manipulated to our disadvantage by abusers of persuasion.*

Knowledge of the arts of persuasion gives us no black magic whereby we can manipulate others as we will, when we will. All the techniques can be applied, but they result in persuasion only if the persuadee changes his thinking or behavior. Most people, by force of sheer inertia, are most reluctant to change patterns of thinking or of behaving; persuasion, all too often, is difficult, if not impossible.

A con man effects changes in the thinking of the sucker to get what he wants, which is cash in his pocket; this is abuse of persuasion. A citizen ringing doorbells in behalf of a school bond issue is also trying to effect changes in thinking to get what he wants, which is a better school system for the community; the more he knows about the techniques of persuasion, the better the chances for approval of the school bonds.

Again and again, throughout a lifetime, each of us will be in situations that call for persuasive efforts to achieve commendable objectives, for self (at no harm to others) and for others. If we are not, to whatever degree, skilled in persuasion, we may lose—unnecessarily and to the harm of ourselves and of others. Likewise, if we are aware of the skills and techniques of persuasion we can protect ourselves against unwanted efforts to change our behavior and thus be much more free to make our own decisions.

Persuasion, if it works, is a potent force—for good or for evil. It is well to remember, as persuader or as persuadee, the old Chinese saying: "Fool me once, shame on you; fool me twice, shame on me."

The nature of persuasion and change

When we examine the process closely, we can see that practically all human speech communication includes some aspect of persuasion. The very nature of the communication act produces at least some change in the behavior of any participant in the event. The change is not necessarily a "compliance" type of behavior; but behavior does change as a result of the confrontation with a speaker, his message, his presentation, and the context of the situation. A persuasive pitch made by the track coach may induce an aspirant to the track team to roll out at six o'clock every morning to work out, instead of habitually sleeping till noon. This would be a behavioral change. He may, however, be convinced that early-morning workouts are advisable but decides to defer action on them till track season begins. He may be convinced that such exercise at dawn is an excellent activity for track stars but that his sleep means more to him than making the track team. He might entertain the thought that early-morning exercise is conducive to health in general. Or, he may never have considered early rising for any purpose, and the persuasive efforts of the track coach may bring to his attention an idea that is novel to him.

The act of persuasion exerts a pressure, an influence, on an individual to effect a change in his thinking and, perhaps, his behavior. Or it may remove a resistance to a change that, when removed, allows you to make the wanted change. That influence or removal of resistance can be channeled through our emotional conditions, through our manner of thinking, through our ability to perceive things, and by a process of relating the change to our wants, needs, and wishes.

Persuasion is a process of inducing change in behavior, beliefs, and attitudes. In speech persuasion, we work with the speech communication of information and messages that so affect the receivers as to bring about changes desired by the initiater. When the persuasive effort is successful, the resulting changes are useful or instrumental for the persuader and the persuadee. The persuasive effort not only seeks to satisfy certain goals of the persuader but also must be perceived by the persuadee as offering some benefit to him.

Change is a condition of living; everything about us is in constant flux. However, the changes that we seek through persuasion are extraordinary, in that they are beyond the ordinary changes that occur. Gradual, inherent changes in processes that occur with the usual passage of time and circumstances are usually hardly discernible. On the other hand, events may create pressures that not only may accelerate the processes of change but also may alter the nature of the change. In the normal course of life, the hair of a human being turns grey or white; intense emotional shock has been known to accelerate the greying process—of course, hair dyes may conceal such natural changes. Over a number of years, a building deteriorates under the best of circumstances and may eventually fall in ruins; a fire or a wrecking crew can accelerate this change to ruin in a very short time.

Behavior changes in response to persuasion vary from nil to forceful action. At the minimum level, a persuader may succeed only in arousing a flicker of attention to his message. The maximum effect prompted by persuasion is some form of action, as, for example, the action of signing a purchase contract as a result of the kind of persuasion known as salesmanship.

| Attention | Perception | Knowledge and Information | Belief and Attitude | Action |

Figure 10–1   Stages of persuasion

In Figure 10–1, the relationship of the nature of changes and the extent of these changes is shown in graphic form.

Behavior and belief

Since the areas with which persuasion is most directly concerned involve human knowing, believing, and behaving, we shall examine these briefly.

Knowing

Our senses allow us to gather information from the world around us. Something must happen to this information, however selective or expansive it may be. The process by which we organize, interpret, and relate the information that our senses gather is the process of knowing. It would follow, then, that knowledge is the organized, interpreted, and related information that each of us has.

Thus, my senses may provide me with information about an object that I encounter. My perceptual processes and cognition allow me to see that it is obviously an instrument of conveyance (I thus classify the information as "instrument" and "conveyance"). I sort out the data my senses reveal into certain characteristics. My previous experience with objects with similar characteristics allows me to identify what I see as an automobile (I have further classified the information, this time in terms of a prior-existing concept of what an automobile may be).

Having classified the information as representing an automobile, I then interpret the information as classified in terms of its connection with other things and with my own needs. This particular automobile is registered in my name and therefore is more useful to me than the one across the street that belongs to someone else.

Having sorted out these data, classified them, and interpreted them in relation to prior experience, I then associate them with my present purposes and being.

The end product of these processes is what we call *knowledge*.

Believing

It is generally assumed that a belief is a total state of being or a collection of subconditions that are bound together in relation to some external referent.

Milton Rokeach has written of beliefs:

> Beliefs are inferences made by an observer about underlying states of expectancy. . . . Belief like motives, genes, and neutrons . . . cannot be directly observed but must be inferred as best one can, with whatever psychological devices available, from all the things the believer says or does.

> A belief system may be defined as having represented within it, [in] some organized psychological but not necessarily logical form, each and every one of a person's countless beliefs about physical and social reality.[1]

When we say we "believe" that another man is "honest," we are saying that we are ready to act toward him and others as we feel we should treat honest men and that he will act toward us as we expect an

---

[1] Milton Rokeach, *Beliefs, Attitudes, and Values* (San Francisco: Jossey-Bass, 1968), p. 2.

honest man to act. If we believe a certain make of automobile is better
than another, we are more likely to choose an automobile produced by that
particular company, drive it when we have an opportunity, buy it when
we are in the market for a purchase, and speak favorably about it to
others.

Beliefs are not necessarily reached by reason. They appear to be determined, to a great extent, by what *we want* to believe, by what *we are able*
to believe, by what we have been *conditioned* to believe, and by those
basic needs that may force us to a certain belief in order to adjust our
behavior to meet those needs.

Rokeach identifies several types of belief and asserts that they are not
equally important.[2] The most pervasive or central type of belief is that
which comes from direct experience and is confirmed by consensus of our
reference groups and persons. Such beliefs represent the "basic truths" a
person holds about himself and his world that are also held by those persons
with whom he relates. These beliefs have a constancy that allows us to
trust. A chair remains a chair no matter how we look at it; also, the experience of people with the chair remains somewhat constant.

This constancy of object and personal relation to it provides us with a
certain stability. Thus, if we discover that our perceptions of objects are
not what we have believed them to be and these new perceptions are confirmed by our friends, considerable concern arises about our ability to deal
with reality. This in turn may lead to strong efforts to restructure or to reor-
ganize our belief systems to make them coincide with the reality we may
be perceiving. Thus, a man may have perceived his woman friend as honest,
loving, and loyal. When someone he respects and admires reports that she is
known for lying, uses men unmercifully for her own selfish ends, and has
been seen with many other fellows, he begins to reexamine his whole world
of perceiving her. Maybe his wish to hold her will cause him to deny his
friend's perception or he will rationalize that she is really not understood.
Or he may simply have to change his whole way of viewing her and on the
basis of the new perceptions change his behavior.

Each of us also has some constant beliefs that are not supported by
consensus. These are derived from our own highly personal and very private
experiences with reality that are shared by no one else. Thus, the first
type of belief can be confirmed by checking with another person while
the second type is not subject to such confirmation even though it is strongly
held. A belief that it is raining can be confirmed by others. But a person's
belief in God, his mother's love, or the love of his girl friend or her boy friend
even though held tenaciously, cannot be confirmed by others.

[2] Rokeach, pp. 1–12.

A third type of belief develops from constant beliefs and is also related to them. In childhood we are likely to accept and trust our parents and their beliefs, but as time goes on this constancy may shift as we discover that others have different concepts. We may accept certain beliefs of our teachers and friends, for example, and then add them to our constant beliefs.

Another type of belief identified by Rokeach includes those that come from persons we accept as having high credibility or authority. These may be called derived beliefs because they come secondhand from others. Such beliefs are more changeable than are constant beliefs. Beliefs may come from our church and political affiliations or from what we assume to be "reliable sources." If we know the kinds of sources a person considers reliable, we can determine many of his beliefs.

A fifth type of belief identified by Rokeach includes those that come from direct experience with objects but that do not require or have social consensus or confirmation and have little or no connection with other beliefs.

When we look at the whole spectrum of beliefs, we find a kind of organization ranging from beliefs with a great amount of constancy to those with very little constancy. Rokeach maintains that a belief system is essential to a sense of identity.

> Taken together, the total belief system may be seen as an organization of beliefs varying in depth, formed as a result of living in nature and in society, designed to help a person maintain, insofar as possible, a sense of ego and group identity, stable and continuous over time—an identity that is part of, and simultaneously apart from, a stable physical and social environment."[3]

Beliefs generally are organized around objects, situations, and people; and they have several components. They involve knowledge or information received and classified. They also involve "affect" or emotional conditions, in that under certain conditions beliefs lead to an arousal of the emotions. Finally, beliefs have behavior characteristics, in that they bring about action and reaction in relation to the objects of belief.

Attitudes

Attitudes have been identified as organized systems of beliefs that predispose us to respond in some specified manner.[4] These complex systems influence almost all human behavior. Thus, we all have attitudes toward self, toward

[3] Rokeach, pp. 11–12.
[4] Rokeach, p. 112.

other people, toward institutions, toward objects; we have a predisposition to respond in a given way to these things. (Or, as we mentioned in Chapter 8, page 146, we have a *commitment* to behave in a certain way.)

Attitudes are identified as being directed toward the object or person and with varying degrees of intensity or power.[5] They are acquired rather than predetermined; that is, a child is not born with a set of attitudes, he develops them. They are also a consistent way of reacting to the environment around us.

Since attitudes represent commitments, we can say that they anticipate much organized action or behavior. Thus, a person with an attitude that is developed around an opposition to, say, labor unions is likely to behave in such a way as to oppose labor-sponsored projects in actual events—many times without really sufficient purely "logical" or informational bases.

Needs and motives

Needs and motivation are important to the process of persuasion. Needs can be described as tensions that develop in relation to our goals. When a need arises and is not satisfied, our biopsychic system increases its internal tensions.

To change the beliefs or attitudes of another person, we must understand at least the other's needs; the situation in which he operates; how he perceives his own situation, those around him, and his own needs; and the types of behavior that he uses to meet his needs. Here, again, our discussions in the early chapters on understanding each other as a base for communication are fundamental. *We must recognize that each of us sees the world in his own way.* A need that we perceive as obvious and self-evident might be a symptom of a deeper and less conscious need. For example, we have all observed persons who seemed to have a high need to win. In most cases, this apparent need is a symptom of a much more significant need for approval or status or acceptance.

By conscious and unconscious design, each of us works out a system of behavior to meet his various needs. In any given situation, each relies on this system to take care of the conditions that may arise.

In general, each of us depends on a number of organized behavior patterns in pursuing our daily lives. The family rituals at meals, special events, and the like represent certain patterns of behavior that have, through use, become expected and represent a norm of behavior for the family. When a ritual or pattern is upset by absence of one of the

---

[5] Frederick J. McDonald, *Educational Psychology*, 2nd ed. (Belmont, Calif.: Wadsworth Publishing Co., 1965), pp. 309–310.

members, for example, or by a change in time of observance, the family group becomes disturbed and seeks another behavior that will meet the needs answered by the first ritual plus the additional need for a similarity to the pattern that has in the past been successful.

Thus, when we anticipate changing the behavior of another, we need to recognize that his present behavior may well be part of some organized system within his life and that the system may strongly influence his performance because it has in the past met his needs or given pleasure. *We need therefore to know available alternatives that would meet the underlying needs satisfied by his current behavior.*

It is no secret that corporations raid each other's executive manpower resources. Money talks, of course, but not infrequently a salary increase does not have sufficient persuasive force to effect a change in the behavior patterns of a "target." In one such situation, the president of an industrial concern finally located "just the man" for an important executive-line position in his company. However, the young man was not inclined to accept the offer of the new position, and he had several reasons. First, the position was very much like the one he had. Second, it would mean moving to another part of the country and away from the area where he had been born and raised. Third, salary and other benefits of the new position were not substantially greater than he was already making. Fourth, he could see no greater promise for advancement. Generally, the behavior system of this man in relation to the new job was not sufficiently challenged to enable him to justify moving from his old position. That is, his needs were being met with the present system and he could see no advantage resulting from change.

The corporation president really wanted this particular man for the position, and he was certain that it offered more opportunity than the other. He analyzed the situation, focusing first on what kinds of needs were dominant in this young man's behavior system. Then he obtained additional information that gave him a clearer understanding of the man's actual work situation in his present employment. Throughout his analysis and development of a persuasion strategy, he kept in mind that the way the young man saw his world was not the way he, as a corporation president, would see that world and that the differences could cause considerable lack of understanding. He tried to see the situation as his prospective employee saw it, and he developed a presentation that showed more value in terms meaningful to his persuadee.

In renewed discussions with the reluctant prospect, the persuasion strategy was put into effect. He was brought to perceive the situation in the new setting as being more adequate to meet his and his family's needs. He was shown and led to believe that the new job would provide for a better long-run advancement than his present job. He was stimulated to take action on the situation by increasing the intensity with which the suggestion of need-satisfaction was made. Finally, he was given a specific proposal for handling the change in position with the least amount of disruption of many of his family patterns. The persuasion was effective in that it led him to change his perception of his needs in relation to the situation. He accepted the position, and both he and his new boss have been satisfied with results.

Human needs, anticipations, and potential for stimulation are unconscious or are hidden beneath the behavior patterns of everyday living. As long as these are satisfied without extreme disruption or effort, we are likely to lose sight of the fact that they are there. Usually, these factors array themselves in a hierarchy of significance; some are more powerful than others. The need for food, for example, is powerful; yet, just after a full meal, our desire, anticipation, and potential stimulation relative to immediate input of sustaining food will temporarily lose their importance as determinants of our immediate behavior. Maslow discusses gratification:

> Gratification . . . releases the organism from the domination of a relatively more physiological need permitting thereby the emergence of other more social goals. The physiological needs, along with their partial goals, when chronically gratified cease to exist as active determinants or organizers of behavior. They have existed only in a potential fashion in the sense that they may emerge again to dominate the organism if they are thwarted. But a want that is satisfied is no longer a want. The organism is dominated and its behavior organized only by unsatisfied needs. If hunger is satisfied, it becomes unimportant in the current dynamics of the individual.[6]

A significant factor to remember is that, as in early chapters, we are again concerned with understanding the other person and his needs as well as our own. Persuasion depends on the depth of this understanding. A person's needs, anticipations, and stimulative possibilities at any given moment determine much of his behavior. Therefore, if we intend to change behavior, we need to know the nature of the system that lies behind any given set of the other's actions.

Human needs have been described by Maslow in two general categories: D-needs are those which, when satisfied, provide for the physical and personal self; they are derived from Maslow's D-love, which is "deficiency love, love need, selfish love." B-needs are those which are met by satisfying the desires of others; they are derived from Maslow's B-love, which is "love

[6] A. H. Maslow, *Motivation and Personality* (New York: Harper & Row, 1954), p. 84

for the Being of another person, unneeding love, unselfish love." Thus, the B-needs represent a higher level of need satisfaction.[7]

Many needs, anticipations, and sources of stimulation are unconscious and are felt only in terms of some external or conscious want or craving—or some substitute that relieves the tension. Our needs and behavior apparently are related to maintaining an equilibrium of the physical, emotional, and mental states of our personality; when something throws the system out of balance, a tension is felt until some new equilibrium is established.

Needs, tensions, and equilibrium

The nature of tension is important to us as persuaders. Generally, we consider it a discomfort that is removed by discharge of activity or relief of some sort. As long as the discharge or the relief does not occur, the state of discomfort continues. Usually, tensions arise when there is an excessive amount of pressure (input) upon us to behave in certain ways and we cannot match the pressure by action (output); when we have conflicting pressures put upon us that confuse us; when our basic appetites or instincts are not consummated; when our anger does not find a satisfactory outlet; when our fear is not relieved; when specific objects that have given us satisfaction are missing in our present environment; and when someone else communicates to us (directly or indirectly) some vague anxiety, fear, or other threatening emotion.[8]

The accomplishment of balance does not necessarily mean that the old balance is restored; it may mean that a new equilibrium has been attained. For example, in a classic experiment, workers in a pajama factory were producing a certain number of shirts per hour, and they considered this production adequate, as long as they were paid. In order to develop change, the experimenters brought some of the workers together and asked them to discuss production goals and possibilities. In doing so, the management implied that the current output was not adequate and this implication created some tension. The groups set new production goals, and the factory soon reached higher production levels. The tension created by the dissatisfaction of management had been transferred to the workers, who provided a release; and a new equilibrium was established.[9]

The materials or ideas that were used to help the persuadees perceive the desirability of change were related to the actual situation in which

[7] A. H. Maslow, *Toward a Psychology of Being* (New York: Van Nostrand Reinhold Co., 1962), pp. 42–43; see also Maslow, *Motivation and Personality.*
[8] Silvano Arieti, *The Intrapsychic Self* (New York: Basic Books, 1967), pp. 32–33.
[9] Lester Coch and J. R. P. French, Jr., "Overcoming Resistance to Change," *Human Relations,* Vol. 1 (1948), pp. 512–532.

these people were operating. As we anticipate working with others to change their behavior, we must be sure that we help them to perceive their needs and tensions *in relation to the actual current situation in which they exist.* A plea for assistance for starving people in a foreign land given after a banquet will not persuade many members of the audience to sign large contribution checks. Some other approach might prove more effective.

As we examine the goals that people seek and the anticipations that press them to behave as they do, we discover the tensions that surround the failure to satisfy these goals and needs. The strategy of persuasion, then, becomes one of bringing the persuadee to perceive the imbalance, to sense the tension, then to lead him to behaviors that will relieve this tension for him and will at the same time accomplish the ends of the persuader. *In a sense, successful persuasion is a process of accomplishing a new mutual balance or equilibrium.*

Motivation

Motivation, as the term is generally used, occurs when a person's feelings are aroused so that he exerts actual physical and psychic energy in attempting to reach an anticipated goal or to satisfy some need. Needs and goals exist; as persuaders, we must learn what they are, then find ways to arouse persons to seek them. It is much more difficult to arouse people to seek goals related to Maslow's B-needs (of others) than those associated with D-needs (of self).

Sometimes the persuader may be seeking a goal similar to the one he is trying to arouse his persuadee to achieve, as when a young man tries to arouse in his father a desire for a new family car, which, of course, is also the lad's goal. At other times, the action aroused will suffice to accomplish the goal of the persuader, as when a television ad arouses my hunger and I go out and buy the advertised product. The persuader, in that instance, was seeking to get me to buy. He had no primary interest in satisfying my hunger; yet he used my need as an avenue to his goal. *All persuasion depends on the arousal of energy in relation to goals,* which seems to be the "push" necessary to bring about the actual change.

Avenues to persuasion

The first step in the persuasive effort, then, is to focus the attention of the persuadees on the situation and its relation to their basic needs, wants, and anticipations that are currently operating with some strength. While we can assume that most people have certain basic drives, we should focus on the particular circumstances surrounding the actual time when we are attempting to influence their behavior.

In assisting a person to confront his needs and tensions, we may use several methods of approach. One way is to bring into direct attention the various events or objects that indicate or reinforce the persuadee's awareness of the presence of his need-tensions. Such may be accomplished by using from his own or related experiences examples that select from the situation the particular needs that are dominant. Thus, a store manager who has been experiencing a high turnover of sales personnel will give attention to discussion of his own problem or to statements about someone who is having similar difficulty.

Another method of opening up the persuadee is to present him with an opinion of a qualified expert. Track coaches and doctors are quoted on the benefits of jogging. Former presidents are quoted on the wisdom or folly of proposed foreign policy. Until children learn better, fathers are quoted on almost anything.

The opinion of a vague concept variously called "everybody" or "people"—or "them"—may be effective with many persuadees. "What will people think?" has for generations been used with telling force. A wife uses this kind of opinion in her persuasion campaigns, as, for example, when she suggests to her husband that "everyone" on the street has noticed the disgracefully old worn-out hat he was wearing.

When possible, we should try to assist our persuadee *to examine his own feelings and behavior* in order to discover the status of his needs and his emotional reactions. To do this, we must create between us a personal atmosphere that will permit free and open discussion of his problems and situations. This atmosphere must be relatively free from threat so that he can feel some support in his effort to look at himself. This kind of experience may come through encounter groups, sensitivity groups, personal growth experiences, gestalt encounters, and personal counseling. In some critical situations that are beyond our competence as persuaders, we may need to provide our subject with special professional help to examine and study his problems. His self-examination may require assistance from a medical doctor or a psychiatrist or a lawyer or a marriage counselor or a priest.

Know what you seek

Establishing the opening perception of the situation is only the beginning of the persuasive effort. Once the matter is opened up, a number of factors must be considered in order to effect the behavior change that may be desired. A primary and very significant factor is the nature of the goal that the persuader wishes to reach. *When you are the persuader, you should have in mind precisely what you wish to have your subject do as a result of your persuasive efforts.*

Successful salesmen must be effective persuaders. My father, I am convinced, was a truly great salesman. He sold goodwill advertising to business houses of one kind or another. Sometimes I traveled with him, and I remember vividly how he approached a sale. As we drove, we would talk over what the prospect would most likely need, like, expect, and respond to in the way of advertising material. When we arrived in the town, instead of going directly to his target business, we would manage two or three stops at places that were likely customers of the prospect; and Dad would size up what those customers might respond to. Before finally calling on the prospect, Dad would rummage through his sample cases and come up with two or three items that he felt would stimulate that person in that business situation. When he approached the man who had the say on buying advertising, Dad would take in a fairly large number of items to be shown, but placed carefully among them would be those that he had selected. As he laid out the items, he would manage to put these in the most conspicuous places. Rarely did he fail in making a sale of the very items he had figured would sell.

Speaker credibility

Much has been written about the significance of the personality of the speaker or persuader in effecting change. Wayne Thompson, however, in a summary of quantitative research in public address, points out that "the available evidence does not support the position that ethos increases persuasiveness in speech situations."[10] In referring to ethos, Thompson uses the classical rhetoric concept of the character of the speaker. Most of the studies he reports were made in laboratory and controlled conditions. It is my feeling that *we cannot isolate the credibility of the speaker from the nature of the situation and the listener(s) at a given moment in time.*

A person's credibility is determined by those who perceive him.[11] Let's put this another way; as a teacher in a classroom I may be perceived by students as having a higher degree of credibility than I would be accorded by nonstudents who had no interest in or concern at all about the subjects I teach. As a mediator, I have found that my official position gives me some degree of attention from my clients, but it does not provide automatic acceptance of my ideas. My credibility must be developed through interaction with both parties, together and separate, on the spot and through

---

[10] Wayne N. Thompson, *Quantitative Research in Public Address and Communication* (New York: Random House, 1967), p. 59.

[11] Carolyn W. Sherif, Musafer Sherif, and Roger E. Nebergall, *Attitude and Attitudinal Change* (Philadelphia: W. B. Saunders Co., 1965), pp. 201ff.

previous interactions. Their confidence in me must be developed from such interaction. Thus, when I am able to be of use to them on one issue my credibility rises in relation to the next issue that we face.

The late Adlai Stevenson brought to any interaction with another person an aura of the respect and admiration generally extended to him. His reputation established a form of credibility for him in almost any situation. Moreover, his ability to interact with his fellows in such a way that they felt he had their concern uppermost gave him an even greater, a more dimensional, credibility in the minds of his hearers. But even for Stevenson, there were situations (as, for example, a meeting of the John Birch Society) in which his credibility would have been low. Credibility is not automatically and immutably a function of the individual; the specific situation may be the essential determining factor.

Sources of credibility

Personal influence is made up of several factors that are involved in the interaction that lead to acceptance of a person by those whom he would persuade. Among them are his *competence* in the immediate situation, his *reputation* in relation to comparable situations, his degree of *projection toward* others, his demonstrated *trustworthiness,* the *consistency* of his appearance and ideas with the standards of his persuadees and his own *standards,* and his *ability* to interact with his persuadees in a fashion acceptable to them.[12]

Listener goals and anticipations

As we have noted, we must understand and relate our persuasion to the goals and anticipations of the persuadee. Whatever the persuasion message, it must contain material that is relevant to the goals and anticipation of the persuadee. He must perceive the ultimate change in behavior as being useful to him (note that we assume Maslow's D-need goals as universal). His perception of "what's in it for him" will depend considerably on the degree to which he is able to associate the ideas of the persuader with his own goals. The successful persuader must help him to see this association.

Remember that each of us develops a system of behavior that serves to maintain a physical and psychological equilibrium. The effective persuader detects the relationship of certain of our behaviors to the needs they meet. The same general type of overt behavior exhibited by two persons is not always symptomatic of the existence of the same need in

---

[12] Ralph L. Rosnow and Edward J. Robinson, *Experiments in Persuasion* (New York: Academic Press, 1967), pp. 2–66.

those persons. Most of us can identify or classify behavior of others (as, for example, hostile or secure or subservient), but we cannot so easily relate this behavior to underlying goals and needs. For example, my companions in a monthly poker session exhibit varying degrees of risk-taking predisposition. But the needs and goals of men who show the same risk-taking behavior are different. Two of the group habitually tend to take more chances than the others. One of them apparently seeks the attention he gets from the others in the group. The other savors the pleasure he derives from the challenge of the unpredictable and the unknown. For either of these men, a persuader might gain some success by suggesting that a new behavior would entail some risk; but for the first man, the risk must be appreciated and respected by others.

Understanding of the relationships among needs, anticipations, and behavior tendencies can provide a persuader with effective means to achieve his purpose. If a persuader can suggest that the desired behavior meets the persuadee's needs and is comparable to the behavior he has been using, persuasion stands a better chance of success.

Message strength

Within the communication event of persuasion, the message itself must have sufficient strength to reach the acceptance level of the persuadee. Message strength is gained through supporting reasons, examples, comparisons, and relevant information. *A persuasive message cannot be useful unless it is directly relevant to the purpose of the persuasion itself.* Some would-be persuaders make the mistake of thinking that it is necessary to fill the message with irrelevant material in order to get the subject into an accepting condition. This is an error in perception of the nature of the persuasive message. If the persuadee is hostile, he is not likely to listen. *The hostility must be dispelled before the persuasion suggestion can reach him.* Efforts to change his hostility are an integral part of the total persuasive effort and are not irrelevant. The work to dispel the hostility must be done with great care and precision. However, if the persuadee is not hostile and seems willing to accept the persuader's suggestion, it is a waste of time to fill the messages with irrelevant material.

Another important function of the message is the presentation of specific information and data. At the proper time, *reliable and pertinent data must be brought into the communication.* In selling a car, for example, a good salesman will have available data concerning the performance of the machine he is selling. The more reliable these data are, the more useful and effective they are in aiding him to accomplish his purpose.

Often persuasive messages include *statements from other people.* We have already discussed credibility, which applies to quoted statements of others as well as to statements of the persuader. When we refer to others, we should be sure that the sources are reliable and credible. Far too many high school and even college debaters quote extensively from "authorities" who know little or nothing concerning the subject on which they expound. The use of the opinion of someone else is at best a delicate process. Some people are fooled by phony testimony of questionable experts; but once a source has been discredited, further attempts at persuasion are pretty limited.

I remember painfully that I once invested in a new insurance company on the strength of the salesman's allegation that some of my esteemed colleagues had bought stock. Later, I talked with those "esteemed colleagues" and found that they had bought stock because it had been alleged that *I* was interested in same. This type of charlatanism is questionable ethically; but, more important, it is not good persuasion because that company and that salesman can never again operate around this territory. *Good persuasion endures and allows people to make intelligent choices; it does not take advantage of people's weaknesses.*

Arrangement of ideas

The Thompson summary of quantitative research in public address suggested that there is relatively no difference between organized and disorganized material in terms of effect upon persuadees.[13] However, for effective persuasion, some attention should be given to the manner in which material is organized. *Persuasive material needs to be organized not in and of itself, but according to the condition of those who are to be persuaded.* If we assume that any persuasion situation is dynamic, that is, constantly changing, we must assume also that materials and presentation of them must change as the audience changes. There is no way to predict precisely how or at what point an audience will change. Therefore, the successful persuader does not attempt to impose a predetermined order of material upon an audience, regardless of its reaction.

If the order of ideas is to be most effective, then, it must be directly related to the particular state of the audience at any given time during the persuasive effort. I used to wonder why my father never twice used the same order of presenting information concerning his product. Each customer was presented the material in a different order and fashion. It now occurs to me that he was making the necessary adjustment to his audience and that not only were his customers different from each other but they were also changing during his presentation.

[13] Thompson, *Quantitative Research,* pp. 65–72.

While there can be no absolute rules governing arrangement of persuasive material, certain general principles may apply:

Static, predetermined organization rarely fits a given audience.

Arrangement must be flexible; it should be part of the dynamic interaction with the audience and the situation.

Formal systems of arrangement, such as the outlines used in writing, do not necessarily have the same usefulness in spoken discourse.

Adjusting to the audience

In most situations calling for persuasion, the persuader will meet in those whom he wants to influence pre-sets ranging from active opposition to his objective to active cooperation in achieving it. To be effective, he must understand the position of any persuadee and must adjust his pitch to that position.

Suppose we are trying to persuade the faculty of a university to allow equal representation of the student body on the university senate. Our goal as persuaders is to influence enough faculty members to take the action of voting affirmatively to assure achievement of our goal. As we buttonhole persuadees or address them in groups, we must adjust to three major behavior patterns that must be changed in some of our persuadees if we are to succeed: (1) active antagonism and opposition, (2) disbelief in or doubt about our proposed objective, and (3) belief and active acceptance.

There are broad general principles that can guide us in adjusting to these categories of audience receptivity to our persuasive efforts. We can apply these principles in our hypothetical university senate campaign and in most other situations in which we must persuade others.

1. For those who are actively antagonistic or less active but opposed, we need *first to establish our own credibility, honesty, and sincere concern* for the welfare of the university, for them personally and for the students. Until we do this, no other persuasive effort can get a hearing. Whatever we say to these people, we should take great pains to speak to them directly, honestly, and tactfully; we should avoid in any way reinforcing their opposition. (Pragmatically, if you have limited time for your persuasive efforts, don't squander it on persons in this category. Be pleasant, don't argue, and move on. As a general rule, persons in this category—be it in politics, sales resistance, or whatever—are not open to persuasion; your time will be more effectively spent adjusting to less negative persuadees.)

2. For the disbelievers and the doubters, we will need to *assemble all the sound and reliable arguments and proofs* we can that such a change

would be to the benefit of the total university. We need to be sure that they believe in our credibility and sincerity. In speaking with them, we should document our information carefully and precisely and make every effort to answer all their objections with clear and unequivocal reasons. Our discussion with them should be calm, confident, and poised, and we should appear easy and assured.

3. For believers and those who accept the idea, we need to *provide some strong motivation to arouse them* to action. At this point, we need to stir up their feelings and emotions in order to stimulate them sufficiently to act, because belief does not automatically bring behavior. In talking with them, we can use more emotional and reaction-stimulating words than with others. Our language can be colorful and vivid. In talking with them, we need to discuss the matter intensely and directly.

The effective persuader can sense the shift through these stages as his audience changes, however slightly, in the desired direction, and he is prepared to adjust to such shifts immediately. When it appears that the group or individual is shifting position from, say, active antagonism toward mere doubt, the persuader changes his material and introduces strong logic and evidence. When the audience moves from doubt to belief, the persuader then introduces the kind of material that promotes action.

Saul of Tarsus, Saint Paul of Christianity, was brought from active antagonism to full active acceptance in one brief encounter—but not by human speech communication. In most situations, we who try to persuade others should be content if we can effect any discernible change toward our desired objective in a single persuasive encounter.

The relative effectiveness of emotional as compared with rational communication in persuasive situations has not been conclusively established by experimental studies, according to Rosnow and Robinson.[14] There probably is no conclusive either-or answer. *An understanding of the condition of the audience at the point of the persuasive encounter is of greatest importance to the decision about which materials to use.* We should approach a persuasive event with many different kinds of materials to be used, or not used, as the situation actually develops. Persuasion is dynamic; as persuaders, we must be flexible.

In adjusting to a persuadee, a persuader should be aware of a few problems related to choice of materials. The actively antagonistic person is not likely to change, and emotional materials will probably only reinforce his position. Those who disbelieve or doubt are most likely to change

---

[14] Rosnow and Robinson, *Experiments in Persuasion,* pp. 127–129.

position but can move in either direction; emotional material suitable for true believers will more often than not damage the persuader's cause by effecting a shift from doubt to opposition. Those who already believe may be bored, even offended, by an approach suitable for antagonists or doubters and may therefore be less inclined to take action.

In persuasion, look before you leap. Determine as best you can the receptivity of a persuadee before you begin your persuasive effort. You cannot adjust to your audience unless you know its position.

In most persuasion situations, action by the persuadee is the payoff. There is no pat formula for assuring this payoff, and its achievement often amounts more to riding herd on mavericks than to persuasion. In politics, precinct workers get their registered voters to the polls on election day; sales manuals are filled with suggestions about "moving in for the close."

Special conditions

Persuasion efforts that most of us will meet in the course of a lifetime, either as persuaders or as persuadees, will fall far short of "brainwashing," which came to national attention as a result of the persuasion exerted on American prisoners of war during and after the Korean War. Hopefully, despite the gloomy prognostications of George Orwell's *1984,* none of us will ever be subject to persuasion by persons who have sufficient physical control over our persons and our situations to effect brainwashing. And hopefully, none of us will ever have the desire, even given the requisite physical control, to subject a fellow human being to such desecration.

In our ordinary, everyday life, there are weak echoes of some of the special conditions that make brainwashing possible, and these may affect ordinary persuasion situations. Among them are the pressures of deprivation, threat, and conformity.

Deprivation Rosnow and Robinson note that "deprivation has the effect of heightening susceptibility to influence. After extended sensory or perceptual deprivation, the subject, in his eager quest for novel stimulation is highly receptive to all kinds of information."[15]

Deprivation may tend to sensitize the individual and thus make him more subject to being aroused; however, deprivation affects some people more than others.[16] Nevertheless, Maslow points out that "the love need as ordinarily studied . . . is a deficit need. It is a hole which has to be filled, an emptiness into which love is poured. If this healing necessity is not

---

[15] Rosnow and Robinson, *Experiments in Persuasion,* pp. 248–249.
[16] Charles N. Cofer and Mortimer H. Appley, *Motivation: Theory and Research* (New York: John Wiley & Sons, 1967), pp. 821ff.

available, severe pathology results. . . . Love hunger is a deficiency disease, like salt hunger or the avitaminoses."[17]

Threat A character in some murder mystery noted that "there's something mighty persuasive about a gun pointed at your head." There is considerable evidence to support the idea that the greater the fear aroused by a persuader in relation to the harmful possibilities of nonacceptance, the greater the chance of acceptance of the persuader's desired goal. But there seem to be some factors that inhibit change when the fear or the anxiety becomes too great.[18] Often too great a threat will bring about total withdrawal from a situation.

Many commercials and advertisements use a form of threat, implying that nonacceptance of a product will mean loss of popularity, loss of status, loss of love. All of us are subjected to overtones of threat in some of the persuasive encounters of day-by-day living: loss of parental approval or even love, loss of acceptance by peer group, loss of grade average, loss of a girl friend or a boy friend.

Conformity The pressure to conform to the group or to other individuals may be present in a persuasive situation. You, as the persuader, may generate conformity pressure by the nature of your material (for example, "Everybody in your class but you has already signed the petition"). Or your persuadee may be responding to your effort as a result of pressures from his reference groups. The effect of group standards, norms, and behaviors on the individuals within the groups has been clearly demonstrated. It would appear that the more we depend on a given group to provide us with satisfaction of our needs, the more likely we are to conform and the more difficult it is to cause us to change.[19]

Delivery

The Thompson studies and many more didactic manuals and essays support the principle that the manner in which one delivers a persuasive effort strongly affects the success of the attempt. Thompson found that "delivery affects comprehension and persuasiveness significantly."[20] The most effective delivery is described as "varied, flexible, animated and fluent."[21] Of course, different audiences respond to different types of delivery.

---

[17] Maslow, *Toward a Psychology of Being,* p. 39.

[18] Rosnow and Robinson, *Experiments in Persuasion,* pp. 147–151.

[19] Dorwin Cartwright and Alvin Zander, *Group Dynamics: Research and Theory,* 2nd ed. (New York: Harper & Row, 1960), pp. 165–345 *passim.*

[20] Thompson, *Quantitative Research,* p. 82.

[21] Thompson, p. 84.

However, since delivery includes both verbal and nonverbal behavior, we should, in our persuasion efforts, give some attention to the body as a communication instrument (see Chapter 6 on nonverbal communication).

Participation

For a number of reasons, persons who actively participate in persuasion are more likely to change behavior than those who are passive. Active participation in the persuasive effort requires closer attention to what is going on and therefore results in better comprehension. *We are more likely to change our behavior under conditions in which we perceive ourselves as a party to the decision.* By participating, we may actually improvise or develop support for a change. When we participate with considerable effort in a situation in which beliefs are different, we are likely to alter our beliefs in order to justify, to ourselves, our active participation.

Summary

A knowledge of persuasion through speech is of great personal significance to each of us. It allows us not only to effect change in others but to be more aware of efforts of others to change us and thus be freer to make our own decisions as to the change itself. Persuasion may be used to change behaviors, beliefs, attitudes, knowledge, and the center of attention. Persuasion is the act of bringing influence pressure upon people to change their thinking or behavior. Thus all speech communication has some aspect of persuasion in it.

Persuasion is most directly concerned with human behavior and belief. Belief is a state of readiness to respond or behave in a specific way. It is not always a result of reason but appears to depend on wants, abilities, conditioning, needs, and anticipations. Thus we must understand as much as possible about the needs and the organized systems of responses, and the like, of those whom we would persuade.

Persuadees need to sense the influence of the need and anticipation. The persuader must know what he wants the persuadee to do, he must speak with credibility in relation to the situation, and he must deal with listener wants, goals, and anticipations.

The persuader must provide messages that have persuasive strength to reach the acceptance level of the persuadee. Supporting materials, specific and relevant information, support from statements of other people are key message forms.

The arrangement of ideas must be directly related to the particular state of the audience at the very time the effort to persuade is taking place. This requires a constant and dynamic process of adjusting to the audience.

Receptivity of an audience may range from antagonism to acceptance in respect to the persuader's purpose. The hostile audience should be met with material of high credibility. Disbelievers and doubters should be presented with sound and reliable arguments and proof. Believers need to be stimulated to act upon their belief.

Persuasion requires varied, flexible, animated, and fluent speech presentation. Particular audiences respond differently to different forms of delivery.

Participation, deprivation, threat, credibility, audience status, and conformity also play a part in inducing change through speech-persuasion.

To bring about change in another person or persons, we must therefore (1) get their attention, (2) bring them to believe and accept us and our purpose, (3) bring them to understand what we want them to understand, (4) cause them to retain or hold on to our direction, then (5) arouse them to action by stimulating their need gratification systems.

For special reading

Albert D. Biderman and Herbert Zimmer, eds., *The Manipulation of Human Behavior* (New York: John Wiley & Sons, 1961). Brainwashing is a subject of considerable controversy and misunderstanding. This book, produced under contract for the Air Force, examines some of the ideas about applying scientific knowledge to the manipulation of human behavior. The process of interrogation is the central concern because of its particular significance to treatment of prisoners of war. The relationship of this material to our work in persuasion is highly significant.

Huber W. Ellingsworth and Theodore Clevenger, Jr., *Speech and Social Action: A Strategy of Oral Communication* (Englewood Cliffs, N.J.: Prentice-Hall, 1967). This brief text is devoted to the study of "the meaningful relation of speaker, speech, and audience, [placing] these factors in a broad social context." While the text is designed for students of public speaking, many of the ideas and principles apply to the whole spectrum of speech processes. The book relates closely to the work of social scientists and to current research findings in persuasion.

Elihu Katz and Paul F. Lazarsfeld, *Personal Influence: The Part Played by People in the Flow of Mass Communications* (New York: Free Press, 1955). The function of persuasion in mass communication is a subject of great interest, in the face of the sophisticated forms of communication to the masses. This book is a solid study of personal influence, prestige, persuasion, opinion leaders, the influence of individuals and mass media on decision-making experiences, and the chain of impact of persuasive communication from one person to another—thought-provoking information developed from wide research. Included in the book is a whole section which examines, as typical, the flow of influence in a Middle Western community.

Ronald Lippitt, Jeanne Watson, and Bruce Westley, *The Dynamics of Planned Change: A Comparative Study of Principles and Techniques* (New York: Harcourt Brace Jovanovich, 1958). Change is the process that the persuader seeks to bring about. This book is written by leaders in the National Training Laboratories who have derived their theory and procedures from the pioneer work of Kurt Lewin. The emphasis is on the role of persuaders, called change agents, and their professional roles as consultants, trainers, and therapists.

Charles W. Lomas, *The Agitator in American Society* (Englewood Cliffs, N.J.: Prentice-Hall, 1968). In this book you will find a collection of speeches representing various aspects of agitation in the United States over the past 80 years. In his introductory material, Lomas discusses the nature of agitation in relation to the conditions, the speakers, and the messages. He then assembles his examples into categories of violence, social reform, civil rights, and anticommunism. In this well-chosen collection, you will find many examples of the things we have discussed in this chapter.

Vance Packard, *The Hidden Persuaders* (New York: David McKay Co., 1957). Here is a book written in the popular vein and filled with examples of how people are persuaded in our contemporary society. This earlier book by Packard pretty much set the exposé tone of much of his work. You will find this one exciting reading as you encounter old persuasions, to which you have responded, viewed from the social critic's eyes.

Goodwin Watson, ed., *Concepts for Social Change,* Cooperative Project for Educational Development (Washington, D.C.: National Training Laboratories, 1967). Following the work of Lippitt and others on the study of change and its inducement methods, this book adds more contemporary points of view. This is a collection of papers by a number of people assembled into a brief monograph form. Such topics as self-renewal as a form of change, dynamics of resistance to change, collaboration for change, utilizing knowledge for change, and examples of strategies for change are included in the papers.

Speech Monographs, Vol. 36 (March 1969). In this issue of *Speech Monographs* are three very pointed studies of personality, source credibility, evidence, and fluency and their effect on persuasion and attitude change.

These studies also include excellent and brief reviews of the significant current research in this area: Gerald R. Miller and John Baseheart, "Source Trustworthiness, Opinionated Statements, and Response to Persuasive Communication," pp. 1–7; James C. McCroskey and R. Samuel Mehrley, "The Effects of Disorganization and Nonfluency on Attitude Change and Source Credibility," pp. 13–21. Robert N. Bostrom and Raymond K. Tucker, "Evidence, Personality, and Attitude Change," pp. 22–27.

Try this

1 In your journal, list your attitudes which you believe affect the manner in which you respond to persuasive efforts.

2 You have seven sentences with which to move an audience (of one or more persons) to action. In those seven sentences accomplish the following things: (1) get the attention of the audience to what you are doing; (2) establish the rightness for them of what you would have them do; (3) convince them of your own credibility; (4) bring the audience to accept the purpose you have in mind; and (5) arouse the audience to perform the action you desire. Your sentences must not be long or involved. In total, you must be direct, pointed, and effective.

3 The way people behave seems to reflect their attitudes and beliefs. Through your own observation and confrontation with others, select several general attitude concepts or terms, such as "militarist," "pacifist," "pro-black," "racist," "hawk," "dove," "anti-Establishment" and the like. For each general attitude term, collect a list of behaviors which you have observed people performing that reflect the attitude term. Example: *Antifraternity*—refuses dates with fraternity men; runs against the Greek organization representatives in student elections; speaks out against fraternal organizations.

4 Identify an important decision of your life that someone persuaded you to make. Can you identify the things that made it possible for you to be persuaded? Enter an account of this event in your journal.

5 List five of your most important beliefs. For each belief, make a list of your friends who share it and another list of your friends who do not share it. (For some beliefs, you may have no entries for the second list.) Check your list by discussing your beliefs with your friends. Were your original lists accurate? Why?

6 Make a list of the beliefs you hold today that you "inherited" from your parents. Compare this list with another list of beliefs you hold that are contrary to those of your parents. What are the sources of the beliefs on the second list?

7 Try an experiment with your own credibility. Prepare a short speech or commentary aimed at persuading others to do something or accept a point of view. Arrange to give it to several different groups. For some groups, appear in rough, soiled casual clothes and give an impression of unwashed unkemptness. For other groups, appear neat and well dressed and clean. Were there differences in the responses of your listeners that you can reasonably attribute to your appearance?

8 Using the same variations in dress and appearance, approach a number of strangers to ask directions. Keep a record of how these people respond and the degree of accuracy of the directions they give you.

9 Prepare to persuade the members of your class to perform some important function or activity. Before you present your persuasion, write down your goal in your persuasive attempt; then estimate the predisposition of your audience, as you perceive it, to follow your suggestion. Use a five-point range for the predisposition: (1) strong agreement, (2) agreement, (3) indecision, (4) disagreement, (5) strong disagreement. Adjust your presentation to your evaluation of predisposition. After your presentation, discuss your evaluation of predisposition and the effectiveness of your presentation with your classmates.

10 Design and administer an experiment to test this hypothesis: *If feedback is a part of the persuasive interaction between the persuader and the persuadee, the persuasive effect will be greater than when feedback is not available to the interaction.* Report the results in your journal.

11 Design other experiments testing some of the assertions and assumptions of this chapter.

12 Prepare a ten-minute slide sequence or film with sound in which you attempt to influence the viewers toward some point of view about which you feel strongly, perhaps in some such area as the inhumanity of modern warfare, the pollution of air and water, the aspirations and needs of dwellers in the ghettoes, the relevance of education to the world we live in.

Chapter Eleven

Rivals, Competitors, and Enemies: Conflict

Objectives

After studying this chapter, you should be better able to do these things:

- Locate any given conflict situation on a continuum from mild disagreement to war.

- Deal with the mutual exclusiveness of goals between persons and between groups.

- Deal with intrapersonal conflicts arising from incompatible wants, goals, needs, motives, and the like.

- Cope with contradictory information or feelings by rationalizing the situation so that they are more compatible.

- Seek intrapersonal bases of interpersonal conflict and vice versa.

- Observe much intergroup controversy as essentially interpersonal struggles of the leadership of the respective groups.

- Control minor win-lose issues before they escalate into major conflicts.

- Prevent a social structure from becoming rigid and not tolerant of the conflicts within its system, thus reducing the chance of that structure being torn apart and destroyed by conflict.

- Reveal information during a conflict or struggle at key points.

- Cope with those who, during a conflict, particularly relish a victory *and are more able to talk than others* and thus exercise more influence over the function in their group during the struggle.

- Keep the channels of communication open as competitiveness develops between adversaries.

- Compel the parties to a controversy to communicate with each other, particularly when there are real barriers to their communication with each other.

- Use the different processes of joint decision-making, negotiation, bargaining, mediation, and arbitration.

- Avoid parties to a conflict moving from mediation to arbitration because they are, at that point, reducing their freedom to make decisions themselves.

A very significant portion of our speech-communication time is involved
in dealing with struggles or conflicts at some level of encounter. Review your
day just past; how many times during that day were you directly involved
in a conflict of some kind? How much of your interaction with others is
either obvious or subtle struggle of one kind or another? One of the most
important but little studied areas of interpersonal speech communication is
the area of conflict and conflict management. The realistic possibilities for
moderation in a world filled with the extremes of conflict lie primarily in the
manner in which people are able to deal creatively with conflict through
speech communication.

Winning, losing, and sharing

Each of us faces decisions that involve making choices from several alternatives. Our needs and desires determine what these alternatives may be. At
the same time, any organized social system contains persistent struggles
between individuals. These struggles characteristically involve decisions followed by actions that put these decisions into effect and stimulate consequences. A decision cannot be said to exist in a conflict system until it
appears as an action or a reaction (or a commitment to action).

Many quite mild disagreements are often called conflicts, but they do
not really qualify as such. In any conflict system, we can distinguish three
degrees of intensity of opposition: controversy, competition, and combat.
A runner in the Olympiad often runs not so much against individuals as
against time. His efforts are, in those instances, more or less unilaterally
directed toward achieving a certain time goal in running the distance. Rivals
may run the distance in less time, equal time, or more time. It is theoretically
possible for any number of runners to break the tape at the exact same
moment—to tie and share the victory. And yet, runners are involved in a
competition that sets up gold medal rewards for those who break the tape
first. There are also degrees of reward for first place, second place, third
place—and each has a value.

In basketball, on the other hand, one team or the other must win the
game. If the score is tied at the end of the fourth quarter, additional time
is given so that one or the other team may emerge victorious. There are
significant differences between the two types of competition. In track, the
players can share the rewards, either equally or in some proportion to their
relative achievement. In basketball, only one team of players gets the
reward of winning. This clear win-lose type of struggle creates special
factors that must be understood in order to fully comprehend the relationship of the players and the acts they perform.

Both kinds of struggles are surrounded by *rules and procedures* that control the behavior of the participants. While in both cases the individuals are competing, they are also cooperating; that is, they are jointly maintaining certain enforced decorum in the conduct of the game. Penalties for infractions of rules of the game are applied equally to all participants.

We shall use the word "controversy" to refer to situations in which there is some joint agreement or joint decision either implied or explicitly devised *to provide a framework for and a control of the controversy.*

In labor-management relations, controversy often develops over grievances. In many organizations, there are grievance procedures, often agreed upon contractually by the parties, which set up the framework of control within which the controversy may take place.

We shall consider *combat* as an extension of controversy or competition into another phase. *In actual combat, or fight, the alternatives or end results are limited:* Either the winner destroys (or harms) the loser and removes him from contention, or the loser is completely absorbed by the winner.

Anatol Rapoport has written of the relationship of the fight to a game:

> It seems that in a fight, the opponent is mainly a nuisance. He should not be there, but somehow he is. He must be eliminated, made to disappear or cut down in size or importance. The object of the fight is to harm, destroy, subdue, or drive the opponent.
>
> Not so in a game. In a game, the opponent is *essential.* Indeed, for someone who plays the game with seriousness and devotion, a strong opponent is valued more than a weak one. [Italics added.][1]

Rapoport also argues that fights do not contain rationality in the interaction of the participants and that games do. In fact, he goes so far as to propose that "a game . . . is idealized as a struggle in which complete 'rationality' of the opponents is assumed."[2]

In the scheme of conflict, then, we view our opponents in three categories. A *rival* shares the rewards or payoff. A *competitor* either wins or loses in a game in which the outcome permits him to pick up the challenge again and again and in which rational processes play a major role. With an *enemy,* one or the other of us must be destroyed or absorbed or removed entirely from the field of action by means of the accumulation and use of every known destructive force at hand, with no rules that can be enforced or followed.

The survival of our culture may now depend on the management of controversy, organized to permit action without loss, and combat that is controlled or eliminated to prevent the effects of its outcome from destroying us.

[1] Anatol Rapoport, *Fights, Games, and Debates* (Ann Arbor: University of Michigan Press, 1961), p. 9.
[2] Rapoport, p. 10.

The areas of conflict

Intrapersonal conflict

Conflict occurs within the individual as well as outside him. We identify internal conflict as *intrapersonal*. We are involved intrapersonally when two or more simultaneous responses are such that if one occurs the others cannot.[3] For example, you may want to go to a party and at the same time want to see a movie that is at its last showing; your wants are in conflict.

Berlyne suggests that responses may be incompatible because of at least two factors: (1) the physiological and psychological construction of the person as a whole and (2) the perceived situation being such that two responses cannot be carried out at the same time; and further that, through learned behavior, responses that may have initially been possible of simultaneous occurrence may become incompatible.

Karen Horney's remarks on intrapersonal conflict are as pertinent now as when they were published toward the end of World War II:

> The kind, scope, and intensity of . . . conflicts are largely determined by the civilization in which we live. If the civilization is stable and tradition bound, the variety of choices presenting themselves are limited and the range of possible individual conflicts narrow. Even then they are not lacking. One loyalty may interfere with another; personal desires may stand against obligations to the group. But if the civilization is in a stage of rapid transition, where highly contradictory values and divergent ways of living exist side by side, the choices the individual has to make are manifold and difficult. He can conform to the expectations of the community or be a dissenting individualist, be gregarious or live as a recluse, worship success or despise it, have faith in strict discipline for children or allow them to grow up without much interference; he can believe in a different moral standard for men and women or hold that the same should apply for both, regard sexual relations as an expression of human intimacy or divorce them from ties of affection.[4]

Dr. Horney makes a clear distinction between those kinds of intrapersonal conflict that are normal and those that are neurotic. The normal person can make a choice between two equally desirable possibilities, even though it means some hardship. The neurotic person in conflict is not able to choose. The two forces are antagonistic to each other and neither alternative is desired; the neurotic, therefore, sees himself as caught in the middle with no way out.[5]

[3] D. E. Berlyne, *Conflict, Arousal, and Curiosity* (New York: McGraw-Hill Book Co., 1960), p. 10.
[4] Karen Horney, M.D., *Our Inner Conflicts* (New York: W. W. Norton & Co., 1945), p. 24.
[5] Horney, p. 32.

Thus, a normal young man may find two women equally desirable as marriage partners, but he is able to make his choice of one even though it means that he cannot have the satisfactions that the other would provide. The neurotic person, on the other hand, may find himself caught between giving *all* his affection to his mother (or a woman who is a mother-substitute) or all to his girl friend and really wants to do neither. He suffers great frustration and anxiety therefrom.

The theory of cognitive dissonance describes another way to understand the internal factors of conflict. When two things that a person knows (cognition) are contradictory or do *not* fit together (dissonance), the person attempts some form of rationalization to somehow make them more compatible. Thus, knowing that cigarette smoking may cause lung cancer and at the same time knowing that the habit of smoking is emotionally satisfying, a person may justify his continuing smoking on the basis that removal of the emotional satisfaction might be more dangerous than the threat of cancer (dissonance reduction).[6]

Also, when the individual becomes involved with others, other forms of dissonance develop that are inherent in the social process. Leon Festinger and Elliot Aronson have suggested that when people with whom a person affiliates and whom he admires have an opinion opposite to his, he experiences dissonance. He then seeks to find some way of working out a course that will permit him to live with the differences or to resolve them. Thus, a person with strong views on racial equality will experience dissonance when others in a group with which he chooses to affiliate have strong segregationist views. Likewise, we experience dissonance when we discover that two people whom we like very much hate each other.[7]

A great deal of dissonance of intrapersonal, interpersonal, intragroup, and intergroup dimensions has been generated in response to the use of violence by militants of the ghettoes, the campuses, the anti-busing campaign, the women's liberation, the Arab-Israel struggle, the Irish Revolution, and others. Many persons who are deeply committed to rectifying the conditions that are so protested are appalled by the violence and cannot condone it. Reduction of the dissonance has not proved simple for most.

The studies by R. Nevitt Sanford show that controversy within an organization may also induce conflict within an individual. The individual's reaction to the group controversy may result in behavior that intensifies the organizational struggle. *Miscommunication and the resulting disruption of*

---

[6] Leon Festinger and Elliot Aronson, "The Arousal and Reduction of Dissonance in Social Contexts," in Dorwin Cartwright and Alvin Zander, eds., *Group Dynamics: Research and Theory,* 2nd ed. (New York: Harper & Row, 1960), p. 214.

[7] Festinger and Aronson, p. 221.

information flow can often be attributed to intrapersonal conflicts of individual members.

On one campus, the executive committee of the student government found itself split over the issue of granting student-fee funds to intercollegiate athletic programs. The chairman of the budget committee was thrown into intrapersonal conflict. As an athlete, he was expected by the athletic department to maintain its position. As an appointee of the student president, he was expected to seek out and administer the will of the majority. In an attempt to get himself away from the "hot spot" of internal conflict, he initiated a special investigation of all student-fee expenditures. This move brought on a storm of protest from the "haves" and loud hurrahs from the "have nots," and the controversy increased in scope and intensity. Faculty and school administration, board members and legislators, hangers-on and the man in the street were eventually embroiled. Statements made by both sides were quoted out of context. The faculty chairman of the athletic council stopped speaking to the faculty sponsor of the budget committee. The president's attempts to mediate the situation privately only contributed to the strife when word of his efforts reached advocates of each position outside the immediately involved groups. All this furor resulted from efforts of an individual to resolve his intrapersonal conflicts.

Pathological needs of individuals within an organization may also lead to controversy and fight. These would include such factors as overactive drive for power, excessive fear of not being liked, and overdependence. Sanford points out that these conflicts are at both the conscious and the unconscious levels.[8]

The existence of intrapersonal conflicts and dissonance may thus be both cause and effect of the whole scheme of struggles between persons and groups.

Interpersonal conflict

The area of social controversy that is called interpersonal is usually identified by overt struggles between individuals for perceived mutually exclusive objectives. These overt struggles are often, but not always, the result of two persons perceiving a situation in different ways. Thus incongruent perceptions play a most significant role in causing controversy. In some situations, the struggle between individuals becomes symbolic or ritualistic, as in labor-management struggles or the presidential elections or in the struggle between a man and a woman. In the labor-management situation both the union leadership and the company leadership are competing for the perceived exclusive loyalties of the rank and file. In the political arena, the competition

[8] R. Nevitt Sanford, "Individual Conflict and Organizational Interaction," in Robert L. Kahn and Elise Boulding, eds., *Power and Conflict in Organizations* (New York: Basic Books, 1964), pp. 95ff.

is for the vote of the people. In the man-woman area the struggle is often for freedom from the perception of being smothered.

Morton Deutsch describes the competitive social situation as a condition in which the perceived goals of individuals or groups in the situation are such that if one individual or group reaches its goal, the other is perceived as unable to reach its goal in the particular situation.[9]

Intergroup conflict

By far the area of conflict that has been most studied (and at the same time remains the most vexing and unresponsive to treatment) is the area of intergroup conflict. The range of intergroup struggle is wide, ranging from sibling sniping within a family unit to struggles between nations. Within this range are at least two types of groups of particular significance: the organized and the unorganized. Organized groups such as unions, management groups, church groups, fraternities, student groups, and faculty groups struggle with other organized groups. Large unorganized groups, that is, aggregations of people who represent certain ideological trends, may also be in conflict; but the real center of the struggle is hard to pinpoint.

Musafer Sherif's studies of creating and resolving conflicts are most revealing. He and his colleagues structured conflicts between children's groups, then through the infusion of superordinate goals, were able to restructure the group relations and manage the struggle. Superordinate goals are those that could not be achieved without both parties cooperating. Thus, if two groups have the basic goal of survival and discover that survival cannot be assured by one group acting alone, but only by both groups acting together, that goal becomes superordinate.[10]

The win-lose trap

The idea that if one person or group achieves the goal that goal is then not available to the other, is the source of the pressures from the compulsion to win and the dread of losing. Many situations in which the goals could actually be shared are perceived as the win-lose, or nonsharing, type, and the contestants (individual and group) get locked into the struggle before they realize

[9] Morton Deutsch, "The Effects of Cooperation and Competition upon Group Process," in Cartwright and Zander, eds., *Group Dynamics,* p. 415.

[10] Musafer Sherif and Carolyn Sherif, *Groups in Harmony and Tension* (New York: Harper & Row, 1953); Musafer Sherif, ed., *Intergroup Relations and Leadership* (New York: John Wiley & Sons, 1962). See also Musafer Sherif and others, *Experimental Study of Positive and Negative Intergroup Attitudes between Experimentally Produced Groups: Robbers' Cave Study* (Norman: University of Oklahoma Intergroup Relations Project, 1954).

the nature of the interaction. Thus, for example, what started out as a minor disagreement between two students became a "live or die" struggle for the presidency of the student association. The escalation of minor controversies or disagreements into win-lose combat situations may be one of the most critical problems of our time.

Robert R. Blake and Jane S. Mouton have examined this escalation process as it relates to management. They indicate that solution to such situations depends in part on the ability of the participants to avoid being trapped unknowingly into win-lose conditions.[11]

The functions of conflict

We all have often assumed that competition, controversy, and combat are undesirable processes and that the prime efforts of social scientists and practitioners should be directed toward *eliminating* struggles from our living situations or at least reducing their frequency and significance. These assumptions may not be sound. Studies of groups under stress and under threat have indicated that *in-group cohesion and solidarity often become enhanced in the face of challenge from an out-group.*

Georg Simmel[12] and Lewis Coser have taken positions supporting the value of conflict. Coser argues that the interest of sociologists of his period was directed at reduction of conflict because they saw it as a disruptive element of society. Thus, he claimed, the central emphasis became "roads to agreement" and mutual adjustment by reducing conflict. This objective, he argues, leads to a tendency to preserve existing institutions and systems through which their own power and influence are felt.[13]

Coser argues that conflict has socially desirable qualities as well as negative values. In his view, conflict creates associations and coalitions by bringing together people who might otherwise have nothing to do with each other. It binds a group together and provides a safety valve which allows a release of pressure and thus aids in preserving the group. The closer the relationship, the more intense the conflict; contradiction and conflict not only precede unity but are operative in it at every moment of its existence. Conflict is an index of the stability of relationships; it binds antagonists and establishes and maintains balance of power.

[11] Robert R. Blake and Jane S. Mouton, *Group Dynamics: Key to Decision Making* (Houston, Tex.: Gulf Publishing Co., 1961).

[12] Georg Simmel, *Conflict and the Web of Group-Affiliations,* trans. Kurt H. Wolff and Reinhard Bendix (New York: Free Press, 1955).

[13] Lewis Coser, *The Functions of Social Conflict* (New York: Free Press, 1956), pp. 26–28.

He contends also that conflict is truly nonfunctional in those social structures in which there is insufficient or no toleration or organized manner of handling conflict. He suggests that the intensity of struggles which tend to "tear apart" a social system may result from the rigidity of the structures. The balance of a system is threatened, not by the conflict but by the very rigidity of the system, which allows for the accumulation and festering of hostility and division. Thus, if a student body or a university administration is inherently rigid in its structure and its system of decision-making, this rigidity in itself may create conflict.[14]

Coser's point was clearly demonstrated in Chicago during the Democratic Convention in the summer of 1968. The rigid police system was unable to tolerate the minor disturbances of the students' crusade or the comparable rigidity of the militant leaders who were spearheading the demonstrations. Such mutual rigidities prevent the development of an equilibrium and riots result. Almost the same type of *polarized rigidity* may be found on every campus where troubles have erupted and in every organized situation where conflict seems to be excessive.

From controversy to combat

These various studies indicate that conflict ranges through all social processes. *Intrapersonal conflict* involves mutually incompatible choices or decisions required of an individual. *Interpersonal conflict* involves a system of relationships between two or more persons who are seeking goals that usually cannot be attained simultaneously under the conditions that prevail at a given moment. *Intergroup conflict* involves a system of relationships between two or more groups of people with incompatible goals.

Conflict, however, has a range of characteristics. Contests, games, disagreements, arguments, disputes, fights, and wars represent a kind of continuum of struggle, described in terms of relationships between the participants, the interactions that take place, the method of making decisions, the goals or intents of the participants, the actual rewards and the outcomes and condition of the participants at the conclusion (see Tables 11–1 and 11–2).

The results of interpersonal and intergroup conflict seem to fall into four categories: (1) when the rewards can be distributed among the contestants, (2) when one party gets its objective and the other is defeated, (3) when the winner not only takes the prize but incorporates the loser into his own system, and (4) when the loser is destroyed and the winner claims all the spoils.

[14] Coser, p. 157.

Table 11–1   Controversy-conflict dimensions and systems

Dimensions	Systems			
	A	**B**	**C**	**D**
1. Participant relationships	Compatible partners (comrades, etc.)	Rivals	Competitors	Enemies
2. Interaction(s)	Cooperation and collaboration through discussion	Controversy contest-type game	Contest-type game and limited war	War
3. Rules	Implied but rarely stated	Cooperation on rules of procedure	Cooperation on rules of procedure	Cooperation minimal on rules
4. Decision methodology	Joint deliberation and integrative activity to a consensus decision	Argument and debate; bargaining to a majority decision	Force, power, manipulation, and suasion to win-or-lose decision	Force to a win-or-lose decision
5. Anticipated goals or intents	Mutually inclusive, complementary, to a mutual solution of problems	Win but it can be mutually inclusive, i.e., both can win	Win but it is mutually exclusive, i.e., only one wins	Overcome, destroy, suppress, mutually exclusive
6. Actual rewards	Shared solution; both can reach maximum rewards	Single or shared rewards	Rewards only to victor	Mastery and control to victor
7. Outcome	Unique decision solution with agreement and joint commitment	One may be ahead or above other or may be equal	A loser or winner	Winner takes all
8. Condition of counterpart at conclusion	Merged; no distinction of rewards	Loser still active and can play another	Ability to continue is preserved	Loser is destroyed, absorbed or removed, or both are destroyed

Communication and conflict

Communication is inherent in controversy, competition, and combat, even with intrapersonal conflict, which is usually triggered by outside events or people who communicate alternatives to the person.

This is not to say that conflicts are a result of poor communication. Conflict, or struggle, apparently is a basic characteristic of the human system. The control and development of the struggle, however, depend almost wholly on communication. Since most communication efforts take place through

Table 11–2 Conflict forms and decision possibilities

Speech-communication form	Concurrent behavior form	Possible procedural systems	Possible decision outcome
Discussion of differences	Doubting	Joint deliberation	Integration of ideas to mutual satisfaction
		Negotiation	
Argument	Disagreement	Bargaining mediation	Mutual satisfaction still possible
		Arbitration	
Persuasion and argument	Controversy		Mutual satisfaction less possible
Psychological pressures and persuasion	Threat	Propaganda	Mutual satisfaction improbable
Orders, commands, and allegations	Fight	Warfare	Mutual harm and destruction of one or both

speech, the dominant area of conflict interaction and control is probably the speech-communication process.

A conflict appears when people become involved in communication acts that lead to countercommunications or feedback that has a special significance to them. Interpersonal or intergroup conflict, per se, does not exist until some form of communication begins to take place. While there may be a potential struggle between two young men who want the same girl, the actual struggle does not break out until some communicative interaction takes place between them. The act of initiating a message to the other sets the fuse for the fight, but the fight does not start until there is feedback.

Since communication is a circular system involving at least two parties, many messages during conflict are planned in such a way that they create countermessages (or feedback) *that can be controlled by the original initiator.* This has been called strategy. Thus when I tell my neighbor that the barking of his dog kept me awake all night, I can expect a range of possible responses. He can say it makes no difference to him or that it wasn't his dog or that he is sorry or that he will do something about it or any number of other responses. If I used strategy to reduce the number of possible responses or to control their nature, I would tell my neighbor that if his dog continues to bark and keep me awake I will complain to the dogcatcher. This strategy communication probably will evoke a spectrum of responses different from the first. Thus, if I am planning a strategy of conflict and want to draw my opponent out I will select those ideas and ways of communicating that will produce manageable results.

Such strategy communications occur frequently in bargaining. One party demands from the other extremes that cannot be met. The obvious reply is either counterproposals of more limited possibility or outright refusal. Many labor-management negotiators deliberately try to make the opposing representatives angry enough to reveal the limits of their position.

Communication forms in conflict

During conflict, communication acts take many forms. Hostile and aggressive comments and statements appear. Arguments arise. Presenting proofs and reasons to the opposition in hope of changing the opposition or the judge (a third party) become involved. Orders and commands appear frequently but are usually ignored or bring negative responses from the antagonists. Charges and countercharges are frequent.

In most interpersonal and intergroup struggles, we may see the use of strategy in the form of propaganda devices aimed at controlling the behavior response of the opponents or of sympathizers. Nations at war rely heavily on propaganda.

Some communication during a struggle may be considered as ceremonial, or "going through the act." We see this in many labor-management bargaining sessions and in the courtroom. Messages of professional negotiators (expressions of violent charge and countercharge, hostility, anger, and the like) are all in keeping with the tradition of the conflict and many times are intended to impress the constituency rather than to advance the negotiation itself.

Similar behavior can be noted in the public communiqués of nations during their struggles with each other. The image of antagonists beating their breasts and shouting epithets at each other is age-old and must be re-created in the ceremonial aspects of contemporary controversy. Why this ceremonial persists may be explored by looking at the effect of ceremonial behavior upon the participants as well as upon the constituents. The contemporary performance of ritualistic hate-the-enemy rites serves basically the same function as the ceremonial war dance of aborigines—it intensifies antagonism toward the enemy.

Information and commitments

During the various kinds of struggle between people and groups a great variety of information is communicated. The revealing of information to the rival, antagonist, or enemy is a significant part of the struggle itself. In chess, for example, the board is completely revealed, and each move reveals additional information about the direction and goals of the player. In contract bridge, however, the information concerning the opposing team's full hand is not available nor is the direction that the hand will be played. Each play reveals further information and reduces the alternative options that may exist for the players. In interpersonal and intergroup conflict at all levels, com-

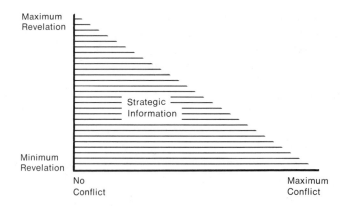

Figure 11–1   Revelation or withholding of information about strategy or intent.

munication of information varies from full information on the status of the
opponents to almost no information concerning the status (see Figure 11–1).

A difficult condition in many conflicts arises when the desire to communicate certain information to the opposite side is counteracted by a fear
that if this information became available to the other side directly from the
source it would be taken as a sign of weakness (see Figure 11–2). Thus, in
many labor-management struggles, one side may wish to make known to the
other side just where its limits may be but fears to reveal the information

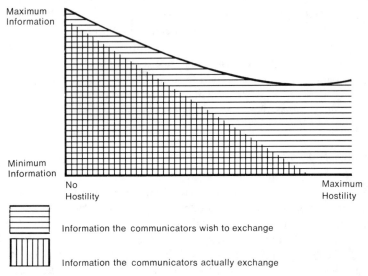

**Figure 11–2   Difference between the desired and actual amount of information com-
municated during a conflict situation. The difference widens as the hostility increases
and information decreases out of fear of reprisal.**

across the bargaining table because of the real danger that the opponent will
assume the information, rather than being real and reliable, is spurious or
contrived in order to test his opposition.

During the course of a struggle, both sides include in their messages
various commitments or concession statements. We have previously defined
a decision as the making of a commitment. Thus, when one party has made a
decision, it faces the problem of communicating that decision to the opposition
without being viewed as a loser by those outside the struggle or being viewed
by the opponent as showing signs of weakness. Several interesting solutions
are used, with many variations.

The parties may simply overlook an item on the agenda for discussion,
thus implying that a decision has been reached. A suggestion that "we can find
an agreement on this" implies a tacit commitment.

The parties may clearly and precisely identify an area of agreement or
understanding, in a blunt avowal of commitment.

A conditional commitment involves an agreement that one part of the
situation is conditional on the development of agreement on another part of
the problem. For example, in dickering over a car purchase, the buyer may
say, "I'll pay your price for the car if you include a new set of brakes, new
transmission and new tires." In a difference of opinion between man and wife,
the husband may agree to take his wife to the new repertory theatre production if she will have steak for supper.

Some commitments are hidden threats. For example, by agreeing to
"explore" the problem of grievance procedures in a company-union situation,
the union may be setting the stage for major charges against the company.
Only the participants to the controversy will be able to detect this. On the other
hand, some commitments are revealed under the cover of threats. For example,
during a controversy over custody of children following a divorce, the lawyer
for the wife finally agreed that the father could take the children for several
months of the year with the following statement: "If you, at any time, take
these children outside of this state for more than twenty-four hours without
permission of the mother, we'll prosecute you for violation of this agreement."
Implied within this threat was the announcement that the father would have
custody of the children for some undetermined amount of time.

Effects of conflict upon communication

What happens to communication under conditions of conflict? Again, we
must distinguish between conflict that ends in polarized alternatives (win or
lose, life or death) and conflict that provides for shared rewards.

Robert R. Blake and Jane S. Mouton explored conditions that develop in
win-lose settings in labor-management situations. Among other effects, they
found that there is an upward shift of cohesion among the group members,

creativity within the group tends to be snuffed out with increases in pressures to conform, those members who are more able to talk than others and for whom victory has particular relish begin to exercise more influence on the group, and judgments concerning the relative quality of the competing positions are colored. They found also that one's own position is inevitably judged superior without regard for actual qualitative differences and that the parties to the conflict tend to attack each other when given an opportunity to clarity the issues and differences, thus increasing the conflict. Stereotype negative hostilities develop toward the other group and these in turn lead to further intensification of the conflict. Any agreements that do exist between the groups are minimized, and differences are highlighted. Knowledge of one's own position is much greater than knowledge of the other group's position. Deadlock seems to be the inevitable result.[15]

According to R. Nevitt Sanford, conflict within organizations or between subgroups of an organization induces conflict within an individual between his loyalties for both subgroups. This intrapersonal struggle leads to behavior that may deepen the organizational conflicts. "He might, for example, suppress his own feelings or say things that he does not mean and thus contribute to the disruption of the communications on which a solution of the organizational conflict depends."[16]

Morton Deutsch has reported his findings on communication and conflict.

> The greater the competitive orientation of the parties vis-à-vis, . . . the less likely will they be to use such channels [of communication] as do exist.

> Where barriers to communication exist, a situation in which the parties are compelled to communicate may be more effective than one in which the choice to talk or not is voluntary.[17]

Deutsch also studied the effect of threat on bargaining results and discovered that "clearly the presence of a threat potential may be deleterious to the ability of bargainers to conclude effective agreements."[18] Threat, in turn, seems to lead to defensive communication systems by persons and by groups.

Jack R. Gibb observed that during defense arousal conditions the listener is prevented from concentrating upon the messages.

[15] Robert R. Blake and Jane S. Mouton, "The Intergroup Dynamics of Win-Lose Conflict and Problem-Solving Collaboration in Union-Management Relations," in Musafer Sherif, ed., *Intergroup Relations and Leadership* (New York: John Wiley & Sons, 1962), pp. 94ff.

[16] Sanford, "Individual Conflict," pp. 95ff.

[17] Morton Deutsch, "Bargaining, Threat, and Communication: Some Experimental Studies," in Kathleen Archibald, ed., *Strategic Interaction and Conflict* (Berkeley: University of California Institute of International Studies, 1966), p. 40.

[18] Deutsch, p. 23.

Not only do defensive communicators send off multiple value, motive, and affect cues, but also defensive recipients distort what they receive. As a person becomes more and more defensive, he becomes less and less able to perceive accurately the motives, the values and the emotions of the sender.[19]

In general, the studies of the effect of conflict behavior on communication indicate that under conflict conditions communication becomes defensive, polarized, and highly controlled. Channels of communication that are available are not used, persistent stereotypes are invoked, the participant views his communication as proper and his opponent's as improper or negative. The total effect is one of confining and restricting the communication of individuals so that the win pattern of the situation becomes dominant. Under such conditions the effort to resolve conflict involves many difficulties.

Conflict management through speech communication

Elimination, resolution, and management

Much has been said in recent years about the necessity to eliminate conflict as a means of making decisions. However, if we are to believe Simmel, Coser, and others, we must make a place in our society for some form of managed conflict. *To resolve a conflict is to solve a problem.* To develop ways and means of resolving conflicts requires a kind of social and political management that has a high viability ("growability") and versatility. This process of managing conflict should retain the social values of the competitive elements, while protecting us from the ultimate resolution forms, which may well be totally destructive.

Resorting to force may resolve a dispute, but it indicates failure of attempts to manage conflict. A number of methods of conflict management are available for the use of skilled and sensitive people, including joint problem-solving, deliberations, negotiation, bargaining, mediation, and arbitration. Each has a particular usefulness depending on the condition of the participants in relation to the goals and the problems. Joint problem-solving and deliberations, for example, may not be useful after conflict has escalated to the level of win-lose but may be effective in the earlier stages of disagreement over solutions to problems.

Joint problem-solving and deliberations

Whenever disruption and disagreement can be anticipated, some form of joint deliberation and problem-solving activity is advisable. In labor-management

---

[19] Jack R. Gibb, "Defensive Communication," *ETC., A Review of General Semantics,* Vol. 22 (June 1965), pp. 221–222.

relations, joint committees of management and union often serve throughout the life of the contract as "watch dog" groups to prevent minor trouble from escalating into a major dispute. These committees, composed of sensitive representatives from all sides, are established to avoid, if possible, break-downs of work and relationships by attempting to solve problems before they become win-lose issues. City planning commissions often function similarly in respect to the development of city facilities and activities. In family rela-tions, emphasis is placed on increasing the joint decision-making of all members.

The process of discussion and joint deliberation is a significant speech-communication system. The more highly skilled people are, in both leadership and participation, the greater is the chance of solving their problems of con-flict through joint deliberations.

Conflict management through negotiation and bargaining

During joint deliberations, the parties develop alternative possible solutions that hold varying degrees of attraction for the members of the joint group. At this point, some members of the group may attempt to bring the solution they favor to acceptance. The lines, however, are not rigid and the possibilities of compromise and accommodation are quite broad.

"Negotiation" and "bargaining" have often been considered synonymous. However, we shall here use the term "negotiation" to refer to that process of discussion between representatives of two or more groups that leads to the settlement of differences or the making of an agreement over matters of mutual concern. Negotiation is not involved in judicial decision-making, in arbitration, or in unilateral decision-making. In fact, true negotiations are impossible unless both parties are restrained from unilateral decision-making. Many teacher–school board dealings have been referred to as negotiations, yet, in many states, the school board retains the right to make the final and binding decision. Thus *discussions between the board and the teachers may have the façade of negotiation but are actually nothing more than information-sharing sessions, unless the board is willing to bind itself to a joint agreement.*

We shall use the term "bargaining" to refer to situations characterized by argument, persuasion, threats, proposals, and counterproposals between two parties as they seek to win concessions from each other in return for favors granted. The key differences between negotiation and bargaining are estab-lished by the elements of argument and persuasion. The bargaining situation brings into play a much higher incidence of argument, persuasion, threat, and the like than does the negotiation atmosphere. Further, negotiation involves much more joint interest and mutual goal-sharing than does bargaining.

At one end of a continuum is the full joint deliberation, involving a discussion of mutual problems. Deliberation blends into negotiation procedures, which in turn blends into bargaining (Figure 11–3).

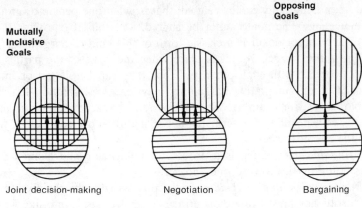

Figure 11–3

Ross Stagner and Hjalmar Rosen have described the bargaining process in labor-management relations:

> Bargaining begins when one side attempts to communicate to the other its perception of the work situation and to induce a change in this situation. Bargaining may be directed toward higher wages, toward less loafing on the job, toward elimination of safety hazards, or toward any other goals that either management or union desires.
>
> Bargaining is necessary because the situation as seen by management does not coincide with that seen by workers and union officers. If the two percepts agreed, joint action would be almost automatic.[20]

Although the labor-management context is most commonly and most generally associated with the process, bargaining also occurs in many other situations. The fruit growers bargain with the food processors over the price to be paid for the crop, nations bargain with each other over many issues of international relations, businessmen bargain with each other over products

---

[20] Ross Stagner and Hjalmar Rosen, *Psychology of Union-Management Relations* (Belmont, Calif.: Wadsworth Publishing Co., 1965), pp. 108–109.

and prices, customers bargain with retailers over prices and products—it is said that students even bargain with professors over grades.

Richard E. Walton and Robert B. McKersie refer to four types of bargaining: (1) distributive, (2) integrative, (3) attitudinal, and (4) intraorganizational.[21]

Distributive bargaining involves the process of resolving an issue that is bound up in a mutually exclusive goal; that is, what one person or group loses the other gains. The goal cannot be shared, and thus if one wins the other loses. The game of poker is a classic form of this kind of bargaining.

Integrative bargaining takes place when the goals of the parties are not in direct conflict with each other and thus they can be shared or integrated with each other. Integrative bargaining may lead to a solution that benefits both parties, as, for example, when a class and a teacher work out an agreement to set a deadline for term papers at a time most convenient for both under the circumstances.

Attitudinal bargaining is a process of influencing and changing the attitudes of the parties toward one another.

Intraorganizational bargaining is the process whereby the representatives of a constituency must bring their principals' expectations into line with those of the negotiator and the situation at the bargaining table. Not infrequently in recent years, union negotiators have returned to their constituencies with settlements that they have urged be accepted; but their intraorganizational bargaining efforts have failed when the membership has voted to reject.

Essential preconditions to effective negotiation and bargaining

Regardless of the social context of negotiating and bargaining, whether it be in a marital rift, a family struggle, a professional problem, a labor-management problem, or on an international level, both parties must be willing to discuss the situation with each other in "good faith." While the definition of "good faith" is always elusive, the term is generally accepted to mean that the parties are willing to and intend to sit down with each other and that they expect to reach a mutually acceptable solution to the conflict. *Both parties must have a basic willingness to agree and to make the negotiation and bargaining process work; that is, each must be willing to exert maximum effort to reach an accommodation with respect to the conflict issues.*

Both parties to the conflict must be "viable," that is, they must be capable of making changes in their present conditions in order to achieve maximum growth and development.

[21] Richard E. Walton and Robert B. McKersie, *A Behavioral Theory of Labor Negotiations* (New York: McGraw-Hill Book Co., 1965), pp. 4ff.

Effective negotiation and bargaining are impossible in a situation of win-lose polarization. The parties must be able to discuss common problems without being trapped into feeling that they must "win" over the other side.

Each party must be willing to reveal its maximum position in the early stages of the discussion. Since the eventual decision will probably be somewhere between the two maximum positions taken by the two parties, these extreme points of reference should be established as soon as possible. Thus, in a labor-management bargaining session, the maximum demands of the union and the maximum demands and position of the company should be made explicit as soon as possible. Until these maximum conditions are known, it is impossible for either party to accommodate effectively to the other. The same is true in working out a settlement during a divorce, a land-sale bargaining, or the like.

Requisites of negotiators

Skilled negotiators in every form of social conflict are communication specialists of considerable ability. Not everyone can perform the function of negotiation effectively on a high professional level. However, since all of us find it necessary to negotiate from time to time, we should know some of the requisites for a good negotiator.

He is willing and able to face the issues directly and precisely. He must be able to cut through the communication fog of the party across the table and of his own constituent, or constituents, and get to the hidden agendas that may be present.

He must be willing to speak plainly and to the point when it becomes necessary to do so. There are times when it is wise to avoid pointed attack because of its untimeliness and the effect it would have on the total negotiations. However, when the time comes for the "moment of truth," the skilled negotiator can react swiftly and surely.

He must be convinced of the proposition or positions he is representing. When a person assumes negotiating responsibility for some other person or a group, he will be more effective in his role if he is able to speak from the depth of his own convictions.

He must be willing and able to make decisions concerning changes in his position. Therefore, he must maintain a close communication with his constituency so that he is able to interpret its will accurately. The good negotiator can make decisions knowing that they are consistent with the policy and will of his people.

He is willing to assume responsibility for keeping his principals informed, as well as for remaining consistent with their policy and for interpreting his constituency's attitudes and opinions accurately at the bargaining table.

He must be a person with considerable self-perception and self-confi-

dence. He must be at least reasonably aware of his strengths and weaknesses. He must have a sound image of himself. He must not be egotistical or overbearing, but he must have considerable poise under fire.

He must enjoy the process of bargaining.

He must operate in terms of "practical possibility" rather than in terms of eventual panaceas. In each situation, the negotiator recognizes that under ideal conditions he could get the maximum for his principals but that no situation is ideal. He therefore is willing to practice the "art of the possible."

He must be reasonably skeptical. He does not take the opinions and statements of the opposition at face value but seeks to understand the hidden intent behind the communications of his counterparts on the other side of the table. On the other hand, he must remain open to being convinced of the soundness or stability of the position of the other side.

He must inspire trust in his constituents and in his counterparts at the bargaining table. Trust is one of those elusive conditions difficult to describe behaviorally. In this context, the negotiator must inspire trust in that he can convince his constituents and his counterparts that they can anticipate his actions accurately. When we trust another person, we feel that we can anticipate his actions with considerable accuracy and have confidence that he will respond as we anticipate. In this sense, it is possible to trust an enemy; that is, we may be able to anticipate accurately how that enemy will behave under certain conditions. Thus trust is a condition that results from insights and perceptions of ourselves and each other.

He desires respect rather than popularity. The good negotiator is not a salesman in a general sense; he is an advocate. His advocacy should be based on sound positions carefully developed and clearly representative. Popularity with opponents often creates doubts at the bargaining table. On the other hand, a solid respect for his judgment and for his integrity is highly necessary.

He can perform his role as advocate and representative of his principals with vigor and imagination. He should be able to reflect to his opponents the emotional implications of the issues being discussed without losing control of his own emotions.

Preparing for negotiations

It is not wise to enter negotiations and bargaining without thorough and complete preparation for what is coming, whether you are representing a client in court or a friend in a family argument. We shall discuss here minimal preparations for effective negotiation.

Know whom you represent. It is not enough to know the broad general nature of the policy of your principals. You should know them as people whenever possible. You should know where their limits are and where their allegiances lie. If you are representing a company, you should be familiar with the nature of that company, its problems, its plans for the future, and how this negotiation relates to them. If you are representing a single person, you should have a very good insight into where that person is in relation to his situation.

Know what your constituents' goals are and the points or issues of the negotiation. As their representative, it is necessary that you be privy to the ultimate objectives of your principals in this negotiation and beyond it. From this base, you should then determine the major conflicts or differences between your position and that of your counterparts on the other side.

Be sure that your line to the decision-makers in your constituency is open and clear. When possible you should get as much authority to make decisions as you can. Realizing that in certain areas this authority may be limited, you should then know how to get in touch with those who can make the decisions and have it understood that you have a priority for their time and attention when needed. In any event, *know what your authority is and what it is not.* If you do not have authority to grant an additional point in a conflict, do not assume this responsibility. Some negotiators prefer to work out a general decision with their principals, with the details to be worked out in the negotiations. When the principals trust the representative, this is an excellent procedure. At other times, the principals may have determined the decisions precisely, and there is little room for adjustment. In such situation, the negotiator should know the nature of these decisions so that he does not reach his limits too soon.

Know your time limits. That is, you should know how long you can maintain the negotiations without agreement and without risk to your position. If a union representative knows that his constituents will not work without a contract, he then knows that the contract termination is an important deadline. He should also know the time limits of his antagonists so that he can avoid time crises except where they may be helpful in bringing about an agreement. In some situations, time is a valuable tool that can be used to bring pressure to bear on the decision-making. In many industries, labor contract decisions are not made until hours or even minutes before a midnight expiration of the old contract because until that time the pressure for getting a settlement is not sufficient to motivate the parties to reach a decision. The same is true for many intergroup negotiations. The guerillas at the 1972 Olympics, for example, tried unsuccessfully to set a time deadline for action.

Know what should not be negotiated. Often negotiators get into areas of decision-making that are not at issue or that are not the province of that particular group to settle. For example, it is not the province of negotiators in collective bargaining between labor and management to set the prices of the product or the service of the employer. If there are existing agreements favorable to your constituents, avoid being forced into a position that requires you to renegotiate these agreements. Likewise, it is not the function of divorce lawyers to perform therapy on their clients nor to negotiate such. Many times advocates representing someone in a grievance procedure waste a lot of time trying to negotiate matters which are truly not at issue. Militants often demand the right to negotiate on items which are definitely not yet their prerogative.

Arrange your goals into several categories: (1) Identify for yourself those things that are absolute "musts" and simply have to be in the agreement. (2) Identify those things that are desirable but that could be traded if necessary to get one of the "musts." (3) Identify those things that would be just tolerable and that you could accept only as a last resort. (4) Identify those things that you cannot possibly agree to under any conditions.

Determine as completely as possible what your opposition will seek. You can get some indication from the patterns of their demands in the past and on other occasions. Exploit any sources of information available to you. You will benefit from research into the situation and evaluation of its ramifications for your opposition as well as for your own principals.

Plan your responses to the anticipated positions of your opposition. This planning is vital. For each issue you may have several alternative response possibilities, ranging in order from the maximum benefit you would wish to the "tolerable." It is wise to start with the maximum and move to the tolerable only under extreme pressure. The order in which you present proposals may have some effect on the negotiations, depending on the manner in which the opposition responds. Some negotiators prefer to leave the very critical and most difficult issues until last, focusing during the early stages on those things that can be agreed upon without much difficulty. This strategy sets the pattern of cooperation; and when negotiations reach the hard problems, there is some rapport between the bargainers. Negotiators often hold positions for which they have considerable strength until last; sometimes these strong positions are scattered throughout the negotiation period so that they give the appearance of supporting the whole structure of demands.

Know the decision-making authority of your opponents. You should know whether agreements reached at the bargaining table can be expected to hold up when the principals have a look at them. If your counterpart cannot guarantee support of the decisions made at the table, you should avoid making key commitments. It is wise to keep from committing all that you may have so that you always have a reserve you can fall back on in case your estimates of the opposition have not been accurate.

Adequately prepared, a person can enter a series of negotiations knowing that his communication effort is going to be received with some respect and significance. One of the first things an opponent can detect is lack of adequate preparation on the part of a negotiator. This is true whether you are negotiating a labor contract, a grade from a teacher, or a date with the girl next door.

Conducting the negotiations

The procedures of the negotiation itself become a set of ground rules mutually agreed upon by the parties to the negotiation. Sometimes the procedural agreement is implicit in the working relationship between the parties involved. For example, the manner of negotiation as to who is going to have the car often follows a formula. Likewise, a contractor negotiating with a builder usually can expect certain ground rules for their bargaining. At other times it becomes necessary to spell out or to work out the conditions under which the negotiations will proceed. In any event the procedures under which the negotiation is to take place must be understood by both parties. Following are some suggestions for handling the negotiations.

Be sure there is agreement on the procedures. There should be clear understanding about such things as who is to call meetings, who is to be the contact person for each side, what the meeting times shall be, where the meetings should be held, who should speak first, and who is to represent each side.

Be prepared to vary your communication approach to your presentation. As a negotiator, you should be able to demonstrate firmness when necessary, to be conciliatory when necessary, and even hostile when it seems vital to get your point across. You should avoid getting frozen into a single attitude or type of behavior. Your opponents will try to force you into a stereotype position or a single frozen position because this is much easier to handle than a constantly shifting attitude. This is not to say that you do not shift your commitment except when it is necessary, but that you keep your method of approach flexible.

It is good strategy to avoid giving in on all items that you consider can be traded for concessions before you have settled the items you consider to be "musts." Keep some of the "give" points to use as bait for the "must" items when the going gets rough. If you have traded away all your "give" positions and still very critical items remain to be settled, you are in a pretty difficult situation. Again, the principle applies to any arena where negotiations take place. It is not a condition only of labor-management bargaining.

Be sure that any interim agreement is understood to be tentative and conditional on the acceptance of the final and total package. It is common practice and of general understanding that an agreement is not complete until all matters have been agreed upon and the matter ratified by the principals. In the normal procedures, each matter of the agenda is discussed and tentatively agreed upon. This strategy is of considerable importance. By making tentative agreements, subject to agreement on the total package, you avoid having your position chopped away bit by bit until you suddenly end up with a total agreement that just doesn't make sense for you.

Try to get the initiative in the negotiations and keep it. Put the opposition in the position of defending a proposal so that as they work out defenses for their position you can be working on ways to penetrate these defenses or finding ways to sift out areas of agreement.

Keep your temper! There are times when tactics call for you to put on a show of irritation or anger in order to pressure your opponents; but any display of temper should be only for effect. If you do feel anger, make every effort to avoid revealing it. A high school boxing coach once said, "The first guy to lose his temper will lose the fight"; and that statement generally holds true for adversary situations. Angry and hostile statements and attitudes do not weaken or harm your opponent, but they do give him the advantage over you. If you find that the pressure is getting so great that your feelings are beginning to get in the way of your reason, you should call a halt to the negotiations and recess for cooling off.

Be sure that someone keeps accurate and complete records of the meetings. It is important to keep a record of what was said as well as who said it.

Treat as completely confidential what goes on in the negotiation meetings. It is particularly important to maintain the highest secrecy concerning the positions and attitudes of the opposition. Too many times leaks from the negotiations have destroyed possible agreements that were beginning to develop.

Yield a concession only in return for something that fits your goals, no matter how small the concession might be.

Always begin the negotiations with stated objectives well beyond the limits set by your "must" items.

Be sure that it is clear who is the spokesman for your team and that only the spokesman talks for the team. In some situations, the chairman or chief of a negotiating team serves as gatekeeper for participation by other members of the team, since teams often divide the responsibility for various arguments and problems. However, *someone must coordinate the effort and no sign of internal differences of opinion or internal strife within your team should ever be allowed to appear at the negotiations.* Your group should present a solid and well-coordinated image to the opposition. Signs of defection are immediately used as evidence that your position is weak. This is a form of nonverbal communication that is watched most carefully in all negotiations by all participants.

When you bluff, be sure that you can be protected if your bluff is called. Naturally, you're going to be pulling bluffs. These are part of the process. If your bluff works, all is fine. If it fails, you should admit your error immediately; but you should have a countermove ready for quick use. To admit error without a countermove leaves you stranded, with a complete loss of face and position.

The key negotiator or negotiators for your group should be kept fully supplied with information for bargaining. To support your positions, there should be at least twice as much material as you will ever use. All materials should be as accurate as they can be, as up to date as possible, and when possible attested to by responsible parties.

Always be ready to meet. If you are not prepared for some items that come up during a meeting, move for a recess. As soon as you have evaluated your position on those items, make it known that you are ready to meet again. Failure of negotiations can often be attributed to discouragement and refusal to meet on the part of one or both of the parties. Of course, if a genuine stalemate exists and neither party can make any moves, there is no point in meeting; but a negotiating team should never veto a meeting if the other side gives any indication that it is willing to meet. Many stalemates have been broken by simply meeting for long periods and going over the frozen positions. On the other hand, the most obvious settlements are often prevented by refusals to meet.

Always treat your counterparts across the table with respect. They are persons with responsibilities similar to yours who are trying to maximize their position against your effort to maximize yours. Efforts to understand your counterparts as persons and as communicators will help you get closer to them and to be more aware of the things that are putting pressure upon them.

And, remember these rules apply in any situation where you are involved in the bargaining level of decision-making.

Conflict management through mediation

When negotiations appear to have broken down and the parties seem unable to reach final agreement, several alternatives are available. As we have shown, either party or both parties may resort to force in order to test relative strengths and see which can enforce its demands on the other. Sometimes the parties may be able to call in a third party who will make the decisions for them. A more useful device, following the failure of two parties to reach an agreement, is *mediation.*

Mediation is a process whereby a third party is brought into the bargaining or negotiations by mutual consent to assist in reaching an agreement. *The mediator has no power to make any decisions.* His function is to assist the parties in a dispute to reach an agreement themselves. He uses persuasion, reasoning, and objective understanding of the forces at work in the situation. The mediator cannot rule or hand down a decision. The parties to the dispute still have the right to make the decisions. The mediator serves fundamentally as a catalyst to the process of reaching an agreement. Mediation can be used in many types of conflict. It has proven useful in marriage conflicts, in labor-management relations, between racial antagonists, between political combatants, and with many interpersonal and intergroup difficulties.

Because he has access to both parties privately as well as jointly, a mediator may determine the areas of agreement and disagreement with more insight than is possible for either party.

Functions of the mediator

The mediator *convenes the parties* at a mutually acceptable time. He takes the initiative for arranging such a meeting.

He *gathers information* privately from each party about its position and the reasons for it, about its perception of the opposing position and the reasons for it, and about the possible terms of a settlement.

He *serves as chairman* of the mediation sessions and maintains control over the procedures used during these sessions.

He usually *brings both parties together in a joint session at the very beginning* and asks each party to review the situation in front of the other party. In this way, he begins to assess the relationships between the two parties and also begins to test the depth and the significance of the disagreement.

While the parties are meeting jointly under his guidance, he *encourages the parties to continue negotiations under his observation and with his assistance*. If at such a joint meeting the parties are willing to discuss matters further with each other, he will encourage them to do so.

If he sees that nothing appears to be gained by continuing the confrontation of the parties in conflict, *he may separate the parties and begin working with each party alone*. In doing so, he may serve in several capacities: He *may carry messages* from one group to another. He also *screens messages* which he carries. If one group suggests that he tell the other group some quite sharp message, he is likely to temper the message before he delivers it. Sometimes he will eliminate much irrelevant material from ideas that he carries between the two parties. At other times he will *introduce new ideas* into the situation by testing them independently with each party. He *may be a message blocker* in that some messages which he evaluates as useless in leading to an agreement will be ignored. The manner of his communication during this process is of supreme importance. Skilled negotiators watch him and listen carefully to the messages he brings. The particular placement of a word, the change of a tone of voice, the attitude he uses when he brings ideas to the group tell each professional negotiator a great deal about the state of the situation.

At many points, the mediator *uses persuasive methods* to bring both sides to change their positions.

The mediator *demonstrates to both parties that he is reliable*. He must have the confidence of the parties or he cannot be of assistance to them in reaching a mutual agreement.

The mediator *listens to all sides at great length*. Among the most important tools that a mediator uses is his ability to listen.

The mediator *can differentiate the "window dressing" demands from the "must" demands*. He must be able to determine quickly the key matters in the position of each party. A negotiator can help him by making clear which positions are incontrovertible.

Throughout the time that a mediator is working with a situation, he *makes suggestions for ways of resolving the differences*. He uses a wide spectrum of suggestions; some seem absurd, others seem obvious. His purpose is to stimulate both parties to start seeking other ways of finding an agreement.

As one of his most important functions, the mediator *intervenes at those times when he feels it will be most useful*. During face-to-face confrontations, he listens to the parties state their positions very carefully and often at great length. He refrains from comment or intervention until he feels that such would be useful in moving the parties further toward agreement.

A mediator often is aware of a situation long before it comes to the point where it needs his specialized services. Usually when he is approached for help, a mediator will assess the extent of the efforts of the parties to solve the problem. If, in his opinion, more can be accomplished before his services are needed, he may suggest that the parties continue their efforts and keep him informed of progress. In this way, he can determine when he will intervene.

This sense of timing is of the greatest significance in a mediator's performance. It determines not only when he will intervene, but also when he will make suggestions or when he will report information he has developed from the parties to each other. The "sixth sense" of a mediator, which guides him to the proper moment for intervention of ideas or presence, is one of his most precious possessions.

A mediator often functions as an agent of psychological catharsis in the conflict setting. In this significant function, he *provides an opportunity for each party to release the tensions built up by the struggle*. Often he allows himself to become the object of hostility simply in order to reduce the hostility between the parties in conflict. At other times, he listens encouragingly as the parties privately tell him their feelings about the situation and their feelings about their opponents. Or he may provide relief with a well-chosen joke or story.

A mediator *suggests to both parties that they reevaluate their positions*. In so doing, he may suggest to both that they begin trading some of their positions or reducing some of their demands.

He *attempts to get the parties to break particularly complex issues into components and to deal with each component separately*.

When necessary, the mediator *makes contact, in a private and discreet fashion, with influential persons on both sides to enlist their assistance in bringing about change.* Sometimes this takes the form of private sessions with the spokesmen of a side. At other times, he may get in touch with one of the principals who exerts a great deal of influence on the situation.

The mediator *exerts as much pressure as he can on both sides to get them to move;* and each side feels the pressure on its own position. It can be expected that, in his private meetings with each of the parties, he appears to be urging acceptance of the other side's point of view. In many instances, it may seem to both parties that the mediator is taking sides with the other party.

He *finds a way for each party to lose an issue or argument and still save face.* This is a most important function. Many times the representatives of a constituency are so frozen into their position because of pressure from their constituents that it is impossible for them to move. The mediator can assist by offering rationalizations, justifications, and clarifications that will provide the representatives sufficient reason to change their position without threat of reprisal by their constituencies. This function strikes at one of the key problems in the win-lose condition that develops in many controversies.

By logic and persuasion, the mediator *attempts to raise doubts in the minds of the representatives of each side as to the value and practicality of their positions.* He makes this effort mostly in the private sessions with each party. If a group begins to doubt the soundness of its own position, he opens it up for examination of other possibilities. This "unfreezing" of the firm hold on a given position is essential to start change leading to eventual agreement.

When it seems that all is of no avail and that no amount of talking will resolve the deadlock, the mediator, even in the face of what appears to be hopeless deadlock, often *keeps the parties talking to each other either face-to-face or through his good services.* In the folklore of the various kinds of professional mediation services there is a saying: "If they don't talk, they can't reach an agreement." When the mediator realizes that no amount of skill or effort on his part will resolve the problem, he usually so informs the parties and removes himself from the negotiations or asks that other mediators be brought in to serve as a panel with him. A mediator may actually remove himself from the immediate negotiations, but technically maintain a surveillance over the situation so that when and if things change and he can be of use in making an agreement he is ready to move in again.

There are also times when the mediator *keeps the parties separated from each other and keeps them talking to him rather than to each other.* Such tactics become necessary when the parties have reached such a state of animosity that confrontation confounds reasoned judgment.

The mediator *does not try to engineer a solution to the problems in one move.* He may take considerable time to lay a groundwork of ideas. He may drop hints or make suggestions early and then not return to them until they are suggested by the parties as their own ideas. He may also begin dropping bits of information that eventually fit into a clear pattern, but he will not begin to fit them all together until he feels that it is appropriate to do so. He may try to get the parties to agree on minor issues at first, then point to these with considerable pride so that the habit and satisfaction of making agreements can develop.

The mediator's speech communication

The mediator's speech communication is his most important tool in performing his work. Throughout his total effort, the manner in which he speaks and listens is of prime importance in his service to the parties in conflict. Most of his communication is person-to-person or in the small-group setting. Very little, if any, is before large groups, which would call for a public-speaking performance.

Because of the close personal nature of much of his work, he must be able to speak informally and confidently. His voice must reflect poise and control. His manner must reflect his patience and alertness. He must be able to state ideas clearly and must encourage the parties to use feedback to him as much as possible and must provide feedback to the parties.

Many of the messages in the bargaining setting are unspoken and unwritten. They come from the facial expressions and the physical behavior of the participants at the bargaining table. The mediator must be able to read the significance of these messages and to use this information efficiently.

A major factor of assistance to the mediator is the trust that the parties have in him and his ability. When the parties agree to bring in a mediator, they must have some reliance on his integrity and his sense of justice. They must be able to anticipate with assurance that his functions and behavior will not work to their disadvantage. This is a big order, yet the mediation of any dispute requires that the mediator have this kind of relationship with both parties if he is to be most effective. By assuming that he will not work to their disadvantage, the parties should not assume that he will not force them to examine their positions carefully and try to show them the advantage of a settlement. In some situations, a possible settlement is not to the advantage of either party. In these circumstances a mediator allows such an agreement to occur only if both parties are aware of the consequences. However, in evaluating a possible settlement, the mediator is aware that any settlement of a controversy has an inherent value if the controversy is costly and debilitating of either or both parties.

The mediator also sets the tone and establishes the standards of communication between the parties by the manner in which he handles the meetings and the discourse. *In a sense, a mediator is also a teacher in that he is attempting to bring about change in the processes and the situation.*

Emotional pressure is not often regarded as useful; yet in the mediation process, mediators may use emotional pressures on both sides in order to stir them toward agreement. In one labor-management situation, for example, the mediator had helped the parties develop the framework of a settlement to the point where everything was worked out but one single point of very minor importance. At this point, both parties stalled and froze up. After nearly eighteen continuous hours of attempting to find a way to agreement, the mediator called both groups into a joint meeting, reviewed the whole situation with them, pointed out that a single very minor point separated them from an agreement. He then told them in strong emotional language that if they were thus willing to let such a small item prevent the triumph of sanity and reason he would have nothing more to do with the situation; then he picked up his briefcase and walked out.

The two groups sat in silence for a few minutes before someone said, "Is he really leaving?" To which a person on the other side said, "I'm afraid so, and I guess he's right. I think we better take another look at our situation." Within a short time the two parties ironed out the minor issue, then sent a messenger to the hotel to request attendance of the mediator at the signing of the agreement.

Remember, *the mediator does not make the decisions; he influences the parties to make their own decisions.* He tries to remove the obstacles to the parties' reaching their own decisions. He serves as a stimulant to the process of joint decision-making and to the process of managing conflict creatively.

Conflict management through arbitration

In most areas and types of social conflict, when the parties are unable to settle a dispute through their own processes or through the assistance of a mediator, they may then turn by mutual agreement to a third person and ask him to make a decision for them. The arbitrator will hear each side present its case and will hand down a decision in respect to the issues defined for him by the parties. *At this point the parties have given up their own right to make the decision on the issue and have agreed to abide by the decision of the arbitrator.* Arbitration plays a significant role in settling or managing conflict only when the parties are unwilling or unable to make decisions through joint deliberation or with the help of mediation.

The arbitrator's function is very similar to that of a judge or a jury but differs from that of the mediator, who does not make the decisions for the parties. We might consider mediation and arbitration as third-party methods at two ends of a scale. At one end of the scale, in mediation, the decision-making of the parties to the conflict is preserved. At the other end, in arbitration, the decision-making of the parties is removed. Obviously, there are situations in which the parties to a conflict cannot or will not reach agreement, and a third party must move in. Such intervention is particularly justifiable when the public interest or the interests of people not a party to the conflict are adversely affected, as in the case of divorce proceedings involving children.

The arbitrator serves in a more official capacity than does the mediator, and his operations are more formal. He *sets the time and place of meetings between the parties.* Usually meetings are hearings, which may range from a very informal review of the circumstances to a formal hearing with procedures much like those of a courtroom.

The arbitrator *presides at the hearing* as both parties present their arguments. He determines who is to be heard and raises questions with the parties as to the nature of their arguments.

The arbitrator *questions witnesses* whom the parties wish to bring in. He also questions the spokesmen and others in order to clarify their positions.

The arbitrator *attempts to get all the evidence pertinent to the matter.* Some labor-management arbitrators who become involved in grievance disputes over working conditions actually go to the work area to view the conditions themselves. In one case an arbitrator was hearing a case where a worker had charged that going up and down 200 feet of stairs to his work position was a health hazard. The arbitrator went directly to the site, walked up and down the stairs himself, then ordered a medical examination of the complainant to determine whether that amount of activity would indeed be a physical hazard to the worker. Not all arbitrators go to this extreme. On the other hand, most arbitrators feel that it is their job to get as much evidence as possible so that they can make as just a decision as possible.

In order to make fair decisions, an arbitrator *must be familiar with previous practices in situations similar to the case at issue.* He must research the case records of other arbitration decisions in the same area to determine precedents and patterns of previous decision-making.

He finally *makes a decision and writes the award and opinion.* The award is the decision as to which side is right or what is to be done. The opinion gives the supporting reasons for the award. Arbitrators' opinions should be objective and sound and should avoid giving advice for the future except as it is germane to the case.

One of the significant conditions that eventually follows arbitration is the irritation of one of the parties. *Only one side can win the case; the situation has been frozen into a win-lose condition before it goes to arbitration.* Research has demonstrated that in these win-lose situations arbitrators' decisions result in the winner exulting and celebrating, while the losers contend that the judgment of the arbitrator was rigged or unfair or unjust. The losers' considerable animosity toward the arbitrator often is transferred to the group leadership, and an adverse arbitration decision is frequently followed by overturn in the group's leadership.[22]

Force

When other means fail and still no decision is forthcoming, the parties often resort to force. In labor-management relations, force may take the form of a strike, a lockout, or other forms of economic pressure. In international relations, force takes the various forms of war. In interpersonal relations, force takes the form of fisticuffs or actual gunplay. *Force usually represents the failure of the parties to reach an agreement by any means other than a test of strength to determine who will dictate the terms of the agreement.*

Joint decisions—mediation—arbitration

One way in which we can view the three control processes is to refer to them as stages in getting a decision. If parties fail to get a decision through the joint decision-making processes, they should then turn to mediation where a third party may help them to make a decision. If the parties fail to reach a decision with mediation, the right of decision should be put into the hands of a specialist, and a third party should be asked to make the decision for them. One can easily see that the degree of freedom of the individual and of the group recedes at each step of the process. But the biggest cut in free decision-making comes when parties cannot find agreement either with or without mediation and must then give up their right to make decisions themselves. *Whether resort be to the courts, arbitration, or force, once parties to a conflict have failed to work out their own destiny, their freedom in a given action is forever abridged.*

Summary

Conflict is an essential or inherent part of living. Intrapersonal, interpersonal, and intergroup conflicts are continual in our social existence. Conflicts between persons and groups usually arise when at least two parties to the situation seek goals that are mutually incompatible; that is, if one party achieves its goal the other cannot achieve its goal. There are other species

[22] See Blake and Mouton, "The Intergroup Dynamics."

of conflict, however. We need, therefore, to provide a scale wherein we can view the spectrum of rivalry, competition, and war. Fights and games have inherent similarities but differ in terms of the outcomes and results to the players.

Controversy, competition, combat, and their derivatives are considered valuable as long as they do not result in the destruction of the social values The problem, however, is to control them so that they do not escalate into wars or destructive systems.

Speech communication plays a key role in most conflict situations. As a matter of fact, communication of one sort or another is one of the prime factors involved in any struggle situation. The control and development of the conflict processes depend almost entirely on the control and management of the processes of communication between and within parties. Communication forms of significance during controversy appear in expressing hostility, aggression, argument, orders and commands, charges and counter-charges, propaganda devices, and role playing. During a conflict, many levels of information exchange are developed. In some conflict situations, agreement on the rules of the game requires some negotiation between the parties. Each party is making commitments and avowals to the other, which carry various meanings in the relationship between the parties to the conflict. The degree of antagonism in conflict usually determines the degree of effective communication; the greater the antagonism, the less inclined are the opponents to reveal their strategy or intent and the more inclined are they to withhold strategic and critical information.

Conditions of conflict affect communication variously. Group cohesion increases, creativity tends to be reduced, those members who are more able to talk than others and for whom victory has particular relish begin to exercise more influence, participants view their own position as completely superior, and stereotype negative hostilities develop toward the opponents. Knowledge of one's own position is much greater than knowledge of the position of the opponent.

Speech communication is one of the most useful means of avoiding or coping with the win-lose condition that seems at the heart of destructive forms of conflict. Among the methods available for managing conflict are joint problem-solving and deliberations, negotiation, bargaining, mediation, arbitration, and force.

For special reading

Kathleen Archibald, ed., *Strategic Interaction and Conflict* (Berkeley: University of California, Institute of International Studies, 1966). A number of

people who have spearheaded the effort to understand human conflict assembled in 1964 to discuss various aspects of their discoveries. This book
is a report of the papers presented, rejoinders, and discussion of these
papers. For those of you interested in greater depth of exploration of the
problem, this material will be provocative.

Kenneth E. Boulding, *Conflict and Defense: A General Theory* (New York:
Harper & Row, 1962). The author of this book is one of the world's leading
students of conflict theory. This book, which combines game theory with
social and psychological theory, is a useful and thoughtful statement of contemporary thinking about the nature and resolution of conflict.

Lewis Coser, *The Functions of Social Conflict* (New York: Free Press, 1956).
This one is not so easy to read, but if you persist some of the more valuable
understanding will emerge. Coser integrates much social-psychological
theory into a series of propositions about conflict in all ranges of society.

Elmore Jackson, *Meeting of Minds* (New York: McGraw-Hill Book Co., 1952).
Here is a book about ways of settling disputes in labor-management affairs
and in international relations. Jackson reviews the manner in which disputes
are handled in the United States, in Sweden, in Great Britain, and in the
United Nations. His main interest is in the mediation process.

Robert L. Kahn and Elise Boulding, eds., *Power and Conflict in Organizations*
(New York: Basic Books, 1964). Another collection of papers by leading
scholars in the field, this book brings together the work of economists and
behavioral scientists. It is a report of the main statements in two special
seminars conducted by the Foundation for Research on Human Behavior.
Here again is hard reading, directed toward discussion of research findings
and theory advances. But, if you are interested in being challenged to seek
the deeper understanding, this is your meat.

Gerard I. Nierenberg, *The Art of Negotiating* (Englewood Cliffs, N.J.: Haw-
thorn Books, 1968). Here is a very readable book, full of excellent examples,
which suggests methods of negotiation. You will find this one very useful in
your own personal and professional development.

Musafer Sherif and Carolyn W. Sherif, *Groups in Harmony and Tension* (New
York: Harper & Row, 1953). Musafer and Carolyn Sherif are real innovative
pioneers in the study of intergroup conflict, and here they write on the development of their theories and researches. This book is prerequisite to any
study of intergroup conflict. They deal with attitude studies, prejudice, social
distance, and interracial struggles and make a plea for the interdisciplinary
approach to the whole problem.

Georg Simmel, *Conflict and the Web of Group-Affiliations,* trans. Kurt H. Wolff and Reinhard Bendix (New York: Free Press, 1955). Georg Simmel was a classical sociologist who wrote extensively around the turn of the century. While his observations and postulates were based on his limited system of observation, his insights seem to have been highly effective in that they have persisted as useful propositions for the later experimental study of struggle. Again, here is a not-so-easy book for those of you who want to start a real exploration of human conflict.

Ross Stagner and Hjalmar Rosen, *Psychology of Union-Management Relations* (Belmont, Calif.: Wadsworth Publishing Co., 1965). In this concise paperbound volume, two highly respected industrial psychologists analyze the conditions of industrial conflict. They pull together much contemporary research and theory to provide a clearer understanding of what may be happening to us.

Aubrey J. Yates, *Frustration and Conflict* (New York: Van Nostrand Reinhold Co., 1965). Most of the books listed here deal with the intergroup dimensions of conflict. This one deals with the intrapersonal problems in conflict and conflict theory, relating frustration and aggression theory to conflict. On the face of it, there appears to be a significant relationship. This book looks at that relationship.

Try this

1 In your journal record some of your more important *intrapersonal* conflicts which you believe may affect the way you communicate with others.

2 Describe how you have relieved some "cognitive dissonance" in respect to an intrapersonal conflict.

3 Assume that you are to represent your class in negotiating with the instructor as to how grades are to be awarded for your class work. What plans and preparations will you make for this negotiation?

4 Find a case study over which there is considerable difference of opinion in your class. Have those with differing opinions try to convince each other of their opinions. When the differences have become quite firm, step into the situation and try to mediate.

5 Divide the class into two groups. With one group representing faculty and the other representing students, try to negotiate a set of bylaws for a joint student-faculty senate.

6 From the many current local, state, national, and international struggles, select one that you feel is significant and examine the following dimensions: (1) Who is involved in the struggle? (2) What is the position of each side? (3) What negotiations have taken place and what happened in them? (4) What, in your opinion, is the potential for managing or resolving the conflict?

7 The following statement by columnist Sydney J. Harris appeared in the *San Francisco Examiner* (July 31, 1968, p. 35, reprinted by permission of Sydney J. Harris and Publishers-Hall Syndicate). Read the statement carefully, then prepare what you consider to be an effective answer either supporting or differing with his point of view.

> The big word this year is "communication." If everyone, we are told, would only get together and "communicate" with others, we would feel closer, our disputes would not be so rancorous, and maybe even some amicable solutions could be found for our disagreements.
>
> Well, I am not that hopeful. Having been what is nowadays called a professional "communicator" for a quarter-century, I don't believe there is any magic in communicating—at best, it simply lets you know what you are disagreeing about.
>
> Increased contact, on the verbal level at least, does not necessarily bring about agreement or understanding; it only works this way among persons or groups who already have a friendly feeling toward one another and who are not sharply divided on basic interests and values.
>
> Whatever scanty sociological data we have available tends to bear out the impression that closer contact between hostile groups only increases the mistrust, kindles the anger, and escalates the enmity.
>
> "Peace talks," for instance, almost never succeed except when the contending parties have already come to them seeking peace as their immediate goal.
>
> The current cant about the need for "communicating" is part of the semantic folklore of our time. While I am certainly appreciative of the value of general semantics in helping us think more clearly and express ourselves more accurately, I do not hold with the loose extension that "most differences are really verbal."
>
> There are, of course, verbal confusions and ambiguities that prevent adversaries from joining the issue. But this is not to say there is no issue to be joined, or that using words in the right way would reduce or heal the breach.
>
> This extreme form of nominalism is as futile and unrealistic as the opposite viewpoint of resolving conflicts by power.
>
> Words deal only with the intellectual level of our being. But it is in the affect—in the will—that we are most motivated in basic areas. It is not what we know or don't know that makes us act as we do—it is what we want and do not want.
>
> With most of us, the appetite directs the will, and the will informs (or deforms) the intellect. The stomach, as Diogenes said, has no brain.
>
> What must be communicated are good feelings, not statements of position, if the communication is to have any force for change.
>
> When bad feelings communicate from group to group, or person to person, they make things worse, not better. The world needs more lovers; then it could do with fewer communicators.

Epilogue: Some Issues and Frontiers

This book will never be complete. Each day our experience will add more to the substance of which we speak here. It is a growing, "becoming" thing because it's about people. Now I want to strike a few exclamation points by saying some things that I think should be said in order to put interpersonal speech communication into the perspective of the here and now. I cannot begin to catalog all the problems of today that can be dealt with by the speech communicator, but several of them seem to be basic to the vital issues of our times.

The generation gap

Some claim that the generation gap is a fantasy. I do not agree. I know that my perception of newer generations is faulty, and that their perception of my generation is faulty. I know that it is very difficult for me to find the time and the energy to try to listen with patience and effort to the excitements of the younger generations. But when I do listen, *I get excited too!* I am painfully aware of parents and others who refuse to allow themselves once again to feel the pain, the stress, and the confusion of being young. On the other hand, one of my sweetest friends is the oldest person I know, in terms of years, and also the *youngest* person I know, in terms of feeling the stress and strain of new ideas and new discoveries. At eighty-nine, she is an unreconstructed rebel. She always has been. For her the gap does not exist—but she is an exception. A real gap exists for most of us, and both *you and I must assume the responsibility for dealing with it*. Just ranting and railing about it will not change it! Reminding our elders that they do not really understand us does not create an understanding. *We must move into action through speech communication to close the gap.* As of now, we seem to know of no other way except complete and destructive schism. Speech communication cannot take place unless persons become *engagé*. Mere confrontation is not enough. The *engagement* must be joined, the bond must be established, and the problems must be pursued at close range. I would rather shake a man's hand than be waved at from afar.

Me and you: loving and hating

When I am at odds with myself, I have difficulty dealing with you. If my cultural heritage has conditioned me to stifle love and affection, I cannot reach out toward you. Our communication *engagement* is thus, at its best, limited and frustrating. When my conditioning has been such that I feel I must draw a protective wall around me, it is practically impossible for you to reach me with your communication efforts. One of the most exciting challenges of our time is the exploration of the nature of me and of you and the invention and discovery of ways in which we can be opened up to each other, can become tolerant of each other, and can be ourselves freely and openly.

Smiley Blanton wrote that we have always feared those destructive impulses in our own hearts and that the emergencies of the present will be met successfully only when individuals in sufficient numbers use love to conquer hate in their personal lives.[1]

Love as a way to peace and security has often been extolled and glorified. Yet the real essence of love has been forgotten. In its place we have assumed a kind of sham love, which centers entirely on self-gratification, is concocted and sold in the marketplace.

After forty years of practice in psychiatry, Dr. Karl Menninger wrote that most of us spend our whole lives without knowing the real nature of love. With the inadequate start in childhood and adolescence, he says, it is not strange that we reach adulthood without love or even a conception of what it might be. Menninger points out that such things as companionship, group membership, infatuation, exhibitionism, dominance or submission, and unselective sexual desire are mistaken for and are called love.[2]

A significant part of speech-communication processes involves an understanding of and relating to the other person. This condition is a principal ingredient of human love, as Dr. Menninger points out:

> What psychoanalysis showed was that true love is more concerned about the welfare of the one loved than with its own immediate satisfactions, that it demands nothing, but is patient, kind, and modest; that it is free from jealousy, boastfulness, arrogance, and rudeness; that it can bear all things, hope, and endure. So said Paul. So said Freud.[3]

We are often tempted to feel that there is insufficient basic love tendency in the human animal to allow for the development of the fullest

[1] Smiley Blanton, *Love or Perish* (New York: Simon and Schuster, 1957), p. 30.
[2] Karl Menninger, *The Vital Balance* (New York: Viking Press, 1963), p. 364.
[3] Menninger, p. 365.

interpersonal communication. Clemens Benda has pointed out that being in love brings on a new and unique relatedness and breaking of isolation, which is a kind of bondage that, while it is sought after, also deprives one of his freedom and independence and may even lead to an involvement that he may hate and wish to destroy.[4]

Thus there is a constant struggle between being consumed and being the consumer. However, Benda describes a higher level of love which dissolves the conflict.

> There is not *one* love but the infinite magnitude of human responses to the experience of being in love. The challenge of love differs according to age and also in man and woman. Each individual expresses his love in his own way. If falling in love turns into loving somebody, the passivity of the emotions is transformed into an attitude in which the whole personality takes an active part. At this point man ceases to be a helpless being surrendering to his emotions and becomes a human personality who is responsible and cognizant of his actions.[5]

The increasing number of divorces and undivorced marriage failures is a certain testimony to the failure not only of communication but also of the fundamental love relationship, which must be co-requisite to the communication experience. The love of one's fellowmen coupled with an understanding of the sorry state in which most find themselves could lead to a better communication between us.

Smiley Blanton speaks of our frustration and cynicism arising from unfulfilled needs for real human love.

> I believe that mankind, secretly starved for lack of love, yearns desperately to have its plight recognized and its emotional claims supported. Men and women are not content to hear their inner aspirations voiced merely in the maudlin accents of mass-entertainment media, for these offer only fantasies which do nothing to alter the essential burden of their lives. They wish to have their needs fulfilled in the world of action—in business, in politics, in everyday human contact. Yet our prevailing social philosophy places a premium upon the suppression of our craving for warm human relations, and ordinarily one does not dare give expression to it for fear of general ridicule.

> We are all oppressed, far more than we realize, by this enforced concealment of our hopes and desires. Its unspoken betrayal of human integrity evokes deep resentments that emerge to plague us in disguised forms, of which the brutal cynicism so often encountered in modern life is but one example.[6]

Are we willing to challenge the allegation that love simply does not exist in sufficient amount to do much good? Is the failure of love not one of the most serious threats to our very existence? Is the blocking of the communica-

[4] Clemens Benda, *The Image of Love* (New York: Free Press, 1961), pp. 4–5.
[5] Benda, p. 5.
[6] Blanton, *Love or Perish*, pp. 194–195.

tion and revelation of love destroying us in the ensuing frustration? Certainly speech communication has a significant role to play in this issue.

The establishment

Groups that challenge our present ways of doing things demand, among other things, that the present establishment be dislodged, if not destroyed. The meaning of "establishment," as the term is used by such groups, is vague; and the word apparently refers to anyone or any group in power. Thus, existing organization on the college campus, mainly associated with the administration of the university, is viewed as one of the establishments. So also are the city, county, state, and federal governments.

The essential problem we face is not whether the so-called establishment should be challenged, *but what is to replace it?* Should we expect to have the current establishment replaced by only another establishment? If so, what is to be the nature of the new establishment? Without some new form of organization, we can expect only a condition of non-organization of anarchy. Is this condition of nonorganization in our personal and collective lives inevitable? Can we lay aside the structures of our present systems, and then proceed to grow and develop without some other form of system?

You and I, as speech communicators must become party to the dialog on these issues. It may be perfectly proper to challenge the present system. In fact, the "current system" has been the object of challenge in every age and in every society. But the unique problems of our here and now rest in the structure of a new system that will provide maximum freedom and will nurture the ability to assume the necessary responsibility to deal with this freedom.

Here, too, is the issue of how we can put our speech communication to use. Is it enough to speak to each other for the purpose of agitation? Must we not also move beyond the agitation to provide some thoughtful and constructive means of dealing with our here and now and with projecting our system into the future?

Social innovators for the development of creative experiments in organization communication are an absolute necessity if we are to overcome the errors and the unresponsiveness of the establishment to the people. Central to their innovation is the creation of speech-communication systems whereby people may work together within an organization productively, freely, usefully, and with pleasure.

Take a look at what is happening on your campus, in your town, in your state, in your country, in your world. Where are you going to stand in relation to the establishments therein? Are you going to become actively engaged in the discourse so vital to your own life and the life of your children? This book presupposes that you will do so and that you will need all the powers of speech communication you can find to enable you to deal knowingly and effectively with the issues you discover.

Knowing too much but not enough

In these times, the total amount of technical information available doubles at least every decade. Computer systems now receive, store, and return upon request billions of pieces of information. This ready access provided by computer technology makes available to any of us more fragments of knowledge, more pieces of information, than any human being can use in his personal system. Despite ready access to this vast accumulation of information, most of us live in a personal world where information is limited by what we need and can absorb.

In preparing ourselves for participation in today's world, many of us have chosen or have been guided into technical, vocational, and specialized programs of education. The engineer may have much information about pollution of the environment by the wastes of man's production and living, but he rarely knows how he could integrate this information into the society so that it can be used for human benefit. Today, our air is polluted with sounds, with gaseous wastes, and with particles of a disturbed earth thrown up by the machines of extraction; our water is polluted with organic waste, chemical residue, and other garbage that destroys all life within and around. We have available to us scientific and technological information with which we could alter these conditions, could restore clean and quiet air to the gaseous and discordant cities, could restore the clear, clean, sparkling stream to its original purity; but the ability to apply this information to practical and realistic human use seems woefully lacking. Many universities are developing research and educational programs in environmental studies; however, few if any of these programs include much emphasis on processes of speech communication, which are essential if advanced information and technical skill are to be transmitted to and used by mankind. It is frightfully possible that we may destroy ourselves before we can communicate the message that might save us.

Managing and manning the technology

No management system can exist without communication. Most of us recognize this statement as a useful assumption. Few persons, however, have the capabilities and training to develop the communication systems within the managerial network that will allow for the maximum effectiveness of system management. Throughout this book, the factors of speech communication have been related to problems in management. This is not accidental; the essential problems in managing the vast technology that we are developing are essentially interpersonal speech-communication problems. *We do not need a separate book on communication for management.* The problems of the manager and his communication are of no different origin or genre than the problems of anyone else or of him in a different setting. No matter what the technical or physical setting, *the beginning of the interaction is within ourselves.* Thus, the style of management depends on the speech-communication process. So does the relative emphasis on product versus persons; movement of messages up, down, and across a system; the interaction between the human system and the mechanical system; and the exploration of the real goals of the enterprise. We must develop a managerial system that can effectively deal with the fantastic technology without an equally fantastic destruction of human values and conditions. Along with the great advancements of the technologies of production must come even greater developments of the human communication systems. Our personal and societal welfare, even our very survival, may depend on such developments.

The struggles between labor and management are undergoing rapid change in pattern and purpose. Certain segments of the labor movement were once considered the leaders of an enlightened liberality, which would bring a more open and productive economic society. These same segments are now some of the most conservative and rigid groups in our economic world.

The labor-management conflict is only a small part of the frontier in our production enterprise. The struggle in the "executive suite" is well known. The problems of relating production to people have been pointed out in this book. Everywhere in the management system there is a great frontier for persons skilled in speech communication. From the foreman to the president of the company, from the worker to the international president of his union, the need for more effective speech communication is painfully apparent. Of particular importance on this frontier is the problem of sustaining the personal nature of a man's relationship to his job in a work setting that is less and less characterized by interpersonal interaction. Management needs people who can communicate with the customer and with the general public in defense of the economic system. Labor needs the same kind of people. Both need people who can communicate with each other and who can deal with differences and controversy so as to prevent the destruction of the enterprise and protect the personal interests of all who are party to it.

On being frozen up, apathetic, and disenchanted

How many times in the civil conflicts of the 1960s did we hear or see "We'll destroy you, baby" tossed with great feeling into the middle of angry

confrontations? Who is the "we"? Who is the "you"? In our chapter on conflict, we talked about the ultimate outcomes of conflict, and noted that
destruction of the antagonist represented the ultimate result of a struggle
at its greatest extreme. Are we, therefore, to assume that those who say they
are out to destroy are, indeed, in the final stages of conflict? Are they (or
we) so frozen into the position of win or lose that there is no outcome for
any of us but destruction? Or can we possibly gain entry into the situation
and restructure the conflict to controversy, which can be mutually productive
rather than destructive? Here, again, we—each of us—must make some
decisions (commitments, remember?) about how and where we are going to
exert ourselves through speech communication. And such decisions we
must make.

In today's world, the greatest evil is to remain uncommitted, undecided,
and passive. A black friend of mine told me once that "We've already turned
the corner in our thrust for freedom and you haven't even decided whether
you are going to do anything about it, much less even be aware that we are
here!" I think that situation is changing. It is certainly no evil to change
commitments, to alter decisions. The ability to change is, in fact, a condition
to be courted. But the basic responsibility we all face is to get *involved.* We,
as speech communicators must be *engagé; engagement* is essential to life.

Since the shootings at Kent State University, the campuses of the
country seem to have simmered down. The tightness of the labor market
facing graduates and the disenchantment with our prolonged involvement in
the Vietnam war seem to have drained much of the urgency out of the young
people who just a few years ago were demanding the right to be actively involved in the decisions of the society. This apathy takes many forms. More
and more students are dropping out to drift hither and yon around the
world. This is a wonderful development, for their basic curiosity and courage
are giving them opportunity to discover themselves in a more international
context. But those who drop out and just stay put—frozen into immobility
and laxness—are growing in numbers and may become the seedbed of
further violence, unless we can help them to communicate about their anxiety
and debilitating disenchantment.

Many issues facing us today demand high-priority attention and action.
Judging by our experience of the 1960s, the action obviously will not be
useful if it is violently destructive. Yet, many structures of our present
society must be destroyed in order for us to survive. One of our greatest
challenges is to design the kind of society that will allow us to survive the
next hundred years—or even the next decade. By 1990, we may have only
one chance in a hundred of surviving as a society. But rather than sit idly
by, waiting for the moment of destruction, how much better it would be for
us actively to seek ways of making that one chance *really work!* This is the

challenge that could lead us out of passive disenchantment, and our speech communication may be our most important tool.

Being apathetic can appear in another form. After a particularly violent discussion in class of some of our current problems in human communication, a student approached me in some anger. The comments of that student went something like this: "Look, you're not doing what we expected you to. This disturbs me and I don't like it. Everything was going along okay until you come along and force me to get upset by insisting that I think about things going on around me. I could care less! Why can't you leave me alone? I don't want to be disturbed! The way of living my parents provided is fine. I like it. Don't bug me!" In spite of the "student power" movements on many campuses, I'm afraid that my young friend spoke for far too large a majority of students in our schools.

There is ample evidence that our cultural norms and standards place high premiums on things as they are. "Be not the first by whom the new are tried, nor yet the last to lay the old aside" is acted out daily by all of us in many areas of living. The dynamic conservatism of Alexander Pope's advice is perceived by many as essential to moderate the destructive explosive force of the new and to prevent the old from petrifying the culture. Too many organizations formed for specific purposes tend to try to perpetuate themselves, petrified, long after their purpose has been accomplished.

You and I, once having found a reasonably effective way of communicating with each other, cease to seek more effective ways of interacting until some crisis forces us to break out of our pattern. While one would not want a kind of society so mercuric that it could not be stabilized and maintained for even a little while, a major issue of our here and now is that our social, personal, and political behaviors have been frozen so hard for so long that even the most limited basic changes seem almost impossible. Our minds can create rapid and gigantic changes in the mechanical and physical world around us, but those same minds seem frozen tight to interpersonal behaviors that have about as much relation to today's reality as an ox cart to a super jet.

Crossing the culture gap

Probably no more important problem faces our total society today than the inability of people of one culture to communicate with those of different cultures. The Tower of Babel still exists, and those who seek to end the babbling are too few. The problem does not arise primarily from differences in language, except as language represents a cultural condition. We hear much about the "black culture" and the inability of "whitey" to understand and to communicate with the blacks. Here, short-circuited communication may be not basic but rather a symptom of failure of both parties to develop cultural understanding. Learning to love our neighbor depends a great deal on being able to communicate with him. Our Latin American neighbors are examples geographically closest to us. Our approach to the Central and South American cultures has been brutal, stupid, and devoid of loving. Instead of first attempting to understand, to engage in real communication with the people in these cultures, we have moved into these areas with money and equipment and tried to impose *our* system, *our* standards, and *our* concepts of living. We seem to have ignored the fact that changes within a culture must come from the inside—from the desire and the character of the people of that culture. I was shocked and dismayed upon visiting the capital of a Latin American country to find that the "Yankee gringo" contingent in that capital city lived in a section almost like a compound, separated from the rest of the city. Very little attempt was ever made by the U. S. residents to relate to or to establish true communication *engagement* with the natives. Those few affluent natives who did associate with the American sector were viewed by the majority of the population as traitors to their own country.

Knowing another language and speaking *to* other cultures with that language does not establish the essential communication *engagement* that brings a meeting of meanings. What is behind those language symbols and signs is the essence of a culture. We have done very little to find out how to communicate about that. Too little of what the anthropologists have discovered about cultural origins and characteristics is ever fed into the mainstream of our international communication. We seem to be preoccupied with the superficial artifacts rather than with the living cultural realities of a foreign sector.

People, ideas, and things
Ours is a world filled with gadgets. Every home contains little machines and devices of all kinds. The getting and keeping of things seems to preoccupy so much of our time that the knowing of people and the enchantment of sharing ideas have become almost incidental to our living. Things made to free us from preoccupation with tedious and unpleasant chores so that we can spend more time with ideas and people defeat that purpose by bringing desire for more things. Instead of freeing us, our gadgets are enslaving us and making us dependent upon them and possession of them for the feeling of fallacious security based on affluence and satisfaction. As we seek to develop effective speech communication, our preoccupation must shift from gadgets to people.

An open society closed
The strength of our kind of political and social system should exist in checks and balances such as we have in the structure of our government, along with the encouragement of innovation that would come from an *open system*.

Indeed, many of us have rationalized by giving great lip service in support of the open system we call democracy. And yet, some who prate most loudly about preservation of democracy mutter in asides that the system will not work if you "really want to get a job done." This hypocrisy is so prevalent and so obvious in our society that *the disenchantment of those who really believe in the open society has been driven to crisis proportions.* Certainly the barriers and breakdowns in our communication systems have prevented the rationalizers from hearing the rising tide of protest against the increasing restriction placed on individuals. We must remember, however, that no open system can really exist until every person in it assumes his full share of responsibility for making it work. Unless the body politic and the social corps can engage in significant and useful speech communication, the first line of responsibility will never hold. The ultimate defeat of the open society is preordained when men fail to assume their responsibilities for preserving their culture, and among these is the responsibility for perfecting their speech-communication processes.

In short, what faces us as we seek to become effective in our interpersonal speech communication is a host of major issues whose resolution depends to a great extent on the development of more effective speech communication in the total society. What we do as individuals is highly significant in this process. We not only become part of the effort to deal with these issues; we also become agents of change to help others learn to deal with them.

Anti-education educators

Our educational system is one of the most significant areas in which change can be generated. In this arena we have witnessed the greatest efforts to generate change met by the greatest efforts to prevent change from taking place. The public school today is the subject of attack from the one side from rigid citizens who are unwilling to permit children (their own and others) to be exposed to anything different from what they suffered in their own schooling. From the other side, the school is under siege by the militant radicals who demand that the system be destroyed—with nothing to take its place. It is hard to say which attack is the more dangerous. Each is a malevolent social virus that can destroy one of the most significant defenders of what is left of our so-called open society.

What we need today is a kind of educator who is unwilling to accept on faith or tradition the procedures and the personnel of the whole educational system. We need vital young men and women who honestly question every educational principle and every method that is used in the system. Our teachers should be well skilled in speech communication, because it is through this process that the greater part of our educative process takes place. Educators must know how to use the speech-communication process to open up the classrooms so that learning and change can be accelerated by more adequate adaptation to the capacities of the students.

The struggle for these classrooms is a vicious one. It is clearly recognized that within the educational system lies the potential for progress, regression, or stultification. Too much of our current educational leadership is frozen into an educational pattern devised in times that have little relevancy to our present. Our educators should not be so indoctrinated with the rigidity of a petrified institution that they cannot challenge it and change it when it fails. Those who can challenge are the anti-education educators. Some of you may have the guts and the stamina to be one of these.

Truth, slippery words, and credibility

One of the most significant developments of the early 1970s is the continuation of the "credibility gap" that was recognized in the late 1960s. In the fall elections of 1972, the principal campaigners spent most of their time accusing each other of deception. When we watch the major figures in our political arena spending millions of dollars and hundreds of billions of man-hours of listeners' time to sling mud at each other, we are justified in wondering where real choices may be. When the information about what is happening and what has happened in foreign as well as domestic affairs is always in question, where do we go for the security of truth? A few years ago, Robert L. Phillips wrote a doctoral dissertation on types of evasive responses discovered in a television series; his catalogue of techniques of evasion indicates that evasiveness occurs in nearly every communication event.[7] Evasiveness relative to questions of crucial importance in our political and social society *when the answers are known* may indeed become one of the most critical issues of our time.

But even more critical than evasion is the apparent necessity to avoid informing the public of the affairs of the nation. Many excuses or explanations are given—national security ranks high on the list; yet, many subsequent revelations show that matters vital to the decision making of the people are deliberately kept secret to protect political power rather than to provide national security. This public irresponsibility demands our attention.

Power and authority

Probably no other issue of our time should be of more concern to each one of us than the problem of power. For example, the person who, unilaterally, breaks off a marriage or an engagement exerts almost total power over the

[7] Robert L. Phillips, "A Typology of Evasive Responses," *Educational Broadcasting Review* (August 1968), p. 38ff.

other who has nothing to say and can do nothing to prevent rupture of the relationship. This is almost raw power on the interpersonal level. Such exercise of power is becoming more and more prevalent as the nature of the marriage relationship is being examined in our society. As people seek ways of acting out the idea of freedom, they can become monsters of power over others. The violation of relationships and the destruction of organizations through actions of single individuals—whether in political, social, religious, or educational institutions—is obviously abuse of power.

Let power be interpreted as the ability to control the behavior and outcome of other persons' behavior. One who uses that ability should accept the great responsibility that goes with it. Today, too many of us are not taking on the responsibility of power even though we exercise its prerogatives; too many of us are unwilling to face the consequences of our own acts. At the same time, too many of us are willing to exert over other people the maximum power available as it protects us. The ethical question is paramount. Our speech communication must concern itself with the creation and the execution of power and with protection from misuse of power on all levels of society.

Seeking the peak experience

Maslow has described the "peak experience" of a human being in a highly dramatic set of propositions. To him the peak experiences represent the ultimate in personal identity and fusion with others. Some of the conditions he describes as characteristic of the peak experience include perceptions of the self as free from blocks, inhibitions, fears, doubts, and the like; more spontaneous, expressive, and natural behavior; more creativity to the degree that expression and communication often become poetic; attaining real joy; becoming free and trusting; feeling mostly in the here and now with little connection to the past and future; being able to listen to others better than ever before; reaching the acme of uniqueness and individuality; being able to function with ease and effortlessness, being at a perceived peak of intellectual and physical power; and being more integrated with others and with the world around us than ever before.[8]

To be able to experience all of these along with the other constructs that Maslow describes as the peak experience would indeed be a high moment of significance in anyone's life. Too many of us live with the illusion that the greatest and the most exciting moments of our life are behind us or that such moments will really never come. The search for the peak experience must be constant and persistent—in the here and now. All of us need

[8] Abraham Maslow, *Toward a Psychology of Being* (New York: Van Nostrand Reinhold Co., 1962), pp. 70–118.

to be on the frontier where we are seeking more exciting, more useful, more pleasurable moments in our relationship with ourselves and with others.

> The duty of life is the sacrifice of self: it is to renounce the little ego that the mighty ego may be freed; and, knowing this, she found at last that she knew Happiness, that divine discontent which cannot rest nor be at ease until its bourne is attained and the knowledge of a man is added to the gaiety of a child.[9]

[9] James Stephens, *The Crock of Gold* (New York: Macmillan Co., 1912), p. 288.

Appendix:
"The Black Bag"

On the first day of the Elements of Persuasion class in the spring quarter of 1967 at Oregon State University an event took place which was to change the lives of several people.* At that first session, a male student appeared in the class completely encased from head to feet in a black cloth bag, commonly known as a stone bag. This extraordinary event had not been planned as part of the course. After talking with the instructor about the course during registration, the student had decided to try an experiment with his fellow class members to see how they would react when he appeared in the black stone bag, which he had received as a gift. The instructor agreed and explained later, "I'm enough of a nut to try anything once." The experience turned out to be more than a casual incident.

Now, how do you think a class would react to the presence of such a figure—a black bag with a human being inside it? According to reports, the members of the class for almost four weeks of the eleven-week term outwardly *ignored* the Black Bag. However, the instructor noted "strange looks" being exchanged between students and directed toward the Black Bag. He also noted that there were always at least two seats between the Black Bag and anyone else. Inside the bag, the young man became more and more irritated and "up tight" in response to the manner in which he was being treated, so one day he sat next to a young man about twice his weight. The husky young man reacted by poking the Black Bag with an umbrella saying "What do you want? I didn't do anything to you." When the Black Bag did not answer, hostility and defensive behavior increased; and with an angry "Get away from me!" his adversary got up and moved to another part of the room. (Keep in mind that no one other than the instructor and the student inside the bag knew the identity of the person inside.)

---

* This brief résumé of a series of events that took place in the classroom of Dr. Charles S. Goetzinger at Oregon State University in the spring of 1967 was reviewed by Dr. Goetzinger and is published here with his approval.

Finally an assigned speech was due. Everyone in the class had spoken but the Black Bag. He rose in his place and stood mute for three minutes. Hostility became intense. Students reported later that they felt he had not met the norms of the class.

Tension mounted and reactions became explosive, even though the students in the class refused to discuss the Black Bag inside the classroom. The instructor gave leads for discussing the situation; and he noted later, "They [the students in the class] just absolutely refused to even consider that there was anything going on in the class. . . . They just weren't about to even concede he was there."

A drastic change occurred when one of the class members gave a speech in which he said, "I don't know what your problem is; the Black Bag isn't bothering *me*." He then spent eight minutes pointing out how the Black Bag *was* disturbing him. In the process, he revealed that he and a friend had been following the Black Bag in an attempt to discover more about him. In fact, he had collected quite a record of things he had observed. This broke the log jam, the subject was finally out in the open, and the class began to examine its own behavior and feelings.

More people started to follow the Black Bag, and he naturally became more of a celebrity on campus. The general tone of the class discussions, according to the instructor, was one of wishing the Black Bag had never appeared and not knowing what to do about him since he had. "We found out later that the biggest frustration was trying to explain to the outside world what was going on," the instructor said.

Once the log jam of noncommunication about the situation was broken, the class began to work out its problem of its Black Bag. Subsequent speech assignments brought the Black Bag to the front where he tried to explain what he was doing and, of great importance, how he felt about the way people responded to him. He responded to questions of his classmates, and an intense and significant dialog began. His classmates went from hating him to loving him to partially accepting him.

Led by the instructor, the class examined why it had responded to the Black Bag as it had. This analysis opened up many avenues of the effect of norms and attitudes upon people as individuals and groups. Here was an unknown. The characteristic behavior of most groups toward the unknown is fear. Fear is expressed by such behaviors as hostility and avoidance. The class began to see how it had followed these patterns quite unconsciously.

The class developed a protective attitude toward the Black Bag as a result of the curiosity of the society that existed outside the classroom. Naturally, such a bizarre event commands some attention. Once the press became aware of the matter, newspapers, television, and radio were full of the situation. At one very critical time, members of the press approached the instructor for permission to attend the class while the Black Bag was there. The instructor referred the matter to the class to make the decision. After some discussion, the class decided it didn't want any intruder in the classroom but agreed to publication of a story about the situation. A well-written story did appear. Then another newspaper published a sarcastic editorial to which a class member responded with a biting letter in defense of the Black Bag. Soon national syndicates became interested. Due to pressures by people outside the classroom, it seemed almost necessary to allow the press in. And so, after another request, the class decided that on a given day the press would be allowed into the classroom provided that the regular class activity would not be disturbed.

On the scheduled day, the press arrived early in the morning for the class, which was to begin at eleven o'clock. Other classes scheduled for that room during the earlier parts of the morning were moved so that the press could have time to set up recording, camera, and lighting equipment. The scene, when the class began to assemble shortly before eleven o'clock, was very much like the mob scenes at a national event or after a boxing match. The small room was filled with high-intensity lights, three or four tripods with large cameras on them were placed at points in the room. Eight or nine cameramen with hand cameras were milling around taking pictures of anything, everything, and everyone. Microphones were taped on the tables in front of each chair. Amplifiers and large recorders were set up in the back of the room. In the hall outside the classroom, nearly a hundred students and faculty gathered to see what was going on. Through this screen and into this arena the members of the class sifted. Students coming late to class had to crawl under cables, tables, and tripods to get to their seats. A copy of a San Francisco paper with big black headlines about the Black Bag was shoved into a student's hands by a reporter, and the student was ordered to be reading it while cameras rolled and clicked. One student was forcibly directed to crawl under a tripod in order to get to his regular seat.

Obviously, the reality of press coverage was not what the class had expected or what the press had promised. Everyone in the class was uncomfortable and angry, even the instructor. One member of the class said that he was ready to go on with the regular class work for the day, which was to give a five-sentence speech that would get some specific action from an audience. The instructor agreed, and the student stood up in the glare of the hot lights and began to speak. The essence of his comments was that he felt the press would not report the situation fairly or honestly, that it viewed the whole situation as a joke which it definitely was not, that he did not like the intrusion of the press into the classroom, and he was *leaving.* Whereupon he forced his way out of the room. This caused some scurrying of the assembled onlookers, during which time a girl student rose to her feet. When the noise subsided, she gave her speech in much the same vein. At that point, the instructor scratched his head, slowly rose from his chair, picked up his books and papers and also left. Whereupon all but three or four of the class followed after.

The three or four students who stayed attempted to answer questions for their classmates. Downstairs in the professor's office, the rest of the class gathered with serious, disturbed intensity. Here the Black Bag was finally accepted as a human entity in the same crisis as they. He was not separate from them then. The students were mad, the instructor was mad, the press was mad. The students and the instructor felt that the media had violated every principle of professional ethics by violating the agreements made with the class and the instructor, and because of this feeling they wanted nothing more to do with any of the media. The husky young man who had jabbed the Black Bag with an umbrella was one of those who stayed behind to defend him to the press.

With deep concern, the group in the instructor's office began to examine what had happened to them and why they had retreated in such panic. The discussion was serious, intense, probing, and each student there began to discover things about himself and his fellow human beings that he had never known before. A few of the press representatives were allowed to eavesdrop on this discussion, and they were shocked and sobered by the depth and intensity of the students' discussion. The seriousness of the situation to the students so concerned one member of the national press that he arranged to stay several days to talk with the students and to get the feel of the actual situation. The result was a quite sympathetic article in a national magazine.

The following weeks were filled with stories about the Black Bag. But none of them came from the class or its members. After the incident with the press, the classroom door was closed to outsiders with the full support of the department chairman. Nevertheless, as the Black Bag continued to come to class, hordes of students gathered daily outside the building and in the lobby to watch his coming and going. Significant was the fact that the campus student community, in part, after its first reaction of hostility and laughter and after the national press had covered the event so widely, began to refer to the Black Bag as "*Our* Black Bag." Even one of the local barbers commented several times to his customers about "Our Black Bag," while shaking his head in puzzlement.

Anticipation rose high as the end of the quarter approached. Would the man in the Black Bag reveal himself? Attempts by the press to find out who he was even went so far as to try to get copies of the official class roll from the chairman of the department. When the class heard of this, it tightened its own security measures. Many times, the Black Bag was asked if he would reveal himself, and each time he answered honestly that he really didn't know.

The executive director of a very popular national network TV show tried to negotiate with the Black Bag to reveal his identity on that show. Although the network offered an astounding reward to the Black Bag to reveal himself, he turned down the offer. (Earlier he had received $50 from a regional radio station for a telephone interview which he had immediately donated to the library to purchase books of poetry.)

The day of the final exam arrived. Again the press was very much in evidence, although the classroom itself was protected and was not invaded. Again cameras and microphones were hooked up in the lobby outside the classroom. Outside the building between 500 and 1,000 students and townspeople gathered to view the event. The Black Bag entered the classroom, the door was closed, and the exam period passed. When the final bell rang, the door opened and the Black Bag came out and was whisked away by bodyguards provided by the department and class members. He never did reveal himself to any other than the instructor, a few friends, and a few of the department officials, who were sworn to secrecy. To this day few people know who was in that bag and many of those who were directly involved—such as class members, reporters, teachers—have said they would just as soon *not* know.

The incident of the Black Bag is a real one. The class, the press, the university community, the local community, and other groups exhibited behavior that tells a great deal about the way people alone, in audiences, in mobs, and in societies behave. The characteristic reactions of a group under pressure—retreat, fear, hostility, protective and defensive behaviors; the significance of feedback by nonverbal means; the manner in which the class and surrounding community cultures moved from rejection to eventual acceptance of the Black Bag—are patterns of interaction that emerged with unexpected impact.

Index of Names

Allport, Gordon W., 49
Appley, Mortimer H., 213n
Archibald, Kathleen, 234n, 253
Arieti, Silvano, 204n
Aronson, Elliot, 224
Asch, Solomon, 149
Ashby, W. Ross, 88, 100

Back, Kurt, 71n
Bakan, Paul, 140
Barker, Larry L., 140
Barnlund, Dean C., 88, 93, 106, 113n
Baseheart, John, 218
Bateson, Gregory, 72, 73, 78
Beavin, Janet H., 100, 108n
Benda, Clemens, 259
Bendix, Reinhard, 227n, 254
Bennis, Warren G., 54n
Berlew, David E., 54n
Berlo, David K., 16, 89, 90
Berlyne, D. E., 223
Berne, Eric, 11, 12, 15
Biderman, Albert D., 216
Birdwhistell, Roy L., 214
Blake, Robert R., 163, 227, 233, 252n
Blanton, Smiley, 258, 259
Bois, J. J., 79
Bostrom, Robert N., 218
Boulding, Elise, 225n, 254
Boulding, Kenneth E., 66, 254
Brecht, Bertolt, 35
Brooks, Keith, 20
Brown, Charles T., 7
Brown, Roger, 79
Burgess, Ernest W., 114n

Campbell, James H., 90n, 106n
Carpenter, Edmund, 9n, 38
Cartwright, Dorwin, 214n, 224n, 226n

Clevenger, Theodore, Jr., 216
Coch, Lester, 204n
Cofer, Charles N., 213n
Combs, Arthur W., 64
Condon, John C., Jr., 77
Coser, Lewis, 227, 228, 235, 254
Culbert, Samuel A., 52

Darwin, Charles, 104
Davis, Martha, 105n
Deutsch, Morton, 226, 234
Dewey, John, 161
Ducasse, Curt John, 38
Duncan, Hugh Dalziel, 80

Eissler, Ruth, 12n
Ellingsworth, Huber D., 216

Fabun, Don, 5
Fast, Julius, 120
Fergus, R. H., 125n
Festinger, Leon, 57, 71, 224
Fisher, Seymour, 45
French, J. R. P., Jr., 204n
Freud, Anna, 12n
Freud, Sigmund, 258

Gandhi, Mahatma, 44
Gendlin, Eugene T., 80
Gergen, Kenneth J., 26n
Gibb, Jack R., 191, 234
Goetzinger, Charles S., 270n
Guilford, J. P., 161
Gunther, Bernard, 28, 104

Hall, Calvin S., 41
Hall, Edward T., 106, 107, 118, 119, 121

Index of Subjects